POLITICALLY ANIMATED

Non-fiction Animation from the Hispanic World

Politically Animated

Non-fiction Animation from the Hispanic World

JENNIFER NAGTEGAAL

UNIVERSITY OF TORONTO PRESS
Toronto Buffalo London

Toronto Buffalo London
utorontopress.com

ISBN 978-1-4875-4442-3 (cloth)
ISBN 978-1-4875-4534-5 (EPUB)
ISBN 978-1-4875-4443-0 (PDF)

Toronto Iberic

Library and Archives Canada Cataloguing in Publication

Title: Politically animated : non-fiction animation from the Hispanic world / Jennifer Nagtegaal.
Names: Nagtegaal, Jennifer, author.
Series: Toronto Iberic ; 84.
Description: Series statement: Toronto Iberic ; 84 | Includes bibliographical references and index.
Identifiers: Canadiana (print) 20230447694 | Canadiana (ebook) 20230447724 | ISBN 9781487544423 (cloth) | ISBN 9781487544430 (PDF) | ISBN 9781487545345 (EPUB)
Subjects: LCSH: Documentary films – Political aspects – Spanish-speaking countries – History and criticism. | LCSH: Animated films – Political aspects – Spanish-speaking countries – History and criticism.
Classification: LCC PN1995.9.D6 N34 2023 | DDC 791.43/340917561 – dc23

Cover design: Val Cooke
Cover image: Still image from *Eva de la Argentina* (directed by María Seoane; produced by Azpeitia Cine, Illusion Studios, and the Instituto Nacional de Cine y Artes Audiovisuales [INCAA]; released on 20 October 2011 in Buenos Aires)

We wish to acknowledge the land on which the University of Toronto Press operates. This land is the traditional territory of the Wendat, the Anishnaabeg, the Haudenosaunee, the Métis, and the Mississaugas of the Credit First Nation.

This book has been published with the help of a grant from the Federation for the Humanities and Social Sciences, through the Awards to Scholarly Publications Program, using funds provided by the Social Sciences and Humanities Research Council of Canada.

University of Toronto Press acknowledges the financial support of the Government of Canada, the Canada Council for the Arts, and the Ontario Arts Council, an agency of the Government of Ontario, for its publishing activities.

Funded by the Government of Canada
Financé par le gouvernement du Canada

Contents

Figures

Acknowledgments

This book has been a singular project, but by no means a solitary one. It has received, just as I have, meaningful intellectual, financial, creative, and moral support. To begin, I wish to recognize the critical insights and questions shared by a number of faculty and graduate students at the University of British Columbia's Department of French, Hispanic and Italian Studies, who have shaped this book in no small way. First and foremost, a heartfelt thank you to María Soledad Fernández Utrera, whose moral support and perceptive suggestions have been constant, from the point of this book's conception to its eventual publication. I also wish to express my gratitude to those who have generously shared their time and expertise by reading and responding to drafts of individual chapters at various points throughout the writing process. To Alessandra Santos, Jon Beasley-Murray, Anna Casas, Sara Barnard, Gianluca Oluic, Xana Menéndez Prendes, and Mirta Roncagalli: thank you.

I am grateful to the Society for Animation Studies (SAS) for the financial support that the SAS COVID-19 Stimulus Fund has offered this animation-related initiative. The SAS has sought to support members like myself in maintaining professional productivity during the pandemic, which was, as it turns out, a time in which animated sectors across the globe boomed beyond expectation. Now, more than ever, it is an exciting time to be researching within the discipline of animation studies.

I thank María Seoane, director of *Eva de la Argentina*, for granting permission to use the still image that appears on the cover of this book. Special thanks are also due to Nathan Thomas for assisting in the reproduction of this image.

Special thanks are also due to my acquisitions editor, Mark Thompson, and my associate managing editor, Janice Evans, who did not let this project lose momentum, and who have made the entire process from proposal to production a smooth and enjoyable one. Simon D. Coll was an integral part of this process, and I am grateful for his meticulous copy-editing services. Likewise, it has been a pleasure to work with Stephanie Mazza in the promotion of this book. Thank you all for believing in this project, and for partnering with me.

On the flip side of the production process, I certainly could not have experienced the productivity needed for this endeavour without the help of family who cared for my three babies during the hours that I laboured over this fourth one. To my parents, Mike and Gerda; to Elise, Heather, Maria, and Anneke: I am grateful for always knowing that my children were in the best hands. Finally, to Joel, Noelle, Henk, and Joely: thank you for walking (and crawling) alongside me as I walked (and at times also crawled) my way along this exhilarating journey. This is because of you, and for you.

POLITICALLY ANIMATED

Non-fiction Animation from the Hispanic World

Introduction: Towards Expansion and Liberation in the Field of Animated Documentary

Politically Animated: Non-fiction Animation from the Hispanic World offers the first book-length study on the convergence of animation and actuality within films, television series, and digital shorts from across the Spanish-speaking world. It does so with the specific aim of interrogating many of the ways in which animation as a stylistic tool and storytelling device participates in political projects that underpin an array of non-fiction works. The phrase *politically animated* refers to, on the one hand, the ideological implications of employing specific techniques and styles of animation within certain socio-historical and cultural contexts, and, on the other hand, the fact that it is a political project that inspires or *moves* the film and television director or digital content creator to action. By paying particular attention to cultural production beyond the realm of cinema, this book continues to stretch the bounds of current animated documentary scholarship, just as it does by pointing to animated journalism and the animated essay as relatively new and definitively exciting areas of study within this burgeoning field that has now seen two full decades of fruitful investigation.

Throughout this same time, Hispanic film-makers have collectively employed various animation techniques to recreate and recast politically turbulent periods of historical pasts and presents. The reconstruction through animation of numerous national histories as well as of both central and marginalized historical subjects has been achieved with as much attention to form as to content, and as much concern for the twentieth-century past as for the twenty-first-century present. We see this, for example, in the way that Jairo Carrillo and Oscar Andrade integrate hundreds of 2D testimonial drawings into the award-winning short turned feature-length film *Pequeñas voces / Little Voices* (Colombia/UK, 2003 and Colombia, 2010, respectively), a child-centred take on Colombia's armed conflict that will be the subject of study in chapter 1.

Specificity of style for storytelling purposes is also extremely evident in Manuel H. Martín's self-proclaimed "graphic novel documentary," *30 años de oscuridad / 30 Years of Darkness* (Spain, 2012), which will be the focus of chapter 3. The significance of this pioneering project can be understood when we recognize its appearance in the context of Spanish comics rapidly developing into a form of "consequential art," as the title of Samuel Amago and Matthew J. Marr's recent book claims,[1] through which questions of historical memory have contributed to a prominent theme of creative exploration. Meanwhile, the interplay between form and content can be seen to its maximum extent in Laura Piaggio and Marcelo Dematei's trans-stylistic, made-for-television documentary series *Cuentos de viejos / Old Folks' Tales* (Colombia/Spain, 2013–19), some of the forty episodes of which I use for analysis in chapter 6.

These films and television series stand as several culminating points in what is now a century-long, rich history of documentary storytelling through animation found within the Spanish-speaking world, a phenomenon that will be systematically outlined later in this introduction. And yet, there persists a lacuna in attention to animated non-fiction originating from the Hispanic world, despite the well-known fact that it is here that the history of animated cinema itself has its deepest roots. It was on Argentine soil, just over a century ago, that cartoonist turned animator Quirino Cristiani (1896–1984) joined creative forces with then nineteen-year-old screenwriter Federico Valle to direct the first animated feature film in the history of cinema: *El Apóstol / The Apostle* (Argentina, 1917). Boasting an impressive runtime of seventy minutes, the political satire consisted of 58,000 frames that featured cardboard cut-outs, a technique later trademarked and patented by Cristiani. The film created by the pair of Italian immigrants portrayed the intervention by Radical Party leader, and then president, Hipólito Irigoyen against the governor of Buenos Aires, Marcelino Ugarte.

Tragically, all negatives and copies of *The Apostle* were lost in a 1926 fire that ravaged Valle's vaults. Equally unfortunate was the loss of Cristiani's second feature-length animated film, not unironically named *Sin dejar rastros / Without a Trace* (Argentina, 1918). Released against the backdrop of Europe's ongoing Great War, the eighty-minute feature depicted a botched attempt by German submarines to deceivingly draw Argentina as an ally into the war. Following a censorship order from Irigoyen, the film was confiscated by national police on its first day of screening, under strict orders that it be permanently stored away by the Ministry of Foreign Affairs. As a result, *Without a Trace* was never properly received by audiences or film critics of the day – or of any day, for that matter.

No doubt consumption by fire and the confiscation of these pioneering films, not to mention a second fire in the 1950s that destroyed the rest of the Argentine animator's tapes, contributed to a lack of recognition during Cristiani's lifetime.[2] It was not until very late in life that the Italian-born Argentine would receive long-overdue recognition for achieving the cinematic milestone with the production of *The Apostle*, as well as another, having directed the first animated film with sound, *Peludópolis / Peludo City* (Argentina, 1931).[3] The chiefly posthumous acclaim that Cristiani receives today is due in large part to the work of the late world-animation historian Giannalberto Bendazzi (1946–2021) in the early 1980s,[4] while Argentina's national news media and beyond continue to hail the cartoonist and animator as the Argentine who was two steps ahead of Walt Disney. Cristiani himself, who once received a personal offer to relocate to the United States and work for Disney's animation studios, famously stated that "Disney fue grande, pero yo llegué primero" (Disney was big, but I arrived first).

Less widely known, however, is the fact that a now century-long tradition of the hybridization of animation and the cinematic practice of documenting past and present actualities also has its deepest roots in the Hispanic world, in the likes of film-makers such as Cristiani himself. Prior to the production of his first feature-length film, the Argentine animator created a micro-short (two and a half minutes) film to close out the newsreel series *Actualides Valle* (Valle News), produced by the eponymous Valle. That is, the working relationship between the creators of *The Apostle* actually began the year prior, when the news video producer sought out the budding caricaturist in hopes of realizing his vision of an "experimental political vignette 'in action.'"[5] The segment, hailed by audiences, was the satirical *La intervención en la provincia de Buenos Aires / Intervention in the Province of Buenos Aires* (Argentina, 1916). Valle's idea was, as Bendazzi explains, to capitalize on the Argentine love for political discussion and satire and create newsreels with political cartoons for the citizens of Buenos Aires, who were especially engrossed in these topics.[6]

At the same moment in time, and across the Atlantic, the artistic pairing of animation, politics, and early documentary forms was also being developed on American soil during the twenty-two-month production of Winsor McCay's propagandistic short *The Sinking of the Lusitania* (USA, 1918). The twelve-minute film, thematically in tune with Cristiani's *Without a Trace* from the same year, is now widely cited (including by scholars of Hispanic cinema) as the first animated documentary in the history of cinema. One could challenge this assumption, however, on at least three counts: first, if we consider that a number of

Cristiani's earliest films were based on current events from national and global political scenes;[7] second, knowing as we do now that "documentary" is not synonymous with "somber social cinema," and it is not uncommon practice for documentarians who make use of animation to "harness the power of dark humor" in their so-called "projects of public pedagogy";[8] and, finally, given that the two main criteria used today to classify animated documentary involve the film being recorded or created frame by frame, and that the subject be the real world in which we live, rather than the film-maker's wholly imagined world.[9]

What matters most, however, is not which animated film was the first to appear in 1918, a fact of which there is no record as detailed release information has not been recorded for *Without a Trace*. What these early Argentine and American films demonstrate is that the political potential of animation was recognized by pioneer non-fiction animators such as Cristiani and McCay at the dawn of the cinematic art form itself. One century later, in the context of animated documentary existing as an established and increasingly pervasive genre within many world cinematic traditions, we are witnessing the realization of animation's power for transmitting political ideas, issues, and myths by a great number of animated documentarians. That is, film-makers, television directors, and digital content creators from around the world are employing the ideological tool of animation either in the absence of archive, to challenge the archive, or to put forth new documentary materials and forms *as* archive. In so doing they rewrite various national histories from perspectives that have long been overlooked, erased, ignored, or strictly told using the written word and other "official" modes of transmission.

The central claim that this book makes is that during the production of an animated documentary, aesthetic decisions that are made at the literal drawing board (traditional, digital, or otherwise) allow us to see a film's politics at play. Although animation technologies have progressed from the rudimentary cardboard cut-outs patented by Cristiani and employed in his films, what we can learn from looking back to just over a century ago is that seemingly simplistic forms of animation should not be equated with the notion of unsophisticated content. As all six chapters of this study aim to show, the political power that animation holds is made possible through a wide array of styles and techniques. This is especially the case when animators embrace other mediums that are already tied to political projects, such as children's wartime testimonial drawings, comics and political myth in the Latin American context, comics and historical memory in Spain, and even propagandistic Web 2.0 content as an extension of narcopower in Mexico's war on drugs.

Of these ideological piggybacking moves, as we shall see, creative connections to comics are a particularly pervasive case. A natural consequence of this is that a study on Spanish-language animated documentary on the contemporary big, small, and digital screens would at times converge with comics studies in general, and Hispanic comics studies in particular. The timing for this is optimal as great strides in scholarship on this subject have recently been made. Aside from Amago and Marr's aforementioned edited volume, *Consequential Art: Comics Culture in Contemporary Spain*, in the Spanish context we can name Collin McKinney and David F. Richter's *Spanish Graphic Narrative: Recent Developments in Sequential Art* (2020). This similarly themed edited collection of essays complements *Consequential Art* with its focus on comics' representations of personal and historical memory, identity and personhood, and contemporary issues such as Spain's 2008 economic crisis, which are likewise assembled within a three-part study. We see the examination of these three pervasive themes again the following year within many of the contributing chapters to Anne Magnussen's *Spanish Comics: Historical and Cultural Perspectives* (2021). In *Spanish Comics*, however, we are also introduced to newer themes for exploration, such as comics and censorship, punk comics and countercultural movements, and the relationship between comics and architectural tropes of construction. This last theme, explored in Benjamin Fraser's contributing essay, "Paco Roca's Graphic Novel *La casa* (2015) as Architectural Elegy," can be seen as an offshoot of a branch of study opened up a few short years prior by the same author with the publication of *The Art of Pere Joan: Space, Landscape, and Comics Form* (2019).[10]

Conversely, sustained attention to Latin American and Latinx comics in the United States happened a bit earlier, but likewise swirled around themes of identity and memory. In 2009, for example, we saw Héctor Fernández L'Hoeste and Juan Poblete's *Redrawing the Nation: National Identity in Latin/o American Comics*. In 2017, which proved to be a foundational year for the study of Latin American comics, we saw the publication of Jorge Catalá Carrasco, Paulo Drinot, and James Scorer's *Comics and Memory in Latin America*, as well as Edward King and Joanna Page's *Posthumanism and the Graphic Novel in Latin America*. More recently, we have been given an innovative look at, as the title of Scorer's co-edited volume says, *Comics beyond the Page in Latin America* (2020), which examines online or digital comics, comics in public spaces such as subway stations and *paseos* (boardwalks), and comics employed for the purposes of education and protest.[11]

Though this is not an exhaustive list, these titles merit mention for numerous reasons, above all for the fact that they provide key reference points for the analysis of comics-infused animated documentary projects (no doubt a significant form of comics "beyond the page," to borrow Scorer's term) that will occur at various points throughout this study. As a result, *Politically Animated* diverges from current scholarship on animated documentary for more than just the fact that it pays sustained critical attention to cultural products from the Hispanic world within and beyond the realm of cinema and the animated documentary "proper." Indeed, a necessary sub-focus that runs throughout half of the chapters of this book is the creative union of animated documentary and the comics medium currently being exploited by Spanish and Latin American cartoonists and film-makers alike. As the borders between comics and animated documentary become increasingly blurred on the big, small, and digital screens, so too will criticism of these fields overlap on the pages of future scholarly papers and books such as the present one.

This inevitable work has already started on the discursive level at scholarly conferences such as the sixteenth annual gathering of ImageTexT, ImageTexT in Motion: Animation and Comics, in 2019, and, in the following year, the inaugural edition of Ink and Motion: International Conference on Animation and Comics. Here, chapters 2, 3, and 4 respectively explore the political function of character drawings inspired by the late *Eternaut* illustrator Francisco Solano López in María Seoane's *Eva de la Argentina / Eva from Argentina* (Argentina, 2011), the explicit graphic novel aesthetic in Martín's aforementioned *30 Years of Darkness*, and, finally, the motion-injected editorial cartoons that characterize Saló's innovative comic book trailer turned viral video *Españistan: de la burbuja inmobilaria a la Crisis / Spainistan: From the Real-Estate Bubble to the Crisis* (Spain, 2011), which is received here as a work of animated journalism. By shedding much deserved critical light on a number of these cultural artefacts, this book dialogues with English-language scholarship on this subject, which, for decades now, has either overlooked or has not been equipped to analyse the boom of (Academy) award-winning short and feature-length animated documentaries emerging within the Spanish-speaking world. Ultimately, *Politically Animated* intends to expand the range and reach of anglophone scholarship on animated documentary to include sustained critical attention surrounding a wide range of contemporary cultural products from Spain, Latin America, and North America (namely, feature-length films, viral videos, and television series), while bridging discussions recently germinating in the hispanophone tradition with those already occurring in the anglophone tradition.

Practitioners of Hispanic film studies are just now starting to show considerable interest in the abundant pool of animated documentaries from which scholarly inspiration can be drawn. The animation-based journal, *Con A de Animación*, for example, has recently published two special issues that explore themes of animation, documentary, journalism, and reality, with articles by field scholars and animated documentarians alike.[12] Meanwhile, a growing number of articles in further animation-based and broader cinematic journals are appearing by the hand of scholars around the Spanish-speaking world, in what can be classified as two distinct threads. On the one hand, there are theoretical works that offer attempts to define animated documentary as an audiovisual genre that is consolidated with the digital culture in the global context,[13] and others that offer a social semiotics approach to understanding the meaning-making process within animated documentary and the genre itself as a symptom of contemporary art.[14] On the other hand, there exist a number of critical explorations of the representation of both Chile's and Argentina's dictatorships in numerous animated documentaries,[15] and the role of animation as a poetic, myth-making tool in the narration of the life and death of Eva Perón in *Eva from Argentina*.[16]

Meanwhile, this book adds to a steadily growing number of foundational monographs and edited volumes in the field. First we saw Annabelle Honess Roe's seminal *Animated Documentary*,[17] and a handful of years later, Jonathan Murray and Nea Ehrlich's *Drawn from Life: Issues and Themes in Animated Documentary Cinema*.[18] While the authors of these works largely spotlight projects from the hand of American, Swedish, and British film-makers, and occasionally those by Finnish and South African animators, the present study expands the current field for its consideration of various works from contemporary Hispanic cinema, television, and its digital public sphere, and liberates research on Spanish-language animated documentaries from within the limits of the hispanophone tradition. This is timely, moreover, as we find ourselves in the midst of a period of considerable growth in animated documentary scholarship, with, for example, the very recent publication of Ehrlich's *Animating Truth: Documentary and Visual Culture in the 21st Century*[19] and Cristina Formenti's *The Classical Animated Documentary and Its Contemporary Evolution*,[20] as well as an expanding pool of journal articles with each passing year.

This growth results in an interesting paradox. As has been stated from the outset of this book, the relationship between animation and documentary film is as old as that of animation and fiction film. When compared to animated fiction, however, the body of works classified as animated non-fiction is much narrower. Nevertheless, the near-limitless narrative capacity of the diverse tool of animation in documentary films and animated documentary itself is now being thoroughly explored while animated fiction has not benefitted as deeply from the same critical attention. In fact, Paul Wells, in his recent animation manifesto, laments the fact that when an animated film is finally celebrated, any recognition and critical attention garnered is largely directed towards the film's storyline and rarely towards its animated form.[21] Meanwhile, a growing and nuanced body of work, which recognizes that "animation is a mode perfectly suited to documentary production,"[22] analyses how animation functions as a tool for representing reality. This tepid debate germinating in the 2000s was no doubt spurred on by the publication of Honess Roe's *Animated Documentary* now one full decade ago. Central to Honess Roe's study, which analyses documentaries that make use of numerous animation techniques, from computer-generated (CG) animation, to Rotoshop, to traditional hand-drawn animation, is the question of how animation functions as a representational strategy in documentary.

Honess Roe proposes a theoretical framework for considering three main ways that animation acts in documentary that the conventional (live-action) alternative could not: non-mimetic substitution (a symbolic representation of real-life subjects), mimetic substitution (a realistic representation of real-life subjects), and evocation (largely symbolic animation that conveys subjective feelings and ideas that cannot otherwise be captured on camera). The central claim that underpins Honess Roe's book is that animated documentary "has the capacity to represent temporally, geographically, and psychologically distal aspects of life beyond the reach of live action."[23] This three-pronged, foundational understanding of animated documentary was reiterated by Honess Roe in her contributing chapter to Kate Nash, Craig Hight, and Catherine Summerhayes's edited volume *New Documentary Ecologies: Emerging Platforms, Practices and Discourses*,[24] and has frequently been cited and adopted by authors of myriad recent independent studies on animated documentary.

Only in the last few years has this discourse on the function of animation in documentary film been more thoroughly taken up and expanded with new voices in Murray and Ehrlich's *Drawn from Life*. The volume also includes veteran animated documentary voices such as that of Paul Ward, who seeks to further the field of research devoted to animated documentary by responding to certain overlooked areas, such as spectatorship. For years, Ward has been speculating on the ways in which we can understand animated documentary performatively.[25] In his more recent contributing chapter to *Drawn from Life*, Ward develops this notion further to understand animation as a performative process – its constructedness – which elicits viewer engagement and an emotional response.[26] Ward's research builds on the topic of spectatorial experience more generally taken up by a handful of early scholars of animated documentary,[27] and likewise responds to Honess Roe's recent assertion that there remains "the need for more research into animation reception and a more robust theorisation of spectatorship in relation to medium-specificity."[28]

Most recently, Ehrlich has noted the proliferation of the animated documentary genre, warning that, in the post-truth era, it risks losing its critical potential, and easily becomes a source of promoting misinformation for unquestioning viewers (which should perhaps not come as a surprise, given animation's age-old didactic purpose). However, for Ehrlich the transgressive potential of animated documentary remains, so long as these productions aim towards portraying reality through defamiliarization, so that "viewers see realities anew through innovative representation that breaks with conventions."[29]

As we embark on a new decade of research in this expanding field, animation's critical and political potential within documentary film, television, and digital productions remains a fertile area for study. This book seeks to add critical groundwork to what is currently being laid in this increasingly productive strand of animated documentary criticism. A handful of studies engage head-on with animation's political potential within the documentary genre. Ehrlich, for example, argues that an animated aesthetic functions as an "informational 'boomerang,'" at first creating distance between the spectator and the real-world representation, only to eventually facilitate an "engagement with the difficult political content" as well as "a potential to draw viewers' attention in a highly visual information age."[30] Also focusing on animation's ability to attract an audience's attention, Honess Roe argues for its ability to "disruptively interject" in otherwise live-action non-fiction film, in order to "highlight and hammer home" political agendas or activist messages. For Honess Roe, this is not a question of technique or style, but one of how animation "is woven, or not, into the live action documentary in which it appears."[31] Ehrlich builds on this in a more recent study, discussed above, examining the political role played in a post-truth era by *disruptive* and *defamiliarizing* animated documentaries, as they transcend from merely reflecting reality to shaping it "as it is in the process of becoming, based on what we make of it."[32]

Meanwhile, simultaneous to the production of this book, more tendrils of research on this topic were making contact with animated documentary scholarship under the umbrella of the virtual two-day symposium "Animation and Politics in a Globalized World" (28–9 October 2021), organized out of Germany. However, it is in the pages of this book that one can find focused and sustained critical attention to how and why works of animated non-fiction, as well as their creators, are *politically animated*. And it seems that there is currently no context more suitable to an analysis of this kind than that of contemporary Hispanic cinema, television, and the digital public sphere, in which animators especially – but not exclusively – find inspiration in other art forms already connected to political projects, as will be outlined in the chapter summaries below.

But it should first be mentioned that this steady rise in – and expansion of – animated documentary scholarship should also come as little surprise if we consider Hillary Chute's declaration in the introduction to *Disaster Drawn* that "we are now in a kind of golden age of documentary, in which attention to myriad forms of recording and archiving is greater than ever, and the work of documentary is central to all sorts of conversations."[33] While this certainly now rings true for animated documentary, pioneering twenty-first century productions such as Vincent Paronnaud and Marjane Satrapi's *Persepolis* (France, 2007), Brett Morgen's *Chicago 10* (USA, 2007), Ari Folman's *Vals Im Bashir / Waltz with Bashir* (Israel, 2008), and, in the Hispanic world, Carrillo and Andrade's *Little Voices* follow not so closely on the heels of canonical non-fiction comics analysed by Chute, such as Japanese artist Keiji Nakazawa's manga *I Saw It: The Atomic Bombing of Hiroshima* (1972); Art Spiegelman's Holocaust survivor's tale *Maus* (1991); and Joe Sacco's works of comics journalism, such as *Palestine* (1993) or the more recent *Footnotes in Gaza* (2009).

What is interesting, however, is that even if comics were "ahead of the game," so to speak, in terms of the cultural production of illustrated documentary accounts of history, war, and conflict, sustained critical attention to these source texts has developed in parallel to, if not slightly following, those of the animated documentary genre. Aside from Honess Roe's *Animated Documentary* from 2013, we have Murray and Ehrlich's *Drawn from Life* from 2018 and Ehrlich's own *Animating Truth* from 2021. Meanwhile, in the comics realm, in addition to Chute's *Disaster Drawn* from 2016, one can find Nina Mickwitz's *Documentary Comics: Graphic Truth-Telling in a Skeptical Age* that same year,[34] and Catalá-Carrasco, Drinot, and Scorer's *Comics and Memory in Latin America* the year following. What this parallelism in the publication of book-length studies on these two related subjects can be attributed to is not, as might be expected, an erosion of the high/low culture divide as it pertains to both the art of animation and comics art. Nor is it necessarily due to questions of institutionalization regarding each art form – that is, following Philippe Gauthier, a process of social legitimization in which an art form's expressive potential inherent to its medium-specificity is unduly recognized.[35] Though surely, as Gauthier reminds us, this concept is problematic, as neither comics nor cinema generally speaking has "been institutionalized in the same way in every corner of the globe."[36]

A straightforward answer, rather, can be found in the simultaneous recognition of an archival turn in both comics and animated non-fiction cinema during the 2010s. The year 2012 saw Chute's article, "Comics as Archive: Meta*MetaMaus*" in the prestigious opening spot of a double issue of *E-misférica* titled "On the Subject of Archives" edited by Marianne Hirsch and Diana Taylor.[37] In the context of comics being recognized by some scholars as a place where an archival turn was being identified, Chute elaborates on Art Spiegelman's *Maus*, which first, and perhaps most forcefully, established the connection between archives and comics. Meanwhile, in the realm of animation, we can again turn to Wells for an insightful commentary on the ways in which animation's narrative potential has been overlooked. "Class Issues" is the title that Wells gives to the introduction of his contributing chapter to *Drawn from Life*, "Never Mind the Bollackers: Here's the Repositories, Sites and Archives in Nonfiction Animation." The opening words from the introduction play with the notion of "class issues" in a way that is too rich, too entertaining, and too spot on not to cite in its entirety:

> Imagine a classroom, say, in the old-school style of Hogwarts or Miss Jean Brodie's, and huddled up in the tightly rowed desks are academic subjects and disciplines. [A]t the front, secure in their superiority, are the Classics and the sciences; engineering, business and architecture take their places just behind. The arts, unsurprisingly, sit by the window gazing out on other lands, nudged by the humanities and design to pay more attention, while sport comes in late, pulling its socks up. Film and media studies constantly put their hands up, eager for more attention, while, ironically, at the same time looking back and down at the sullen figure of animation studies sitting in the corner. This morning, however, animation studies is smiling. Its homework has been returned, and the red ticks in the margin have accumulated into three "A"s – "ani-doc," "art" and "archives" – its place in the Academy is thus secure.[38]

It is important to highlight these increasingly in-sync pathways of creation and critical reception in the documentary comics and animated documentary realms, for, as I will argue within a number of chapters in this book, they are not only synchronized, but also increasingly intertwined, especially in the case of Hispanic cultural production. Beyond the three aforementioned films and digital shorts to be studied here, we can name *El Crazy Che / Crazy Che* (Argentina, 2015), co-directed by Nicolás Iacouzzis and Pablo Chehebar. The eighty-three-minute film combines live-action interviews with a graphic novel–style animation to narrate the story of Guillermo "Bill" Gaede, an Argentine engineer who became a Cold War spy. There is also the innovative audiovisual project *La batalla de Mosul / The Battle of Mosul* (Spain, 2019), a so-called "videocómic" (videocomic) that is a short animated piece of (video) comics journalism about the 2016–7 Iraqi government military campaign to liberate the title city from the grasp of Islamic State and the Levant, a project directed by Ángel Sastre and illustrated by David Hernández that features a marked mainstream adventure comics aesthetic.[39] Most recently, we see a second animated documentary directed by Martín, *El viaje más largo / The Longest Journey* (2020), which employs within its parallel narrative threads an adventure-comics-like aesthetic to fittingly tell of the first round-the-world voyage made by the Magellan-Elanco expedition five centuries ago, as well as the first manned lunar landing only five decades ago. This rising trend is sound proof that, including in the animated documentary genre, animation is, as Wells finds it necessary to argue in the conclusion of his animation manifesto, *the inclusive art* that holds the "capacity to embrace all of the other arts within its production process."[40]

On-screen hybridization of both documentary forms aside, I aim to further show that a more general overlap of ideas surrounding these two artistic mediums can occur on paper. That is, dialogues germinating within comics scholarship can be of use to animated documentary in general, and vice versa, given the shared image-and-word form with which each genre comprises itself, their shared use of cinematic language, and, given the fact that these are two contemporary artistic forms simultaneously involved in more than a century-long work of, to borrow the words of Chute on comics, "practices of witnessing" that, although in distinct ways, "innovate the parameters of documentary" and expand documentary's reach.[41] This potential method of approaching animated documentary in the academic realm would not only expand the possibilities of the field, but also loosen up the constraints for the interpretation of the genre from the tradition of defining it within and against live-action documentary film more broadly, a genre from which scholars have long aimed to disentangle and liberate animated documentary. And, an interdisciplinary and comparative criticism is precisely what film scholar Suzanne Buchan calls for in her contributing chapter to *Animating Film Theory*,[42] in which she reminds us, citing Deluze, that "the only true criticism is comparative."[43] But before discussing the specific ways that an interdisciplinary and comparative approach between comics studies and animated documentary studies unfolds throughout a significant portion of this book, it is important to take a brief look at a history of the animated documentary genre itself within the Spanish-speaking world.

A Brief History of Animation and Documentary in the Spanish-Speaking World

The aim here is not to provide an exhaustive list of titles from Spain and Latin America and other parts of the Spanish-speaking world, which either combine animation with live-action documentary or can be classified as animated documentaries themselves. I do, however, seek to trace a relatively clear picture from animation's incursion into early documentary forms at the turn of the twentieth century to the consolidation and subsequent boom exactly one century later of animated documentaries within these different geographical and cultural regions. Thanks to Bendazzi's recent encyclopedic work in publishing the world history of animation, we now have an especially clear picture of the beginnings of animation's incursion into documentary cinema within the Spanish-speaking world. We know, for example, that from the start of the 1900s in Colombia, animation first appeared on the big screen through the vehicle of news reels. We also know that for Chile, like Argentina, animation was from the beginning tied to political satire. In this case, it was at the hand of Alfredo Serey, an illustrator turned animator who was behind Cristiani by a handful of years as well as in matters of technique when he produced the ten-minute short *La transmisión del mando presidencial / The Transfer of the President's Power* (Chile, 1921), which, as Bendazzi explains, depicts the new president, Arturo Alessandri, in the act of watching a safe with cobwebs that illustrate the nation's fiscal deficit, through a series of still frames.[44]

At the start of the next decade, a time considered to have marked the beginnings of a global golden age for animated cinema (1928–51), we see very little use of animation in documentary films. An exception can be found in the Acevedo brothers, documentarians from the Colombian city of Medellín, who included animated military ships in *Colombia Victoriosa / Colombia Victorious* (Colombia, 1933), and hand-drawn routes, tracks, or interesting spots on maps in various instalments of their newsreel *Noticiero nacional* (National News), which covered aristocratic events from sports celebrations to bullfights and ballets, plays and processions, and even student demonstrations.[45] The Acevedo brothers appear to be outliers during this time, when animation largely prospered in fiction film, serving to fuel the "Dream Factory," which offered momentary escape from the harsh realities of what has been called "one of the worst ages in Modern history."[46] Bendazzi notes events such as the Great Depression, a civil war in China, the Second World War, and the start of the Cold War, and to this list we can add the Spanish Civil War; the pre-Perón era in Argentina, marked by economic depression and armed coups; and the start of Colombia's *La Violencia* (the Violence) in the late 1940s.

It would in fact be a number of decades before animation would regain considerable visibility in Spanish-language documentary film, with the 1980s being a critical year for these cinematic encounters across Latin America. In Mexico, the American-born documentarian and film editor Enrique Escalona made the fifty-six-minute film on pre-Columbian Mexico, *Tlacuilo: El que escribe pintando / Tlacuilo: The One Who Writes by Painting* (Mexico, 1987). As Escalona himself explains, he sought to make "an illustration of the values at the basis of our Mexican identity, both social and cultural. I wanted to describe the Náhuatl culture, typical of the Aztecs, by using their writing [their illuminated manuscripts], one of the most important and under-valued manifestations (of their culture)."[47] The same year, Bolivian director Alfredo Ovando employed animation in *Cañoto* (Bolivia, 1988), a short documentary about the independence hero José Manuel Vaca, who fought the Spanish colonialists.[48] And the following year, worth mentioning is Benicio Vicente Kou's *Animatógrafo / Theatograph* (Peru, 1989), in Bendazzi's esteem, an entertaining documentary about the process of creating animated films.[49]

The next notable moment in the hybridization of animation and documentary in the Hispanic world can be pinpointed to the early 2000s for more than a single reason. First, it is here that we see another surge in the incorporation of animation into otherwise live-action documentary, and second, it is at this turn of the new century that we also see the switch to the creation of contemporary animated documentary, as it has come to be known. In terms of the former, we can look again to Peru, where Roberto de la Puente produced *Las tabas* (The Shoes, 2005), a film about an amateur all-female rock group that runs for just under one hour, and features anime-esque animated segments largely around the thirty-minute mark and thereafter.[50] This same year we see the emergence of a short animated documentary in Venezuela, whose pro-socialist government under recently elected president Hugo Chávez was investing heavily in cultural sectors such as the film industry. Under these conditions appeared the eighteen-minute animated documentary *Mi historia es tu historia / My Story Is Your Story* (Belgium/Venezuela, 2005), produced by Belgian-born Jean-Charles L'Ami. The film, which tells of the floods and earthquakes that occurred in Venezuela between 1999 and 2005, is comprised largely of children's drawings and narrated by dozens of children and teenagers.[51]

In form, *My Story Is Your Story* no doubt reflects Carrillo's *Little Voices*, the eponymous, early version of what would in 2010 become a seventy-three-minute animated documentary after the Colombian director teamed up with Bogotano animator Andrade. What is more noteworthy, however, is that Carrillo and L'Ami's pair of short animated documentaries can be considered to mark a definitive switch from the ongoing tendency to weave animated segments into live-action documentaries to the start of a new trend of creating animated documentaries themselves. It seems that the feature-length *Little Voices* would be the next animated documentary production to emerge, which perhaps should come as no surprise, as just prior to its release in 2010, the Colombian animation industry would undergo a rapid transformation from a humble start-up into one of the region's most promising industries.[52]

Accordingly, the fifty-six-minute extension of the award-winning short film of the same title twice marked an important moment for Hispanic cinema as one of its pioneering short animated documentaries, and, most notably as its very first feature-length animated documentary. *Little Voices* offers an unconventional take on the Colombian armed conflict, as it is exclusively narrated by children that were displaced by the violence and is illustrated in part by their testimonial artwork, which is supplemented by CG animation that mimics their childlike drawing style. At the same time this was taking place in Colombia, preparations were underway on the southernmost part of the Latin American continent for Seoane's *Eva from Argentina*.

It was the year 2012, however, that proved to be pivotal for the animated documentary across the Spanish-speaking world. For starters, we can name Victor Orozco's eleven-minute animated short *Reality 2.0* (Germany/Mexico, 2012).[53] A product of the Web 2.0 in more than a single way, *Reality 2.0*, which will be the subject of study in chapter 5, is comprised of a montage of viral video fragments that capture violent acts related to Mexico's drug war and the rise of narcoculture. Meanwhile, notable work was being done overseas in Chile. Claudio Díaz Valdes's short *Chile Imaginario / Imaginary Chile* (Chile, 2012) employs a combination of rotoscope and abstract hand drawings to visualize nine testimonies surrounding the turbulent period between the 1973 Pinochet military coup and the 2010 Bicentenary of the nation's independence. The year 2012 likewise saw for Chile the appearance of the collaborative short, *Trazos de memoria / Strokes of Memory* (Chile, 2012), a fourteen-minute, multi-voiced testimonial account of post-coup political repression within Santiago's infamous detention, torture, and execution centre, Londres 38, directed by Pablo Cespedes and Víctor Hugo Cisternas and illustrated in black and white by a handful of skilled artists.

Simultaneously, across the Atlantic appeared Matt Richard's feature-length *To Say Goodbye* (UK/Spain, 2012), a film that retrospectively narrates the story of the four thousand Basque children evacuated to the United Kingdom in 1937, through fourteen personal testimonies brought to life by full colour 2D and 3D animation. Most notably, the year 2012 also saw for Spain the release of Martín's *30 Years of Darkness*, a novel account, as we will see, of decades-long political repression and the lingering of Franco-era spectres in twenty-first-century Spain. Here, it is worth noting that while 2012 saw the appearance of animated documentaries in full force, at this time we continue to see animation being incorporated into live-action documentary. This is the case, for example, of the Catalonia-based production *Comediants, amb el sol a la maleta / Comedians, with the Sun in Their Suitcase* (Spain, 2013), directors Elisenda Dalmau and Héctor Muniente's theatrical recounting of forty years of the titular theatre company's history.

The year 2014 can also be named as a decisive year for the animated documentary in Hispanic cinema, with the making of the Academy Award–winning *Historia de un oso / Bear Story* (Chile, 2014), Gabriel Osorio Vargas's allegorical account of his grandfather's exile during the Pinochet dictatorship (1973–90). *Bear Story* was awarded the Oscar for Best Animated Short Film in 2016, making history as the first Latin American animated film for not only its nomination to the Academy Awards but also for the fact that it took the trophy back home overseas. Upon its release and reception, Osorio Vargas's eleven-minute film became the culmination of animated representations of the Chilean dictatorship dating back to 2002. In this year, Vivienne Barry directed the short film *Como alitas de Chincol / Like Little Sparrow's Wings* (Chile, 2002), which embraces the art of *arpilleras* (patchwork pictures sewn onto burlap) to denounce repression and censorship under the Pinochet dictatorship. Just a handful of years later appeared Díaz Valdes's *Golpe de espejo / Coup Mirror* (Chile, 2009), a twenty-three-minute documentary that offers a collective testimony of eight young Chileans who were born between the 1973 coup and the year 1989, a film that preceded by four years this director's better known *Imaginary Chile*, as well as the aforementioned *Strokes of Memory*. As Vicente Fenoll outlines in his recent article "Animación, documental y memoria" (Animation, Documentary, and Memory),[54] these documentaries were followed by Osorio Vargas's aforementioned *Bear Story* in 2014, along with three important projects in 2016: *Trazos de memoria 2 / Strokes of Memory 2* (Chile, 2016), *Salvador Allende* (Chile, 2016) and *Los últimos días de Víctor Jara / The Final Days of Victor Jara* (Chile, 2016). Between these, we can recall the previously introduced *Crazy Che* by Iacouzzis and Chehebar.

Finally, it is in Spain that we find the most recent pair of animated documentaries: first, in 2019, Emilio Martí López's thirty-minute *MAKUN (No llores): Dibujos en un C.I.E. / MAKUN (Don't Cry): Drawings in an Immigrant Detention Center* (Spain, 2019) which renders into 2D prisoners' testimonial drawings left on the walls of the IDC in Fuerteventura to tell of the many injustices and human rights violations committed in places such as this, and, the following year, Martín's aforementioned *The Longest Journey*. Having arrived at this point, objections may arise at an apparent act of overlooking any history of documentary and animation in other Spanish-speaking regions such as the Caribbean and Central America. The truth is, however, that the omittance of such information is not selective, but circumstantial. No such pairings appear to be recorded across a variety of media and sources. That is, until very recently.

Through current cultural production from countries such as the Dominican Republic and Panama, the Caribbean and Central America are working their way into the annals of this cinematic history. At the time of writing, the feature-length animated documentary *Milvio: Ojo de la revolución / Milvio: Eye of the Revolution*, about the exploits of celebrated photographer Milvio Pérez during the Dominican Republic's 1965 Constitutionalist revolt, is in post-production, under the direction of Milbert Pérez, nephew of the famed photographer. Also anticipated is an animated documentary from the successful female Panamanian documentarian Ana Endara, who is reportedly directing *Panamazing*, a film that relies on collage animation and documentary to chronicle the attempts of numerous Panamanians to bring big fame to their small country by earning their way into the Guinness World Records through bizarre feats such as rapidly peeling coconuts with one's bare teeth. Although nothing on this project has been reported since 2017, occasional documentation of its participation in numerous developmental workshops in national and international festival circuits from this same year leaves hope for its future release.

This extensive but incomplete list of documentary films and series indicates that contemporary Hispanic cinema and television, and the digital public sphere offer fruitful grounds for a study of animated documentary. This thought follows a final declaration point made by Wells in his "Animation Manifesto," in which he asserts that "animation should be more recognised for its achievements, impact and continuing significance in the contemporary world."[55] Thus, *Politically Animated* can be seen as a direct response to this call, and likewise a project that aims to build on the foundational work that Honess Roe, among others in the anglophone tradition and beyond, have established in the field of animated documentary.

In its entirety, this book rigorously analyses animated documentaries produced within Spain and Latin America and beyond, between the years 2010 and 2019. These are, with the exception of chapter 4's analysis of the digital short *Spainistan*, presented chronologically by year of release. The six chapters are principally ordered, however, to facilitate a formal progression from feature-length productions (chapters 1 to 3) to short digital videos (chapters 4 and 5), and finally micro-short televised episodes (chapter 6), as well as a thematic progression from child narrators and children's politics (chapter 1) to women's and men's political leanings (chapters 2 and 3 to 5, respectively), to the political underpinnings of animating "old folks' tales," to borrow a term from the title of Piaggio and Dematei's made-for-television documentary series. Further details regarding these and other structural qualities will be outlined in the chapter summaries below.

The Present Study

Politically Animated opens with an examination of the Hispanic world's first feature-length animated documentary, Carrillo and Andrade's *Little Voices*, and an exploration of politics surrounding some of its youngest subjects. The main aim of chapter 1, "Animating Agency: Children's Articulated and Embodied Politics in Jairo Carrillo and Oscar Andrade's *Pequeñas voces / Little Voices* (2010)," is to challenge current criticism that labels the film, which is constructed around children's hand-drawn and recorded testimonies of their wartime experience, as a depoliticized appeal to peace and its child narrators as apolitical. By contextualizing my reading of Carrillo and Andrade's animated documentary within an emergent discourse on the politics of children in Latin American cinema, I show that *Little Voices* transgressively challenges the predominant post-2000 trend of using the image of children as politics by providing, rather, an image *of* children's politics.

This conclusion emerges out of a deeper engagement than currently exists with the visual-verbal aesthetic in *Little Voices* and is the result of the fleshing out of two main claims that run throughout chapter 1. First, *Little Voices* is a site in which children's so-called "politics of articulation" play out. That is, beyond recognizing the narrative potential of children's drawings as testimony to their wartime experiences, my filmic analysis also sees their political potential, especially when these testimonial drawings are paired with the children's vocalization of their lived experiences. The second claim arises from paying critical attention to this testimonial soundtrack. I argue that *Little Voices* is an important text for further empirical observation of the ways in which children can and do engage in what the interdisciplinary field of childhood studies calls "embodied politics." That is, through listening to the children's narrations of their internal displacement, their shifting roles and responsibilities within their affected family units, and their concern for these in times of conflict, and their recruitment – or not – into guerilla warfare, we can decipher the many acts, behaviours, and tactics, albeit mundane ones, through which children can resist or sustain subject positions offered to them.

The groundwork laid in chapter 1 regarding how political projects can and do emerge through aesthetic decisions in the creation of animated documentaries is built upon in the following chapter, which provides an examination of Seoane's *Eva from Argentina*. Here, discussion remains within the territory of feature-length Latin American animation. Chapter 2, "What's in a "cómic animado" (Animated Comic)? Poetics, Politics, and Personal Myths of Peronism in María Seoane's *Eva de la Argentina / Eva from Argentina* (2011)," seeks to shed further critical light on the animated-archival dynamics in Seoane's biographical reconstruction of the events that marked the life and death of Eva Perón (1919–52). Unlike critics' dismissal and even outright rejection of aesthetic decisions surrounding Carrillo and Andrade's *Little Voices*, the appropriateness of animation as a tool for reconstructing the life and death of Argentina's former first lady has seen more appreciation, even if only slightly so. The small handful of studies that have analysed the prominent Argentine journalist, writer, and now director's film, see the choice of animation very generally speaking as a myth-building, poetic tool in the reconstruction of history and historical subjects.

Without dismissing these claims, chapter 2's analysis of *Eva from Argentina* pays attention to the particulars of the animated aesthetic, which Seoane designed in collaboration with now late Argentine comics artist Francisco Solano López (1928–2011). I underscore the importance of the film's production during the two-term presidency (2007–11 and 2011–15) of Cristina Fernández de Kirchner, current Vice President of the Latin American nation (2019–), during a time when the symbols and iconography of *The Eternaut* comics saga became a component of the discursive appeal of Peronism in power. I read the participation of Solano López as a means for Seoane to illustrate Kirchnerism as a continuation of classical Peronism through a reading of key scenes such as the highly poetic Loyalty Day scene. Accordingly, in dialoguing with current scholarship on Seaone's film, chapter 2 offers a deeper understanding of *Eva from Argentina* by acknowledging that the reconstruction of Argentina's past also has present-day political implications, which are particularly apparent through its connection to Argentina's national comics scene. Accordingly, chapter 2 initiates a secondary discussion that runs through much of the book, about the ways in which Spanish and Latin American animators are embracing the comics medium as a vehicle to aid in the reinterpretation of history. Ultimately, I highlight how the comics-related animation's myth-building poeticism is aided by resignified archival materials that "disruptively interject," following Honess Roe,[56] the Flash-animated narrative to hammer home what sociologist Juan José Sebreli would call Seoane's *peronismo imaginario* (personal myth of Peronism).[57]

Chapter 3, "Animating Autobiography: Historical Memory and Catharsis in Manuel H. Martín's Graphic Novel Documentary *30 años de oscuridad / 30 Years of Darkness* (2012)," furthers our understanding of how animation as a tool for reconstructing the past can also illustrate sociopolitical issues of the present. Here again we see the creative union of animated documentary and the comics medium currently being exploited by a growing number of Spanish and Latin American cartoonists and film-makers. The pages of the third chapter will explore how the comics medium bears on the reconstruction of the past in Martín's *30 Years of Darkness*, as well as the "cathartic function," following comics historian Antonio Martín, that the graphic novel documentary plays into for present-day audiences.

I contextualize Martín's graphic novel documentary first within Spain's comics memory project, which has seen a plethora of private memories surrounding the events of Spain's civil war relayed through image/text autobiographical and biographical narratives, to argue that *30 Years of Darkness* claims new cultural territory for this trend beyond the bounds of print-based publications. Second, I highlight how the Spanish film skirts a predominantly realistic documentary or *costumbrista* style that has characterized three decades of a Spanish Civil War memory boom. I show that the film's overall thriller graphic novel aesthetic strays even further from this familiar realism by re-employing the trope of haunting, a device common in the highly allusive representations of Spain's turbulent past released prior to the 1990s, to reflect Spain's so-called "spectral past." A close reading of the film's narrative and formal elements (namely, character construction and a ghostly *mise en scène*) suggests an implicit dialogue with the Derridean concept of hauntology to reflect this spectral nature of

Spain's twentieth-century past. Lastly, I read the shift from animated to archival bodies in the film's final scene as an emblematic, cathartic *unsuturing* of past from present.

Chapter 4's analysis of Aleix Saló's six-minute *Spainistan* rounds out this book's discussion on the relationship between animation, documentary, and the comics medium, while likewise serving as a pivot point from its focus on big screen, feature-length productions to works of animated non-fiction on the digital and small screens. The chapter, titled "Simply A-musing: Aleix Saló's *Españistan / Spainistan* (2011) as Animated Journalism in Spain's Comic Public Sphere," aims for a deeper understanding of Saló's iconic comic book trailer turned viral video. I read the six-minute film as a piece of animated journalism that dialogues with news media coverage of Spain's 2008 financial and economic crisis, as well as crisis-related cultural representations that rely on themes of gastronomy and nourishment to illustrate Spain's "malnourished" state.

In so doing, chapter 4 responds to one criticism of Honess Roe's *Animated Documentary*, which is that attention to journalism is a missing component.[58] In reading *Spainistan* as journalistic, I dialogue with nascent discussions regarding convergences between comics journalism and animated documentary in general, and animation as a new form of journalism in particular. To understand the animated journalistic video's relationship with Spain's news media, I turn to Honess Roe's understanding of highly stylized and didactic animation within live-action documentary contexts to argue that *Spainistan* "disruptively interjects" the steady stream of news media from Spain's counter-hegemonic digital public sphere.[59] Furthermore, given the satirical tone that characterizes Saló's short, from the didactic segments to the scenes that I classify as "motion-injected political cartoons," I argue that *Spainistan* is also a signifier of what James E. Caron has recently called the comic public sphere.[60] This will all lead to the conclusion that the six-minute short ultimately emerges as a text that is simply "a-musing"; providing us entertainment while provoking our thoughts.[61]

From here, we will turn our attention to this book's penultimate object of study, which is as similar to Saló's *Spainistan* as it is dissimilar. Likewise housed on Web 2.0 is Orozco's *Reality 2.0*. For the production of his digital short, Orozco likewise finds inspiration in an established and predominantly literary tradition, in this case the essay. However, unlike the satirical tone that permeates Saló's short, *Reality 2.0* is marked by a great solemnity, and while both filmic projects were made for the Internet, disseminated through social media, Orozco's video is comprised largely of existing social media content, as it features a montage of viral video fragments that capture violent acts related to Mexico's drug war.

Accordingly, the fifth chapter, titled "Tracing Cultural Continuities: Rotoscope, Archons, and Archive 2.0 in Victor Orozco's Essayistic *Reality 2.0* (2012)," provides an exploration of how the young Mexican animated documentarian takes a compare and contrast approach to what I call his "two Mexicos": one that is based on traditional culture, and another where narcoculture has become the new daily reality. Through a close reading of Orozco's ten-minute essayistic video, I show that the hand-drawn technique of rotoscope, given its inherent layered structure, becomes an apt tool to illustrate the *continuities* of one reality to another. Thus, further pushing the bounds of animated documentary studies to include further forms of non-fiction, I evaluate the ways in which the Germany-based Mexican animator treats the live-action footage to, on the one hand, trace the evolution of traditional entertainment values into those of narcoculture and, on the other hand, comment on a desensitization to its violence by viewers and a dehumanization of its victims by obscuring from sight or *defamiliarizing* the content through a thick "veil" of animation.

Ultimately, I show that Orozco's animated essay draws certain conclusions on narcoculture's so-called "new visual regime," by reorganizing, resignifying, and redistributing its own social media content. As we will see, the consequences of this power move are twofold: on the one hand, Orozco supersedes the cartels in their role as archon, in the Derridian sense, of this Archive 2.0 content; and, on the other, he is proof that animated documentarians occupy a privileged place among the wider group of documentarians, considered by some to be "archons of the audiovisual," given their ability to undo the "fixed" record of live-action footage in order to (re)determine what will be remembered and how.

Finally, chapter 6, "In Uncharted Waters and Totally Unmoored: The Transmedial Documentary Project *Cuentos de viejos / Old Folks' Tales* (2013–19)," sheds critical light on an innovative anomaly in the realm of animated documentary. Piaggio and Dematei's collaborative, transmedial documentary project has four seasons of 2D-animated episodes as well as hundreds of raw (live-action) videos uploaded to a user-generated online platform. An analysis of the *Old Folks' Tales* series is timely, given the recent critical attention to the convergence between memory, documentary, and animation. Zeroing in on the project's televised component, the sixth and final chapter will ask how *Old Folks' Tales*'s trans-stylistic approach illustrates the difference of individual lived experiences that form a transnational collective memory, one that challenges, broadens, and at times counters Spain and Latin America's official twentieth-century histories. My analysis of a handful of key episodes will argue for animation's unparalleled ability to illustrate the textures of private memory, here largely childhood memories of war and conflict, and will thus bring this study full circle in many ways. It will further be highlighted how the mnemonic medium of animation also has the ability to draw traceable lines – both literally and metaphorically speaking – from one memory to another, doing the work of what has recently been called "visual collective memory."

Ultimately, the final chapter of this book works against a not uncommon claim that animation is a place unmoored from history, emerging as evidence that it is, in fact, firmly moored to not just one history, but to many histories across the Spanish-speaking world. And yet, it will be my aim to show that the transmedial documentary project as a whole is characterized by multiple unmoorings: memorialization from the state, memory from the collective – especially when we consider, as has Andrew Hoskins, that the term "memory of the multitude" better suits the participation of masses in memory activity within the online realm[62] – archive from the institution, animation style from the hand of the animator or the brand of the studio, and, finally, animated documentary from the vessel of cinema.

From start to finish, *Politically Animated* is written with the intent that it be accessible to both students and professors with research and teaching interests in Hispanic studies specifically, though it also aims to attract the attention of scholars of animation, animated documentary, and comics studies more broadly. For this reason I have consistently translated into English the many Spanish-language titles and quotes, as well as non-English scholarly criticism, throughout. I also envision this book to be appealing to animated documentarians themselves, as we witness their incipient intervention in and contribution to animated documentary scholarship in both the Spanish-speaking and the English-speaking world.

Finally, this book responds to many current debates taking place in a variety of fields, making it a keen point of interest for scholars across the humanities and social sciences. Chapter 1's positioning of *Little Voices* as a case study for the empirical observation of children's articulated and embodied politics, for example, makes a significant contribution to this ongoing work by a wide variety of scholars within the interdisciplinary field of childhood studies. Meanwhile, chapter 3's discussion of Spain's historical memory debates on the level of both society and culture through the graphic novel documentary *30 Years of Darkness* will provide much needed insight from the artistic and scholarly margins relating to the media of comics and animation to scholars of Hispanic cultural studies broadly. Further, chapter 6's analysis of *Old Folks' Tales* will also draw the attention of researchers working at the crossroads of aging studies and film or television studies. In short, this book seeks to expand and liberate the bonafide and burgeoning field of animated documentary, and also aims to attract the attention of scholars in a wide array of fields that may or may not be familiar with animated documentary and the important connections and opportunities for interdisciplinary study that these cultural products can bring to myriad fields within the humanities and beyond.

1 Animating Agency: Children's Articulated and Embodied Politics in Jairo Carrillo and Oscar Andrade's *Pequeñas voces / Little Voices* (2010)

It may seem inconceivable that a film that marked two milestones for contemporary Hispanic cinema, being its first fully animated documentary on either side of the Atlantic and one of the first Latin American 3D full-length animated movies, would struggle to find approbation from the box office to the scholarly book page. Yet this has been the unfortunate fate of Jairo Eduardo Carrillo and Oscar Andrade's animated documentary *Pequeñas voces / Little Voices* (Colombia, 2010), an innovative take on the nation's prolonged armed conflict from the child's perspective.[1] The seventy-six-minute film is the result of a project ten years in the making, and a fifty-six-minute extension of Carrillo's own award-winning short film from 2003.[2]

Little Voices looks back on a conflict that persisted within Colombia throughout the second half of the twentieth century, since its outbreak in 1964, and well into the present century. The decades-long conflict has greatly impacted human rights and security conditions in the Latin American nation, and has left over 10 per cent of the population internally displaced. At the time of *Little Voices*'s release, this figure was just over five million citizens;[3] a number according to government statistics that grew in the years shortly following to six and a half million,[4] and was more recently reported to be eight million.[5] During this time, Colombia was the only Latin American country with an armed conflict, although an ongoing dialogue originating in Cuba in 2012 between the Colombian government and the Revolutionary Armed Forces (Fuerzas Armadas Revolucionarias de Colombia, or FARC for short) signified that the country was at last poised to enter a post-conflict era. Following four years of negotiations, and a series of revisions, a final agreement to end the conflict and build a lasting peace was announced on 12 November 2016. As the decade came to a close, however, Colombia's peace process was thought to be fragile and under stress and, as national media reports frequently state, the conflict is said to be heating up again. Today, the armed conflict continues to make headlines, as its consequences, such as forced displacement, torture, assassinations, and gender-based violence, are on the rise when compared to the year 2020.

Although the main players in this armed conflict include guerrillas, paramilitaries, army, and state, the singular protagonist of *Little Voices* is the collective group of displaced children that accounts for over one million persons in the above statistics. Carrillo and Andrade's animated documentary is one of the few portrayals that address the Colombian armed conflict from the child's point of view, and becomes even more notable for straying from the common portrayal of children as innocent bystanders by also depicting them as direct players in and victims of the conflict. To create this perspective, the co-directors visited various Red Cross camps around Bogotá to interview children between eight and thirteen years of age that were displaced by the violent conflict from their villages in the interior of Colombia to the nation's capital city. The film-makers asked one simple question to upwards of 180 children: "Why are you here?" Their collective responses were twofold: five hundred hand-drawn testimonies and over four hundred hours of recorded interviews, both of which are heavily integrated in the production of *Little Voices*.[6] Carrillo and Andrade's animated documentary blends the testimonial artwork with CG animation that mimics their childlike drawing style. The visual and verbal testimonies that shape the animated documentary are diverse, recounting threats and armed attacks against their families, bombings of their villages and farms, forced disappearances of family members and authority figures, and recruitment by guerrilla forces as child soldiers.

Carrillo and Andrade's animated documentary did enjoy modest success in the festival circuit run, taking home the award for Best Documentary Film in Colombia's Cartagena Film Festival in 2011 and receiving numerous honourable mentions and funding awards from a handful of national and international festivals. When it came to its run in Colombian theatres, however, the animated documentary was a box-office flop. *Little Voices* attracted less than ten thousand spectators over three weeks of screening across more than a dozen cities, with numbers falling by 98 per cent from a meagre 8,853 spectators the first week to 167 spectators by the end of week three.[7] To put this into perspective, only weeks earlier Carlos César Arbeláez's Oscar-nominated *Los colores de la montaña / The Colours of the Mountain* (Colombia/Panama, 2010), a live-action fiction film likewise offering a vision of the conflict from the child's perspective, was one of Colombia's most watched films that same year, and saw upwards of 350,000 spectators within its first month in theatres. We can assume from *Little Voices*'s poor critical and popular reception that the choice of animation to depict the reality of the Colombian armed conflict may have been perceived as highly unusual to audiences, who, as Judith Kriger reminds us, at the time more readily associated animation with entertainment and escape from harsh realities of life.[8]

Kriger's generalized statement perhaps rings more true for certain styles of animation than others. Here it is worth noting that a similar misapprehension and even disapprobation was not necessarily seen by other pioneering documentary films from around this same time, which employed animation in the reconstruction of events such as the demonstrations at Chicago's 1968 Democratic National Convention (Brett Morgen's *Chicago 10*, USA, 2007), the 1982 Lebanon war (Ari Folman's Oscar-nominated *Vals Im Bashir / Waltz with Bashir*, Israel, 2008), or the Islamic revolution (Marjane Satrapi's autobiographical comic turned film *Persepolis*; France, 2000 and 2007, respectively). Although the reasons for this are likely many, one main speculation regarding this discrepancy in reception can be made about the style and technique of animation employed by these diverse animated documentarians. *Chicago 10* blends archival footage with highly realistic rotoscope animation while the other two box-office hits released in the context of the rising popularity of graphic novels feature a marked comics-like aesthetic, both of which styles likely appealed more to either the adult spectator specifically or the mature spectator of all ages.

It is precisely for the stark underappreciation regarding *Little Voices*'s formal properties that Carrillo and Andrade's animated documentary provides an especially interesting case for study. It is no secret that the childlike drawings that characterize the film have been a point of contention as well as confusion for spectators beyond general audiences and film critics from the cultural realm. Recent scholarship on *Little Voices*, for example, reads the infantile aesthetic as an erasure of the "political densities" of Colombia's countryside,[9] and a means of creating "a 'depoliticized' appeal to peace" in which children are located outside the political realm.[10]

Broadening this debate, my own analysis of *Little Voices* carried out in this chapter argues for the testimonial drawing/CG animation blend as foundational to the film's estrangement from entertainment and direct engagement with social and political issues in the context of the Colombian armed conflict. On a formal level, *Little Voices*'s animated aesthetic becomes a site in which what Sarah Elwood and Katharyne Mitchell call children's "politics of articulation" are played out.[11] Meanwhile, on a narrative level, the selected children's testimonies offer a means of perceiving the ways in which children engage in what is now, in the interdisciplinary field of childhood studies, commonly called "embodied politics."[12]

To this end, the first chapter of this book draws on a recent body of childhood studies scholarship that theorizes how politics manifests in childhood. One main conclusion, following what has been called a "decade of youthful political geography scholarship,"[13] is that children's politics manifest in more mundane ways, issues, and contexts. By "mundane" Kirsi Pauliina Kallio and Jouni Häkli refer to children's practices that occur in their everyday environments and on their own terms as a means of consciously – or not – developing their subjectivities and "political selves."[14] This can look like, on the one hand, a politics of articulation: Elwood and Mitchell, who draw on Michel de Certeau's notion of spatial stories and Mikhail Bakhtin's concept of dialogic relations, hold that children's drawings and narrations of their everyday lives are sites in which children's political agency and formation can manifest. In other words, as highlighted by Elwood and Mitchell's study, the practice of children's politics may be found beyond their "acts, behaviours, and bodily resistance."[15] These meaningful but mundane phenomena are what were earlier theorized as "embodied politics," best defined as "bodily actions (tactics), through which children are able to resist most attempts to control, manipulate and rule their lives."[16] These tactics are often used to resist "subject positions offered by parental (peer) cultural or institutional forces of socialization,"[17] or, conversely, to sustain them as Jacob Lind suggests.[18] These opposing "tactics" of *resist* and *sustain* are referred to by Lind in the title of his study as the "duality of children's political agency."

A second common conclusion in the study of children's politics is that the focus on the "how" rather than the "what" is key; one should not ask "*what* is or is not political, but rather *how* things are political."[19] Appropriately, proponents of these debates have begun to note that it was time to move beyond talking about children's politics to focus on more explorations between "children, activism, and political work in more explicit ways."[20] This means studying children's lived worlds as potential fields of political action in order to discern their role as political agents in their practices of everyday life.[21]

Little Voices provides the perfect case study for building on the recent work of empirically observing children's politics. This task has been initiated through, for example, an ethnographic study of children's hidden politics of resistance and struggle for play in a Swedish asylum centre,[22] an analysis of Swedish media representations of children in the mobilization for supporting Finland during the Second World War,[23] ethnographic observations of children belonging to families of irregular immigration in Birmingham, UK,[24] children's graphic representations of and dialogues about their everyday lives in Seattle, USA,[25] and empirical observation of Finnish evacuee children's life stories through documentary film.[26] Moreover, Carrillo and Andrade's animated documentary also provides an apt case study for further developing one understanding of the political potential that animation holds in documentary films, particularly what leading animated documentary scholar Annabelle Honess Roe calls animated "disruptive interjections" in live-action documentaries. Honess Roe describes these as "sudden and unannounced change in visual register [that] metaphorically shouts at us, 'this is important,'" meant to "highlight and hammer home" political agendas of films that often already display strong political or activist messages.[27] *Little Voices* in its entirety can be viewed as a metaphorical shout, emitted by a collective young voice (but not without the help or intervention of the adult production team, as will be discussed). Carrillo and Andrade's film offers an abrupt change in the visual register from other films on the same subject, including child-centred conflict narratives like *The Colours of the Mountain*. That is, if live-action film has long been a reference point for offering a vision of the devastating effects of Colombia's armed conflict, the generic difference that *Little Voices* displays can be read as a purposeful *displacement* of this theme to new generic territory. Nevertheless, rather than find themselves drawn into the film by its distinctive aesthetic to find new meaning, the aesthetic decisions seem to have had the opposite effect on spectators, who disregarded animation's (and the testimonial, childlike drawing's) importance.

This opening chapter, which builds on this body of work in childhood studies, and dialogues with animated documentary studies, addresses this paradox. It will be concluded that, through the verbal and visual testimonies of its child narrators, *Little Voices* reveals tactics through which children resist or sustain a rural identity within the city of Bogotá, their dismissal of the hegemonic discourse of "child in need of protection" through affirmations as self governing agents; what Kallio and Ann E. Bartos call "practices of care,"[28] and, in dialoguing with this, what I call here "practices of concern." Likewise, my analysis of Carrillo and Andrade's film emphasizes the fact that a number of these testimonies problematize the image of the child soldier solely as innocent victim, which, as Helen Brocklehurst points out, likely prevails due to society's perpetuation of the "prior relationship of children to the political," in which "almost all definitions and concepts of children are premised on a notion of childhood as an experience which has or should have little in common with the political."[29] This last case is particularly important as, despite the growing recognition of children's politics in their everyday lives, the political agency of a child soldier remains a marginalized perspective.[30]

Accordingly, this first chapter unfolds around the following two questions: How can one understand the animated aesthetic in *Little Voices* as reflective and representative of children's political practice? And in what ways can the "mundane" politics of children's lives be observed within Carrillo and Andrade's documentary film?

Little Voices: The Image of Children as Politics?

The notion of *Little Voices*'s politics arising from its collaborative child subjects themselves, rather than from the subjectivity of the children's characters (that is, from the politics and ideologies being constructed by an adult production team) exhibits a recent shift in critical thinking. This assertion goes well against the predominant post-2000 trend in Latin American cinema highlighted by María Soledad Paz-Mackay and Omar Rodríguez in their introduction to the recent edited volume, *Politics of Children in Latin American Cinema*.[31] These authors point out that when a film makes the representation of children its focus, as have many recent Latin American fiction films that spotlight the child and adolescent voice within a wide variety of genres, it gains a political dimension, "becom[ing] a form of political action – in so far as children do not actively participate in their own representation."[32] Politics, we are told, enter the filmic text in two related ways: first, on the level of content, through the election of common themes such as displacement and marginality, gender and cultural discrimination and recollection of the past; and, on a formal level, in terms of the children's self-representation (or lack thereof), and similarly the children's (lack of) control over the creative process, meaning that ultimately "children remain on the fringe of cinematic representation."[33] These often – but not necessarily – child-centred cinematic portrayals from the last two decades parallel a period of political turbulence and extreme sociopolitical changes, and reflect the views, anxieties, fears, and/or desires of the adult directorial team imposed upon the child object of the narrative, ultimately subordinating and displacing the perspective of the child.[34]

The result of this trend is a phenomenon specific to Latin American cinema that Paz-Mackay and Rodríguez call "the image of children as politics": portrayals of children and adolescents that are always controlled by adults with the purpose of engaging adult audiences; productions in which, save for a few minor exceptions, "the creators of these films are not interested in the point of view of a child."[35] However, like the films studied throughout the twelve chapters of *Politics of Children in Latin American Cinema*, it can be said that Carrillo and Andrade "challeng[e] the displacement created by the conventional subordinated role of children in cinema," and, similar to the objective carried out by the contributing authors in Paz-Mackay and Rodríguez's edited collection, this study brings "attention to the political dimension that implies to choose children as protagonists while including cinematographic mechanisms to recognize and incorporate their voices."[36]

The recognition and incorporation of children's voices is especially true of the aptly titled *Little Voices*, which exclusively features the child's voice through a soundtrack of recorded testimonies. When an adult subject does speak, it is through an indecipherable gibberish, a jargon also used at times by the child subjects themselves to, in the words of Andrade, "quitar la sensación de narración muda que la voz en off le imprime" (to remove the sensation of silent narration left by the voice-offs).[37] These voice-off testimonies that form the basis of the documentary are woven together in four narrative strands throughout the film: "Margarita" witnesses the kidnapping of her father by guerrilla forces; "Pepito" and his family are forced to abandon their home and relocate to Bogotá due to the threat of violence, the same that costs "John" – literally – an arm and a leg; and "Juanito," enticed by the promise of money for his family and drawn to the flashy weapons, chooses to leave his mother's care to join the front lines in the jungle.[38]

Given these events that shape the narrative of the Colombian-made animated documentary, Carrillo and Andrade's film can be located within a recent trend referred to by some as "unfairy tales": testimonial animated films protagonized by children of war that are created for an older audience.[39] Yet the children's testimonial drawings, which partly comprise the visual aesthetic of the film, set *Little Voices* apart from other so-called "unfairy tales" that use a more traditional style of animation solely influenced by the animators. That the film's aesthetic mimics one of the most common forms of child's play – drawing – sets up play in *Little Voices* as an integral part of childhood, and even as a harbinger of childhood itself. This motif of child's play is echoed on the narrative level of the film with its prevalence in the children's verbalized and visualized memories of their homes. Child's play permeates every aspect of their daily lives, from mealtimes to chores to bathing and bedtime, as well as every facet and institution of their society: church, school, the marketplace, and the home. The children narrate their memories of hide-and-seek, playing *cosquillas* (tickle fights), riding horses, and participating in soccer matches. Play is further emphasized by the co-directors, who fill in the testimonial narrative silences with scenes of the children playing tag, roughhousing, interacting with their pets, and schoolroom antics. Play's subsequent absence in the events surrounding their displacement indicates a loss of innocence and childhood as a result of forced relocation.

In this vein, and in the same way that many documentaries begin, *Little Voices* opens with a series of interview segments responding to unpronounced questions. However, in lieu of trademark talking-head interviews typical of adult subjects, the opening scenes are constructed to show the entire body of the child subject. Wide-angle shots emphasize the small frame of the child and allow the viewer to unequivocally get a sense of childhood as protagonist. The wide-angle shot also allows for the children to be seen either at play or notably not at play. To this end, the absence of play in a number of the opening interview segments, chronologically the most recent point in the narrative, suggests that these children have become cut off from a major portion of childhood

Little Voices makes a point about the fragility of childhood through the paradoxical representation of the displaced children as 2D childlike drawings. In this sense, then, the testimonial artwork in *Little Voices*, along with the animated aesthetic that mimics these, functions as what Honess Roe calls "non-mimetic substitution": a creative rendering of historical events in a case where only audio archival materials are available, which adds something, and suggests things through its style and tone.[40] By depicting the real narrators of these testimonies as infantile characters in the film, Carrillo and Andrade at first appear to suggest childhood's incorruptibility despite the conflict. Yet as the narrative plays out, tension builds as it becomes clear that war has had an inalterable effect on childhood. Indeed, children living through an armed conflict see their relationships and family structures affected and permanently altered, resulting in "un desajuste importante" (an important imbalance) in their development.[41] With this in mind one can see how the infantile visual aesthetic becomes inconsistent with the truths of the testimonial voice-offs, and instead, the children's drawings become an uncomfortable – uncanny, even – reminder of what has been lost at the hands of war.

Carrillo and Andrade were aware that the ambitious project of preserving the spirit of the children's spoken testimonies and conserving the simplicity of their testimonial drawings would require differing animation techniques.[42] The solution was to use three distinct types of animation, all of which are unified by showing some semblance to the children's handiwork. Based on the hundreds of drawings, the co-directors created the main characters with hard and focused outlines using vector-based animation and then rendered them into 3D. The bodies representing the four anonymous child narrators, though they are distinguished by their height, hair colour, and clothing still portray an ambiguity that would allow them to be any number of children, tacitly reaffirming that it is childhood that is at stake in the film, and childhood – not any specific child – that is the film's protagonist. By not giving a recognizable face to the four children whose testimonies are featured, the animated avatars become more readily representative of any one of the millions of displaced children.

The main characters and their families, though undeniably the work of the animators, remain faithful to a young child's drawing capabilities

Figure 1.1. "Pepito," "John," and "Margarita" (left to right) at the conclusion of *Little Voices*, created using vector animation (01:04:12)

(see figure 1.1). This is notable in their disproportionate head-to-body ratio, their simple facial features, their jointless limbs, the incorrect number of digits on their hands and feet, and the look of having been coloured by hand.

However, the oversized heads visible in the main characters are notable for more than being a mere characteristic of children's drawing capabilities. Various studies on the human figure as drawn by young victims of war and conflict converge in their conclusion that the exaggeration of the head region or face most clearly expresses and represents the psychological effect that conflict has had on its young victims.[43] In this seemingly subtle detail, we can begin to understand the expressive potential of animation that Honess Roe emphasizes: the exaggerated head size of the main characters in Carrillo and Andrade's animation style aligns itself with the idea that the conflict has had lasting psychological effects on these children. The same could be argued for the opaque colouring of the head region, as the solid fill makes this body part stand out from the rest and emphasizes its prominence.

A number of secondary characters more closely maintain the aesthetic similar to the children's original drawn figures, many of which are displayed during the film's closing credits, for their noticeably undefined features and softer lines compared to the main characters (see figure 1.2).

Figure 1.2. The undefined features and softer lines of the secondary characters (08:03:00)

The majority of these characters are the military, paramilitary, and guerrilla forces, victimizers who are notably portrayed with a more proportionate head size, tacitly re-emphasizing the psychological effect experienced by the young victims, who are depicted with much larger heads. Just as the film stresses one common protagonist, so too does it feature one antagonist. The fact that the animation style of the armed forces features less distinguished lines fittingly communicates that the distinguishing lines between the separate forces for the children are blurred in the film. To them, the armed players are all viewed as one common enemy, or conversely, as one common armed "Other."[44] Accordingly, the film does not clearly distinguish between military, paramilitary, and guerrilla action, but rather suggests that it is the conflict itself – not the individual players – that has had the greatest impact on these children. As they reveal through their testimonies within the film, "Todas las fuerzas que tengan un arma siembran terror" (All forces that carry a weapon incite fear; 00:40:50). Andrade, the film's director of animation, affirmed in an online interview for LOOP animation festival that the children "no distinguen un guerrillero de un paramilitar y solo ven que el dolor y muerte que ellos causan no tiene color alguno" (do not distinguish a guerrilla from a paramilitary and they only see that the pain and death they cause does not have any colour).[45] Thus, the unclear lines in the animation of these characters speak to the lack of distinction between these players within the war.

Figure 1.3. The "extras" generated from untouched 2D cut-outs of the children's drawings (00:02:42)

On a third level, there are what appear to be untouched 2D cut-outs of the children's drawings; their limbs and faces remain immobile and their movements are limited to the travelling of the entire cut-paper figure laterally across the scene (see figure 1.3). These drawings mainly comprise the "extras," along with numerous background images and scenery within the film.

Honess Roe identifies a leeriness voiced by animated documentary's critics, who regard animation as a "layer" that inhibits direct engagement between the audience and the (factual) participants of an animated documentary.[46] Nevertheless, the children's drawings also work practically to solve the problem of a lack of archival footage of their experiences in the Colombian conflict; that is, their incorporation should not be read as merely symbolic of the loss of childhood, as outlined above. The testimonial drawings, when paired with the verbal testimonies, also act politically and expressively in a way that a live depiction of the children could not.

Children's Testimonial Drawings: A Politics of Articulation

The narrative potential of children's drawings as testimony to their wartime experiences has been recognized and exhibited in various forms, notably in relation to conflicts arising in the Spanish-speaking world. Anthony Geist and Peter Carroll's *They Still Draw Pictures: Children's*

Art in Wartime from the Spanish Civil War to Kosovo was published in conjunction with a travelling exhibition of the same title.[47] Geist and Carroll's exhibition showcased children's drawings as historical documents that speak to the children's experiences of air raids, brutality, destruction, and homelessness with a particular focus on the Spanish Civil War. The testimonial artwork, considered "deceptively transparent,"[48] was created in the *colonias infantiles*; refugee camps designated for displaced children during and following the Spanish Civil War.

Little Voices addresses similar themes as Geist and Carroll's project, and through the same medium of children's testimonial drawings. Nevertheless, the film's infantile aesthetic was a source of confusion for audiences and critics alike, both of whom were quite possibly unfamiliar with the rising trend of the animated documentary, or accustomed to the idea of documentary animation for adult audiences, which, in the following years, would be theorized and commented upon by the likes of Honess Roe, Ward, and Kriger, among others. This means that the film was largely dismissed as children's entertainment, resulting in the low audience attendance noted above, and caused confusion among critics who were seeking to understand the animated documentary. Yet, more importantly, *Little Voices*'s release in 2010 meant that the film appeared in parallel to the emerging recognition and exploration of children's politics. Nevertheless, the limited critical attention that the film continues to receive has either been unaware of these debates or unwilling to recognize the more mundane children's politics taking place.

This should perhaps come as little surprise as, until very recently, childhood has been conceived of as a more or less apolitical field of social and cultural practices. We can attribute this to the mundane nature of the issues and contexts of children's politics, which means not only that they are often dismissed as apolitical, but also that it presents an empirical challenge for researchers. As Kallio and Häkli point out, this mundane nature in fact makes children's politics more difficult to study as "children do not express or play out their politics in the forms and terms familiar to adults, nor identify their own action as political. This pertains particularly to very young children whose politics are studied the least."[49] Ultimately, rather than perpetuate the above mentioned *image of children as politics* cinematically, Carrillo and Andrade's animated documentary offers the image *of* children's politics.

Here, a first caveat is in order regarding the authenticity of the child narrators' agentic expressions in *Little Voices*. The documentary itself suggests through a statement in its opening credits that "esta película fue dibujada y narrada por ellos" (this film was drawn and narrated by them; 00:00:48). We know, however, that despite Carrillo and Andrade's insistence that the drawings and narrations come from the displaced children, the film, on both its visual and its verbal narrative level, is also undoubtedly – and unavoidably – influenced by the adult animation team. It can be difficult, as Johanna Sköld and Ingrid Söderlind state, "to disentangle the genuine commitment of the children from the adults' initiatives and political motives."[50] However, these authors, following Alexis Artaud de La Ferrière, go on to say that "children are not necessarily politicized against their will."[51] Even if adults are active in producing children's testimonies on war, de La Ferrière argues, we should not conclude that "children themselves have no political intent or awareness within this pipeline."[52]

On the one hand, the question of authenticity within Carrillo and Andrade's animated documentary is a lot less problematic than that of the twentieth-century Swedish wartime propaganda and media representations analysed by Sköld and Söderlind. *Little Voices* has a double-testimonial nature and the children were forthright and willing participants. However, there is still work of "disentangling" to be done as the adult animation team has the final say over how the drawings and testimonies are presented. In her contributing chapter to *Art as a Political Witness*, Susanna Hast proposes a useful understanding of this dynamic when she argues that "there are practical and ethical problems in engaging children in presenting their experiences of violence in public, so for quite obvious reasons we have the adult intermediary between the child-witness and the audience."[53] Although Hast is speaking about a theatre, her ideas directly relate to the filmic text *Little Voices*. She proposes that Carly Wijs's play *Wij/Zij / Us/Them* (Belgium, 2014), about the Beslan school siege told from the child's perspective and centring on the war experience of children, takes into account not only children's victimhood but also their agency, "encourages an adult's engagement with the child's world, rather than adults imposing their world upon children."[54] Children's testimonial drawings are literally foundational to *Us/Them*, as the opening scene features two young narrators in the act of inscribing the setting of their story onto the stage on which they stand, "demarcating the lines of the blueprint of the building where the school siege took place" yet simultaneously drawing "a site of violence,"[55] in a factual, corporeal and imaginative act of storytelling that "stands out as children's agency."[56]

The adult engagement with the child's world, especially through their recreations of it, is at the heart of the articulated politics that Elwood and Mitchell speak of, as children's conversations, these authors state, are "fundamentally their story *to us* about … their own self-perceptions, and their critical awareness of how others see them."[57]

If, as Elwood and Mitchell argue, "children's representations and dialogues comprise a significant space of their political agency and formation, in which they can make and negotiate social meanings, subjectivities, and relationships,"[58] then one cannot possibly view the quasi-testimonial visual aesthetic in *Little Voices* as an erasure of Colombia's political densities and a means of creating a "depoliticized" appeal to peace in which children are located outside the political realm. *Little Voices* is, in fact, bookended by two metatextual moments that self-reflexively point to the film's constructedness as fundamentally based on the children's testimonial drawings.

In the opening sequence, amid the dark and rainy skies that frame the cityscape of Bogotá, and from within the crowd of hand-drawn characters depicted in figure 1.3, a small piece of paper is swept up on a gust of wind, seemingly emerging from the pocket of the young soldier-like subject (00:02:33–56). The soldier's drawing becomes the focal point on screen as the camera abandons the crowd to follow the creased sheet of paper on its trajectory from street level upwards to great heights marked by the city skyscrapers and subsequently inland through a corridor of buildings to the brighter skies and greener backdrop of what presumably represents the nation's interior. As the sheet of paper lifts and turns on each gust of wind, it is at times caught facing the camera in its entirety, revealing for a brief second a map-like drawing with its grid of dark roads and a number of visible landmarks, around which stand what appear to be numerous armed actors. The illustration at last flies out of the shot as the camera emerges through the final row of skyscrapers and, with a slower pace and smoother movements, scales ranges of high forested hills as it finally arrives at the populated rural areas of Colombia's interior, suggesting at once a geographical as well as a temporal leap inland and back in time to the origin of the story.

From this moment in the film's opening sequence to the closing credits during which a number of the testimonial drawings are again revealed, *Little Voices* – whether knowingly or not – "underscore[s] the persistent political significance of representations, particularly cartographic representations."[59] Fourteen drawings fade in and out on the left-hand side of the screen as the closing credits scroll upwards on the right-hand side (01:06:25–01:09:40). Each image lingers for a full ten seconds as a chilling, hypnotic tune is carried out by a single child vocalist, who is accompanied by pluckish string music and, eventually, by harmonized a cappella vocal percussion from a number of adult voices. As the first song ends, and the drawings continue to appear on screen one after another, the soundtrack shifts to a more jovial tune to close the credits sequence, one with similar vocal percussion and pluckish string music, but which features an uplifting melody tapped out on an electronic keyboard. Notably, one-half of the fourteen testimonial drawings demarcate family dwellings and farmland as places central to the children's experiences of war, and simultaneously represent these places as "site[s] of violence," to borrow Hast's term.

Echoing the more peaceful turn in the concluding soundtrack, a pair of these final cartographic representations features more serene scenes, which reflect happier times before the conflict entered the children's lives, but can also be read as one practice of representational agency highlighted by Elwood and Mitchell, where children opt to omit from their representations the places and experiences they do not like, erasing the people and activities connected to them from their representations.[60] Bright yellow suns, fruit trees, and green mountain ranges fill both scenes. Though these are common characteristics to children's art across nations and cultures,[61] and bearing in mind that Colombia is without a doubt a very fertile country, the cheery tone of these images – echoed in the film's early scenes – depict a deeper meaning, especially when set against the dark tone that permeates the city scenes, which precede and follow them. The Garden of Eden–esque way the children have drawn their home makes it appear as a utopia. The idealistic vision of their life before displacement occurred is echoed in their testimonies. As "John" explains of life on the family farm before the bombing incident that left him maimed, "Pues teníamos la fortuna; nunca nos faltó nada" (We were very fortunate; we wanted for nothing; 00:14:10).

Beyond these, seven pre- and mid-conflict cartographic representations feature numerous scenes of violence in the broader rural environment (two), children participating in, or directly experiencing, the violence (four), and one illustration that solely features dozens of explosive weapons (one). Together, these opening and closing sequences underscore that the documentary is constructed in part – and modelled in whole – on the representation-narration axis through which children's articulated politics manifest. And, whether consciously or not, the animated documentary suggests that children's narrational representations "are an extremely important site of political agency."[62] In this way, through its formal properties, *Little Voices* strays from the post-2000 tendency in Latin American cinema that perpetuates the image of children as politics, and provides instead the image of children's politics. The documentary film essentially animates agency, bringing to life the children's testimonial drawings and narrations through which they articulate, to borrow the words of Mitchell and Elwood, "their identities, perceive how they and others are being positioned, and engage these positions and relationships implied by them."[63]

These issues are especially perceptible on the verbal narrative level. Through the testimonial soundtrack, the animated documentary also dialogues with children's politics, revealing much about the mundane ways, issues, and contexts in which these manifest. Before moving on to an exploration of this idea, however, a second caveat is in order. Documentary films are inherently subjective by nature, and, being an animated documentary the question of reality versus fiction becomes even more apparent. I argue, however, along the same lines as Kallio, who also attempted an observation of children's politics through Erja Dammert's (live-action) documentary film *Sotalapset / Children of the War* (Sweden, 2003), that "the documentary film that is used as a source of material is not understood as a factual transmitter of either wartime policies or children's politics. Instead, the extracts are used to carve out the essence of children's politics, the fact that, regardless of their positions in policy fields, children do act as 'political selves.'"[64] Along these lines, in their discussion of twentieth-century Swedish media representations Sköld and Söderlind state that "sometimes children do speak and act within historical sources. As outlined in the critique of the agency ideal, it would be naive to interpret such accounts as authentic representations of children's perspectives. However, it is just as problematic to not consider what the sources might reveal about children's political and social agency."[65] This is especially the case when, although the adult animation team unavoidably interjects in the visual narrative, the verbal narrative consists in whole of the children's testimonial statements and stories.

Revealing Children's Embodied Politics at the Verbal-Visual Narrative Level

Beyond revealing and representing children's articulated politics on the formal level, from its opening scenes to its conclusion Carrillo and Andrade's animated documentary also becomes an important site for the empirical observation of children's mundane yet significant embodied politics. The pervasive testimonial statements reveal the very real ways in which children do act as "political selves," to use Kallio's term,[66] while their adult-constructed animated avatars and the animated *mise en scène* reflect many possible ways in which these or other children have or might have or might possibly exercise their political agency. Through its verbal and visual narration of the (cinematically) interwoven lives of the four child narrators, *Little Voices* exposes tactics through which children's embodied politics can arise. We see a resistance to or sustaining of rural identities within an urban home, a dismissal of the hegemonic discourse of "child in need of protection" through affirmations of children as self-governing agents, young children's capacity for caring agency and practices of concern, and the ways, issues, and contexts in which children can acknowledge subjectivities of innocent victim or actively committed child in the armed conflict.

To begin, the aforementioned opening interview segments strongly communicate a resistance to urban identity and an adherence to a rural identity through the children's speech acts; a sentiment dramatically emphasized by the adult animation team as they visually reiterate and exaggerate such opinions by visually depicting these child narrators as engaged in play that symbolically points to their home in the countryside while they verbally communicate their preference for rural life. This feeling is clearly expressed by the archival voice-off ascribed to the character of Pepito, who appears in the film's opening scene: "No me gusta Bogotá porque, por ejemplo, en el barrio donde yo vivo, donde vivo con mi mamá, en ese barrio pues por nada pelean. Por ejemplo, cuando se emborrachan, pelean y se apuñalean" (I do not like Bogotá. In the neighbourhood where I live with my mother people are fighting all the time. They get drunk and fight and stab each other; 00:00:55). Pepito's distaste for his new urban environment, or rather, his longing for life on his family farm, is reiterated by the fact that his animated avatar, a young, dark-haired boy who sits atop a bed inside his new home, still sports a traditional *sombrero vueltiao* (turned hat) despite his indoor and urban location, and plays with various animal figurines. In the background of the shot, behind Pepito and on his bedroom wall, are five haphazardly hung drawings of the same horse and two dogs occupying forest and mountain scenes.

In this opening scene, Pepito's hat, his toys in his hand, and the drawings featured behind his figure can be read as an illustration of the child narrator's awareness – despite his young age – of his displaced status, as well as a rejection of this subject position through his avid imaginings and recreations of home and, as Lind argues of children in the UK who are aware of their status as deportable, as a means of "offer[ing] their own definitions of who they are and where they belong."[67] The animated *mise en scène*, which surrounds the boy with bucolic images and symbols, visually echoing the verbal sentiment that he "does not like Bogotá," shows a verbal resistance to urban identity while also visually communicating a will to sustain a rural one. The resulting effect is that Pepito at once embodies the "dual aspect of children's agency" of resist and sustain that Lind explores.[68] With these assertive words and potent imagery that form the opening visual-verbal narration of the documentary film, one can see animation's communicative potential, being an aesthetic that is entirely made rather than resulting from registering a pro-filmic reality. Animated visuals are, as Charles Forceville notes, "to an unusually large extent under the control of the creator."[69] Building on this idea, Paul Wells, in *Understanding Animation*, argues that animation permits the film-maker "to be more expressive and thus more subversive."[70]

Although these scholars are theorizing about animated works of fiction, their understanding of animation's communicative power no doubt also extends to the animated documentary genre. From this initial scene in *Little Voices*, one can feel a tension between the archival and the animated – that is, the voice-off and the visual aesthetic – or rather, between reality and fiction. Little doubt is left in the viewer's mind as to the veracity of the young boy's verbal testimony, while the animated *mise en scène* as well as his avatar are undoubtedly constructions – whether based on his real appearance, home, and habits or not – manufactured by the adult animation team. However, the question in animated documentary, as Honess Roe and now many others have so clearly pointed out, is not of animation's veracity, but rather the way (or multiple ways) that animation functions as a representational strategy in the portrayal of certain subjects, events, and settings that a documentary film depicts.

It is clear from this initial interview segment in Carrillo and Andrade's *Little Voices* that, beyond reflecting the children's testimonial drawings, the animated aesthetic should be understood as a visual expression and exaggeration of the archival, essentially becoming emblematic of the embodied politics being expressed. "Pepito's" knowledge of the urban violence, which he describes in a rather detached, matter-of-fact voice using the third-person plural and thus demarcating an us/them, reveals an urban consciousness that has already been instilled into him, while Pepito's resistance to the city – or sustaining of a rural identity – which is reiterated by his imaginative play, highlights how, in the words of Lind, "children in an irregular situation have to manage … multiple subject positions."[71] In the case of this first child narrator, as well as the others, this includes subjectivities such as displaced rural citizen and outsider city-dweller, while the scene also verbally and visually narrates how children in this irregular situation navigate a tension between being an informed rather than ignorant – or innocent – child. Moreover, the way that "Pepito" is drawn, and likewise the way that he is drawn into a world of imaginative bucolic play, symbolically suggests an everyday struggle "to assert the right to decide on [one's] own identity and belonging."[72] Here it should be noted that I, like Lind, do not aim to idealize children's dual political agency of resisting and sustaining certain subject positions, but rather highlight "that it comes about as a reaction to the repressive context of [displacement] that no one should have to experience."[73]

In short, this opening scene reveals that, while the testimonial sound track permits one to empirically observe, or more appropriately perhaps, perceive, the very real ways in which children verbally practise embodied politics, the animated aesthetic allows the spectator to envision these or other forms of embodied politics that may or may not have really occurred, but which are undoubtedly very real – albeit mundane – forms of children's political expression and participation. A similar case of resisting and sustaining subject positions like that of the displaced child can be seen in a following segment within the opening interviews scene. The voice-off of a young, female child narrator, whose testimony is visualized on screen by the character of Margarita, begins her opening statement in a way that echoes that of "Pepito." The young girl reveals of her mother and sisters that "es que en la casa estamos contentas pero en el barrio no. Porque por allá van los señores y matan muchachos. Mi mamá está buscando a veces si se puede ir, pero la casita ¿cómo se hace?"(at home, we're happy, but out in our neighbourhood it's different. There are men there that kill children. My mom would like to leave, but where would we live?; 00:01:25). It is evident from the words of the young girl that belonging depends as much on place as it does people, while her identity remains tied to the countryside. While "Margarita" expresses the complacency her family members feel within their new home, she also reveals a disenchantment with and fear of her surrounding environment. This is a complete reversal – as the spectator will soon learn – of her childhood and upbringing on the family ranch. The second part of the film reveals that the farmer's daughter is always at play outdoors, the family orchard her playground and the livestock and her sisters and parents her playful companions.

The dark, urban location that forms the setting of her opening interview statement is a far cry from the tranquil pastures that "Margarita" would leave behind following the family's displacement after the forced disappearance of her father. While the testimonial soundtrack plays, on screen a long shot reveals Margarita perched on a swing that hangs from a dilapidated swing set. The long shot reveals the location of the play structure to be adjacent to a busy urban traffic zone. Passing buses and numerous other vehicles in the background reinforce the notion that this is a rather precarious place for a park. Arguably, the image of a swing set evokes the notion of carefree childhood, yet the setting of a high-traffic street corner, especially after nightfall, calls to mind the notion of being "out of place" while also evoking Sandra Karlsson's notion that children's "everyday political acts of resistance are manifested through their struggle to access play."[74] The *mise en scène* suggests this struggle, while the way that "Margarita's" animated avatar does not interact with the swing set emphasizes the fact that the young girl is no longer characterized by a playful nature. Rather, in this initial scene, which is chronologically the most recent point in the filmic narrative, Margarita is characterized by grown-up preoccupations and knowledge that juxtapose her infancy suggested by her pigtails, hair bows, and pink, well-worn play dress and apron.

Mia Schöb notes that the impact of the city is twofold: on the one hand, it allows them to recuperate their childhood, while, on the other hand, they have moved from one violent reality to another. They experience re-victimization within the city; this one being more dark and crowded than their rural home.[75] "Margarita's" confession reveals that she now faces a double dose of violence: that which led to her displacement to the city, and the new dangers the city life brings. As one study explains, Colombia's urban areas have suffered from violence in the form of homicides, whereas the rural populations have suffered from violence in the form of armed confrontations, massacres, and displacement.[76] Caught in a cycle of violence, displaced children become re-victimized in their post-conflict environment not only for discrimination, poverty, and exclusion that can accompany displacement but also new forms of violence characteristic of their new surroundings.

On the one hand, the animated *mise en scène*, as well as the fact that there is no adult present in the scene to either watch over or even push the young girl on the swing, tacitly foreshadows the disappearance of her father, which is documented later in the filmic text yet also suggests one common form of children's political agency highlighted by Kallio and Häkli: "children's self-governing political agencies."[77] As the pair of researchers note, children, by resisting dominating power structures and uncomfortable orders can act as self-governing actors "nearly anywhere: At school, at work, on streets, in parks, in public and private vehicles, in shopping centers, at refugee camps, in virtual communities – that is, *in* childhood."[78] Here again, however, I want to emphasize that children's self-governing political agencies are not idealized, but rather seen as the result of the effects the violent conflict has had on their family structure, as well as on an unfortunate and undesired displacement. Kallio and Bartos note "the fragile life situations that make [refugee children] extremely vulnerable" but, as these authors continue, their status as refugees "in no way detracts from their opportunities for political agency. Rather, these children develop political subjectivities that are both a result of their vulnerabilities and are also fundamentally a result of being human."[79] While these two authors specifically theorize about child refugees, the same can certainly be argued for the internally displaced.

In fact, beyond the visual suggestion that the young girl must take responsibility for herself, the young narrator's final opening statement – "Pero la casita ¿cómo se hace?" (But where would we live?) – reveals an identification and understanding of political aspects, as well as a reflexivity that characterizes, according to Kallio, a "turning period" in their politics in which children can be understood to become adults, in terms of their political agency rather than their age.[80] From where Margarita sits, her lacklustre effort to swing, the broken swing beside her, and the absence of other playmates suggest that the young girl is in fact on the precipice of adulthood, a nuanced visual nod to the film's overarching message that childhood is lost in the face of war as symbolically communicated by the non-mimetic infantile animation style, as previously discussed. This same sentiment is later played out in the documentary film – which is chronologically an earlier point in the testimony of her life – at the moment of her father's forced disappearance. As the voice-off recalls, "Llegaron algunos señores con pistolas y tapadas la boca … y me dio un beso y me dijo que no me preocupara y que nos fue … porque no nos pasara nada" (00:47:30), on screen Margarita gives her father an embrace as he symbolically places his hat on her head. The hat appears too large on the girl's small frame and out of place on top of her pigtails, an exceptionally childlike hairstyle (see figure 1.4).

Yet the hat symbolizes the idea that it is time for Margarita to don her grown-up clothes, so to speak, albeit too soon, and this scene, like many others in the documentary film, challenges common correlations between age and agency. In this moment, the girl's youth is emphasized as she screws up her face in a defiant childlike pout. However, the fact that her pout does not escalate into a tantrum but rather into a controlled frown as she waves goodbye to her father, who is led away at gunpoint, can be read not as a child with a complete lack of power or agency, but rather as an agentic expression "of the silent child, or the conformist child acting in line with adults' expectations."[81] In this moment, while donning the symbolic hat, what is unspoken but clearly illustrated for the spectator is the fact that Margarita knowingly assumes the role of head of the family. The suggested shift from receiver of care to what Kallio and Bartos calls "practitioner of care" reflects a significant yet under-acknowledged aspect of children's agency signalled by these authors: children's relationship to care.[82] As Kallio and Bartos further assert, children daily "negotiate moments of dis-ease, inequality, suffering and conflict, which sets the stage for caring practices

Figure 1.4. Donning adulthood (00:48:16)

to develop."[83] These practices can involve care for siblings, parents, grandparents, and other family members, as well as fellow displaced travellers, and can manifest in practical ways, such as the sharing of food or the running of errands, but also in "more subtle, long-term ways of maintaining and creating caring relations with other children, youth, adults and the elderly."[84]

Prior to this shift, however, "Margarita's" testimony reveals the more mundane and childlike ways in which children act as political selves within their everyday environments, in part doing what Bosco calls the "micro-political work" that many children carry out in their daily contexts, such as family help.[85] The very first sequence following the aforementioned geographical and temporal jump inland and back in time unfolds as "Margarita" explains daily life on their family farm. The three young sisters, who have just awoken, start their day after their father has already milked the cows and brought home fresh milk for breakfast. The animation communicates a meal happily shared, after which, habitually, as "Margarita" narrates, the girls would wash themselves as their father would bid them farewell to return to work "a sacar el ganado" (to let out the cattle; 00:05:45–00:06:28). As the girl's voice-off goes on to narrate how their father would rejoin the family for lunch, his animated figure walks past the sisters as they playfully bathe in the yard with the water running through a hose connected to the wash basin their mother is preoccupying herself with, and subsequently out of the shot towards – we are led to believe – the livestock.

The camera then cuts to the following scene, where the father emerges from the background and enters a coffee field that fills the foreground of the shot. With this cut occurs not only what is presumably a jump forwards in time but also a shift in the testimonial voice-off ascribed to Margarita. In this scene, the testimony of the first young girl narrator is amalgamated with that of another, who is, presumably, the daughter of a coffee farmer. As the new voice-off narrates the happenings of the harvest, the animation takes on a didactic function, showing a personified coffee bean humorously drying and roasting itself, while alternating narrative shots reveal Margarita and her younger sister at play among the harvesters (00:06:40–00:07:18).

Although not a prominent tactic employed by Carrillo and Andrade throughout the film, the weaving together of multiple children's testimonies in this moment allows for the perception of children's politics from a variety of anonymous subjects that share, we are to understand, experiences that are quite universal to a child's upbringing against the backdrop of Colombia's armed conflict. As the father drives a truck towards the unnamed town, loaded up with the harvested coffee as well as Margarita and her sisters, the party passes through an armed road block. This is one of the first visual cues, following the opening interview scenes, created by the directors to signal the proximity of the conflict to these children's lives. Sure enough, a third child's voice is woven in to the soundtrack of this scene, as a means of telling us that the farm vehicle's destination is "el pueblito que se llama 'Pueblo Arrecho'" (a little town called "Savage City"), a place that, as the voice-off goes onto reveal, "se llama San Luis de la Isla, pero le dicen así porque casi todos los domingos matan gente" (is named San Luis de la Isla, but people call it that because every Sunday people are killed there; 00:08:24).

The scaffolding of the three testimonies shows a progression from children's awareness of the work of others, to their own micro-political work and, finally, to what I call their "politics of concern." While nearly all of the child narrators express their duty and obligation to helping out the family before and after the conflict directly interrupted their lives, many also express how their role in and knowledge of the family's economic stability has changed amid the conflict and following their displacement (as seen in the case of "Margarita" above), ultimately reshaping their practices of practical and relational care into practices of care in the psychological sense as they develop and express concerns for family wellbeing.

Certain narrative threads even allow us to perceive how, under the weight of the conflict, children's micro-political work and caring practices carried out within the family home are supplemented and/or supplanted by a politics of concern. We see this in the case of "John," for example, who retrospectively narrates his obligations to the household leading up to his accident, where he would help his mother to prepare dinner, take care of the sweeping and mopping, as well as many other daily household chores (00:48:26). While prior to his displacement, "John's" micro-political work and caring practices were carried out within the family home, his opening interview statements reveal a shift in the magnitude of these to become a concern about the family home itself. The voice-off narrates that the young boy's parents "vendieron la casa a casi regalada" (sold the house for so cheap they almost gave it away) and goes on to reveal the boy's awareness of and preoccupation with the fact that "no era el dinero que se merecía esta casa porque era una finca hermosa. Hoy quedamos casi en la calle" (it wasn't the price that the house deserved because it was a beautiful farm. Today we're almost homeless; 00:02:09).

To emphasize the boy's knowledge of the likelihood of a life on the streets, the directors draw John into a dimly lit streetscape, symbolically placing him on the luminal space of the kerb. The carefully constructed setting emphasizes the loss of his family's cherished farmland, once again demonstrating that in animated films, the communicative power of the *mise en scène* is, in the words of Forceville, "to an unusually large extent under the control of the creator."[86] This scene, like the one featuring Margarita, with its absence of adult subjects and a dark and precarious setting, once again emphasizes the reality but also heightened necessity for displaced children to act as self-governing agents.

A third testimony from the opening interview sequence reiterates children's self-governing capabilities and their politics of concern in the context of displacement. The testimonial thread tied to a nameless young boy on screen does not advance, save for one scene mid-film that employs a subjective lens and shaky cam to depict the armed combat entering his town as well as his family home. In one of the film's most understated and tragic moments, an explosion and an abrupt fade to red on screen, coupled with the silencing of gunshots and the boy's frightened whimpers, signals the death of the armed intruder and, ultimately we are led to believe, of the boy too, who was watching the action from his hiding spot inside a wardrobe (00:35:18–00:36:20). This fictional scene at the midway point of the film can be read as the co-directors' tacit nod to the little voices that were silenced by the conflict, and the creation of the boy's character can ultimately be read as a foil to the four main child narrators, who survive the violence to tell their stories.

With the boy's implied death, however, we find an inconsistency in the documentary film, as the same character's appearance in the opening interview scene suggests (but does not confirm) that he has in fact survived this event and has relocated along with the other children to the city. It is in this opening segment where a young voice-off tied to this character narrates how "mi papá a veces que trabaja y echarle al facto y a veces no le sale trabajo. Muy a veces que llega a las nueve porque si uno, si él llega a las nueve gana más plata y si él llega más temprano gana menos plata. Pues, si con esto estamos haciendo el mercado para comer" (my dad sometimes works in construction. He does not always have work. And sometimes he does not return until nine o'clock. On those days, he earns more money than when he returns earlier. When he comes home early, he earns less money. It is because of this that we are able to go to the market and buy food; 00:01:43). Similar, then, to the way that "John" employs the third person to express concern about how he and his family are nearly homeless, this young child's use of *estamos* (we are) in relation to making ends meet reveals a comparable politics of concern. Ultimately, this type of testimonial statement perceptible throughout Carrillo and Andrade's documentary film, together with their animated iterations, reveal a dismissal of the imagined or expected "dependent child in need of protection," most often realized, as Brocklehurst notes, in images and literary sources,[87] and acknowledge not only the micro-political work, following Bosco, or children's care agencies, following Kalli and Bartos, but also what has been called here a "politics of concern."

As a final area of exploration I want to turn to the less-theorized perspective of the child soldier's political agency. This is one aspect that makes *Little Voices* a particularly transgressive cultural product. Carrillo himself states in an interview for the prominent Spanish-language global news source *El País* that "para mí era importante ver tanto a niños víctimas como a victimarios" (it was just as important for me to see child victims as victimizers).[88] Carrillo's comments regarding his intention to show the other side of the conflict – the recruitment of children as armed agents – are specifically said in response to a question of what makes his documentary film different from Arbeláez's *The Colours of the Mountain*.[89] As Carrillo simply puts it, "Lo otro es ficción, esta es la realidad" (The other is fiction; this is reality).[90]

Little Voices is no doubt highly reminiscent of Arbeláez's film, told from the child's perspective with scenes taking place on the *fincas* (farms), in the local markets, family home, and schoolhouse that are one and the same, save for their differing veneers of live action and animation. In fact, drawing and colouring play an important role for *The Colours*'s young protagonist Manuel, as the film's title suggests. Other forms of play, namely soccer, also play a prominent role. However, in Arbeláez's take on the conflict, while violence is perceived by the children it ultimately does not hinder them from being children. The adult figures, namely the guerrilla forces, teachers, and parental figures are directly affected by violence and displacement, while the children are bystanders. Carrillo and Andrade's film, though more childlike in form, does not hesitate to show the high stakes of childhood in times of conflict.

Meanwhile, the storyline of "Juanito" in Carrillo and Andrade's animated documentary provides a very intimate and forthright look into the reality of children's participation in armed conflict, which remained an especially pertinent issue until the 2016 Peace Accord between the Colombian government and FARC officially began the demobilization process of minors aged fifteen years and under from the guerrilla camps as one it its humanitarian aims. In the opening interview, a medium shot features the adolescent boy's animated avatar leaning forwards onto a kitchen table, the weight of the psychological burden that he carries symbolically represented by the animated figure's hunched back and the way that he rests on his elbows as he fiddles absent-mindedly with a spoon before slumping further forwards to rest his chin on his forearms. The main action in this scene surrounds a cloud of steam rising from a pair of pots on a stove, which, thanks to the slightly left and low-angle shot used in lieu of the traditional head-on angle for talking-head interviews, appears directly behind the subject's dark-haired head. Together, the action of the spoon handled by the character and the boiling pots in the background evoke the popular Spanish idiom *Nadie sabe lo que hay en la olla más que la cuchara que la menea* (roughly translated as "No one knows what's in the pot except the one who stirs it"). The animation, in other words, becomes highly symbolic – even poetic – as it conveys the idea that the boy holds in his mind the psychological trauma that his subjective experience in armed combat has left him with. The popular saying, as famed philologist Jesús Cantera Ortiz de Urbina reminds us, is meant to signify an intimate experience that is understood or known only to those extremely close to the subject.[91]

At this moment, the voice-off begins to narrate that "no tengo ni amigos ya, porque no debe estar ni uno vivo ya … porque los que éramos buenos amigos siempre lo mandaban solamente a batallar" (I don't even have friends anymore because not one should be alive anymore … because they always sent someone to fight from those of us who were good friends; 00:01:11). The animated avatar's listlessness in this present moment features in sharp contrast to the young boy's playful nature pre-combat and even his initial attraction and excitement towards the idea of participating as a soldier in the conflict. Ultimately, the testimony revealed through the character of "Juanito" reveals that, despite the fact that sixteen is the international age limit for a soldier's voluntary recruitment, many participants are in fact much younger than this, as noted by Brocklehurst in *Who's Afraid of Children?*[92] "Juanito's" testimony also coincides with the fact that, of a statistic of hundreds of thousands of child soldiers, the majority are active in government armed forces while the youngest ones are often found within armed (or guerrilla) groups.[93] In the case of the Colombian armed conflict, the boy's testimonial voice-off reveals that "muchos niños entraron. Habían, bueno, como trienta y seis o trienta y siete. Y eran menores que yo, el mayor tenía quince años y el resto diez. Nos enseñaron como tirar al blanco y todo eso" (many children entered [the fight]. There were, well, like thirty-six or thirty-seven. And they were younger than I was; the oldest was fifteen years old and the rest were ten. They taught us how to shoot targets and all that; 00:28:00).

As Brocklehurst, following Carol Bellamy, notes of Colombia specifically, child soldiers had specific roles "designed for them based on pejorative assumptions about their physical and mental underdevelopment and opportunities these afford."[94] Their nicknames reflect these roles, as children used as expendable sentries are designated by the military as "little bells," and as "little bees" within guerrilla forces for their ability to "sting" their enemies before they know they are under attack. Brocklehurst continues this with the statement that "in war, the 'choice' for many children has been to shoot or be shot."[95] As "Juanito" divulges, "Sí, estaba en combate, pero no … me dio mucho miedo … me metí de otro lado de un palo … y todos tirando menos yo … hasta que llegó un [comandante] y me dijo, 'si no disparas te mataré.' Quité el seguro de eso y comencé tirar, gasté dos cargadores y corrí" (I was in combat, but I was afraid to fire, to expose myself … I hid behind a big tree. Everyone was shooting except me … until a corporal came to me and said, "Shoot or I'll kill you." I did not want him to kill me, so I obeyed. I went there, I left my tree and I started shooting. I emptied two chargers and I ran; 00:37:40).

The boy's sobering words juxtapose the initial attraction and interest shown, not only in joining the armed forces, but also in the weapons themselves: "Y llegó el comandante llegó a la casa bien tranquilo y bien, como siempre llegan respetuosos … Me mostró una revista muy bonita con las armas que tenían, decían que no me preocupara si era pobre porque con ellos ganaría mucho dinero. Y por si acaso, me dieron 50.000 pesos para que me fuera" (And the commander arrived at our house quite calmly and well, the way that they always arrive respectfully … He showed me a beautiful magazine with the arms that they had, and he was saying that I should not worry if I was poor because with them I would earn a lot of money. And, just in case, they gave me 50,000 pesos to get me to go; 00:17:57).

The boy's words reflect what Michael Wyness, following Mats Utas, calls a "tactical agency" in which "children make an assessment that in some cases military involvement is a life-saving or at least a life stretching possibility."[96] In other words, they not only "contribute to their material and social survival" but also "demonstrate their capacity to take political action."[97] In fact, this attitude of tactical attraction towards combat is reflected in another interwoven testimony; a voice-off ascribed to Margarita's otherwise unvoiced older sister. In a scene taking place within the town of San Luis de la Isla, to which the coffee farmer and his three daughters have arrived, Margarita and her sisters enter a billiard hall, occupied by a mix of civilians and uniformed combatants (00:08:40–00:09:40). A sequence of mid and close-up shots reconstruct a rather flirtatious interaction between Margarita's elder sister and one combatant. As he leans in close to place his cap on her head, the voice-off explains, "Entonces me lo ponían me median la boina y me decían que me sea una mona linda, esa mona linda se debe ver el uniforme y con la boina" (They put the beret on my head and said to me, "You're cute, but you'd be even more so in uniform"). What happens near the end of the narration is that the objective shot abruptly shifts to a subjective one in which a radiating spotlight in the midst of a cheerful yellow background highlights the image of the young girl as the skirt of her sexualized combat uniform blows upwards while she leans forwards in a Marilyn Monroe–esque pose, laughing as she tries to keep the fabrics of her skirt under control. Here, the camera switches to an objective shot once again with a close-up in which the adolescent girl's face fills the screen, her slowly blinking eyes emphasizing her contemplation of the combatant's words. The voice-off continues, "Entonces yo no les decían nada y me decían ¿Por qué yo no me vaya con ellos? Porque si yo me vaya con ellos quizás me haría mucho mejor porque ellos ofrecían de todo de cierto" (I said nothing. They wanted me to follow them, they told me that my life would be more pleasant, that I would have everything I needed). Following this we see a shot from the exterior of the building, framed through the doorway of the hall, which shows the combatant lifting the girl onto a pool table as she in turn emits a subtle smile. Simultaneous to this, alternating shots that show Margarita caring for the youngest sister, who wanders towards the oversized AK-47s leaning against the wall of the billiard hall.

The singular subjective scene can be read as an animated iteration, albeit an exaggeration, of the fact that the girl considers the young soldier's offer, also verbalized in her statement "Gracias a dios que nunca me convencieron ir con ellos" (Thank God that they never convinced me to go with them). The use of the verb *convencer* (to convince or persuade) in the girl's testimonial statement reflects the fact that, as Wyness notes, children exercise "economic" agency; that is, "their ability to make adjustments to their lives in contexts of severe material uncertainty," including considering the military a viable option.[98] Accordingly, her utterance, exaggerated by the visual narration, reads as a resistance to the hegemonic subjectivity of child soldiers "viewed as relatively passive victims with little control over their lives, unable to understand and interpret their social conditions and unable to respond or adjust to them."[99]

In opposition to this potential recruit, "Juanito" chooses to enlist and is drawn into a group of young recruits playing soccer en route to the base camp. Their carefree attitude despite their destination suggests that they are naive to the horrors of war for which they have signed up. This especially in light of reported statistics that 43 per cent of deceased guerrilla members and 41 per cent of captured guerrilla members were minors.[100] Further, as the trio of boys clamber into the back of a pick-up truck, their demeanour reveals that the recruits view the experience as a joyride, and their enlistment an adventure, a sentiment reiterated in the boy's words upon their arrival at camp: "En el campamento nos bajamos y nos recibieron bien, ¡que bienvenida! Y nos recibieron con buena comida" (We got out at the camp and they received us well. What a welcome! And they received us with good food; 00:21:50–00:22:45). This scene suggests that even the conflict itself for some of these children was conceptualized as a game.

However, a sobering moment and turning point in the film occurs when play is physically replaced by violence. The young recruits' soccer ball is sequestered and deflated by a soldier upon their arrival at camp, and in the following scene "Juanito" and the other boys are handed guns as a stark replacement to their former toy as they are instructed on how to shoot. Although the aim of both games is to shoot, the ball and the bullet have markedly different impacts on their target, as well as on the marksman. The deflated ball at the hands of the recruiter is symbolic of a transition from boyhood to manhood. Play – that is, childhood – becomes victim of war, and war has irrevocable effects on these young boys' childhood as indicated by the boy's testimony in the opening interview sequence. The testimony of the child soldier reveals the shift towards a disenchantment with the reality of warfare when base-camp drills turn deadly and "a los que estaban bien lastimados mataban, Si no sálvese quien pueda" (they would kill those who were badly injured. If you couldn't save yourself, no one could; 00:31:56).

Eventually "Juanito" tells of his desire and decision to desert: "Un día entre nosotros pusimos un plan, todos los pequeñitos y nos pusimos un plan de librarnos" (One day between all of us we made a plan, we and all the little children made a plan to liberate ourselves; 00:56:39). Although the plan fails, and ultimately proves fatal for a few young recruits, "Juanito" does manage to secure his freedom – officially – when a cousin comes to liberate him, saving the boy from, as the voice-off reveals, a life in hiding (01:01:40).

In the end, and in opposition to the many, narrow depictions of child soldiers in twenty-first-century popular Western media, what *Little Voices* achieves is, in the words of Myriam Denov, a representation of "the children behind the guns [and] the complexity of their wartime and post-war experiences."[101] The tendency has been to "'pathologise' children in armed conflict" through portraying them as largely threatening, and uncivilized, or "dangerous" and "disorderly," or, in stark contrast to this as either "victims" or heroes. Such depictions, as Denov notes, "draw from some of our most romanticised contemporary western conceptions of childhood and its association with innocence and vulnerability. Children are cast as dependent, helpless, victimised and incapable of rational decision-making."[102] *Little Voices*, conversely, reveals the ways in which children's experiences in the Colombian armed conflict defy these three categorical representations. Instead, and again in the words of Denov, they embody "greater ambiguity and complexity ... turn[ing] simultaneously around the shifting realities of victimisation, participation and resistance."[103]

Little Voices opposes the more conventional live-action aesthetic for narrating children's very real and complex experiences amid and against the backdrop of the Colombian armed conflict. The distinctive blend of children's testimonial drawings, CG animation and live testimonial material in this film not only make this take on the Colombian armed conflict stand out from previous live-action portrayals, but further this animation style expressively speaks to the effect that conflict has on its youngest victims. Carrillo's two-pronged interview technique of verbal and visual testimony acts in a therapeutic way similar to the nightmare-mastery technique *Draw Your Bad Dream* developed by Nancy Boyd Webb. Webb purports that the act of drawing the nightmare helps children reduce their fears. Once the picture transfers from mind to paper, it becomes an external object that can be controlled, mastered, and ultimately destroyed in a way of the child's choosing.[104] In this case, however, rather than being destroyed as a means of gaining power over the traumatic memory or experience, the children's drawings are narratively *deployed*, in so doing revealing agentic power that children have within and despite these very experiences. Further, graphic depiction and play based dramatization allows displaced children of an armed conflict to process much of the anguish associated with episodes of war.[105]

It has been argued here, however, that beyond serving as a means to process their experiences, the narrative representations of wartime experience, featured in part and modelled in whole in the filmic narrative, can also be read as a form of children's politics. The formal composition of *Little Voices* mimics how children are able to "ascribe, communicate, and re-write social meanings in narrations and visual representations of everyday spaces and experiences."[106] Further following Mitchell and Elwood, these visual/verbal narrations and representations "matter as sites of political formation where they form and know themselves and others as situated actors in the world."[107]

This present chapter has also highlighted how Carrillo and Andrade's feature-length documentary stands as proof that, in the current landscape of twenty-first-century Latin American cinema, it cannot be assumed that child-centred narratives about conflict or otherwise are either apolitical, or that adult production teams appropriate the image of children as politics. Rather, *Little Voices* evidences one way in which Colombian cinema challenges this predominant trend. Because of its significance, Carrillo and Andrade's documentary film should be viewed as an important cultural artefact in which we can continue the work of observing and exploring the image *of* children's politics.

A discussion of an animated documentary's politics arising from aesthetic decisions is further developed in the next chapter, while remaining focused on Latin American directors and twentieth-century Latin American history, and while staying within the realm of feature-length animated documentary film. Chapter 2's analysis of María Seoane's Flash-animated biopic of Argentina's famed former first lady, *Eva de la Argentina / Eva from Argentina* (Argentina, 2011), will explore two additional ways in which animation fosters a political gaze when taken up as an aesthetic tool in documentary film: on the one hand, as backwards-looking historical revisionism (i.e., a myth-building tool) and, on the other, as a forward-thinking medium through which sociopolitical ideologies of the past can be drawn (both literally and figuratively) into the present, with politics of the future in mind.

2 What's in a "cómic animado" (Animated Comic)? Poetics, Politics, and Personal Myths of Peronism in María Seoane's *Eva de la Argentina / Eva from Argentina* (2011)

María Seoane's *Eva de la Argentina / Eva from Argentina* (Argentina, 2011) is a 2D Flash-animated film that reconstructs the events surrounding the too-short life and death of Eva Perón (1919–52), born María Eva Duarte and affectionately called *Evita* by her Peronist supporters.[1] As the second wife of three-time Argentine president (1946–52, 1952–5, and 1973–4) Juan Domingo Perón, Eva earned a named for herself during her brief stint as first lady before succumbing to cervical cancer at the age of thirty-three. Though all of these names are highly charged with emotion, not all are affirming. To some, Evita was the defender of the poor and advocate for women's suffrage. To others, especially members of the Argentine bourgeoisie, she was a social climber, a prostitute, and a Nazi-fascist sympathizer. Now, over half a century following Eva's passing, and over one full century since her upbringing in the village of Los Toldos as an impoverished, illegitimate, and "humiliated child," as Julia Kristeva notes,[2] the memory of the B-grade film actress turned "Spiritual Leader of the Nation" continues to stir up strong emotions as the most beloved and hated figure in Argentine history.[3]

It is no small wonder then that the memory of Eva Perón continues to inspire myriad products of Western visual culture, from the theatre stage to the big and small screen. The best known of these is undoubtedly Alan Parker's *Evita* (USA, 1996), a filmic adaptation of Tim Rice and Andrew Lloyd Webber's Tony-winning rock opera from exactly twenty years prior, in which Madonna gave a Golden Globe–winning performance in her portrayal as the young Argentine philanthropist and leader. When it comes to the cinematic genre of documentary in particular, there are too many films to name. However, we can cite a unifying tendency as the attempt by film-makers to show Eva Perón in a new light through deliberate decision making regarding a film's formal elements and aesthetic features.

For example, in Tristán Bauer's *Evita, La tumba sin paz / Evita, the Tomb without Peace* (Argentina, 1997) we see live-action re-enactments using actors and a period *mise en scène* rather than strictly relying upon available archival materials. Meanwhile, María Mazzorotolo's *Evita, otra mirada / Evita, Another Look* (Argentina, 2010) is composed on the basis of a collection of personal photographs of Eva taken by twentieth-century photographer and father to the film-maker Alfredo Mazzorotolo. Back on American soil we find a second film simply named *Evita* (USA, 2008), this one a documentary by Argentine-American film-maker Eduardo Montes-Bradley, who incorporates previously unseen historical footage and documents into his film that runs just over one hour.

None, however, had attempted to approach the polarizing biographical subject through the art of animation. That is, until the making of Seoane's film, which relies on the technique of cut-out animation for the (minimal) movements of its 2D characters, whose figures are outlined in strong black lines lending to them a caricaturesque appearance and creating dimension between these and the realistically drawn backgrounds. The result is a not-so-subtle comics-like aesthetic, a filmic style the director herself refers to as the "cómic animado" (animated comic).[4] Ultimately, *Eva from Argentina*'s aesthetic underscores the creative collaboration that Seoane sought with the late Argentine comics artist, Francisco Solano López (1928–2011), famed illustrator of the science fiction comics epic *El Eternauta / The Eternaut*, considered by many to be the most significant comic produced within the nation.[5] The post-apocalyptic humans-versus-extraterrestrials narrative, whose battle scenes play out in the streets of the Argentine capital city of Buenos Aires, has been hailed as the nation's best-loved science fiction comics series,[6] and broader still, one of the most significant cultural texts arising from Argentina's turbulent mid twentieth century.[7]

Interwoven into this "animated comic" aesthetic are archival materials in the form of photographs, newsreel clips, and reconstructed newspapers. These often appear in the hands of the film's narrator, Rodolfo Walsh, a fictionalized version of the prominent investigative journalist who was disappeared in Buenos Aires in 1977 (along with, it should be noted, Héctor Germán Oesterheld, original writer of *The Eternaut*). Rodolfo's verbal narrative reconstructions of history are delivered through a documentary-style voice-over, through which Argentine actor Carlos Portaluppi (1967–) participates in Seoane's film. In tune with *Eva from Argentina*'s hybrid visual aesthetic, these reconstructed narrations are supplemented by archival audio recordings of the real Juan and Eva Perón in their various speeches and public addresses from throughout their time in office while their otherwise voiceless animated figures re-enact these and other historic moments on screen.

Undoubtedly, from *Eva from Argentina* we should expect nothing other than the documentation of Eva Perón's life through the lens of investigative journalism, given that this is a major component of Seoane's successful and multifaceted career as economist, director of national radio channels and cultural magazines, and author of numerous works of historical fiction. By employing Rodolfo as an extradiegetic narrator in the retelling of Eva's story, Seoane not only creates a layer of distance and objectivity between herself and the subject whose life story she analyses and interprets, but the film-maker also skirts a traditional (i.e., singular, linear narrative) documentary approach. The first-time documentarian tasks Rodolfo with the narration of two separate threads; neither one a sub-set of the other, but rather competing main threads.

On the one hand, Rodolfo chronicles the twenty-year journey of Eva's embalmed corpse, beginning with the event that is chronologically most recent to his fictional character's timeline: the cadaver's second kidnapping in 1976 by the military forces that took over the nation's government at the dawn of Argentina's "Dirty War" (1976–83). That is, in one move, the new military government deposed Perón's third wife and presidential successor (1974–6), Isabel Martínez de Perón, and, in another move, disposed of a powerful revolutionary Peronist symbol (00:4:56–00:6:03). This tumultuous period in Argentine history, which lasted for the better part of a decade, saw the disappearance of tens of thousands of its own as one method of political repression under military rule. Accordingly, Rodolfo recounts the facts surrounding Eva's death as he nears his own premature death by assassination at the hands of the same military government, an event that plays out near the film's end (00:58:08–50).

Later segments from the cadaver thread piece together the years-long task of embalming Eva's corpse, a rite performed by Dr. Pedro Ara prior to its original kidnapping in 1955 from Buenos Aires's General Confederation of Labour at the hands of the self-proclaimed "Revolución Libertadora" (Liberating Revolution). The *coup d'état* brought an abrupt end to Perón's nine-year presidency and resulted in his exile, while the body of his deceased second wife, we are told by Rodolfo, endured a five-year guardianship under the watchful eye of accused necrophiliac Colonel Carlos Eugenio Moori Koenig for fear that, should the body fall into the hands of Peronist supporters, it could incite rebellion (00:30:00–00:33:00). These events are eventually recapped for the viewer with a series of brief (one to three seconds) recycled shots (00:53:16–47), this time in chronological order beginning with the embalmment by Dr. Ara before new details are added through the visual/verbal reconstruction of history. Likewise towards the film's conclusion we see and hear that

Eva's cadaver remained in an Italian cemetery near Rome for over a decade, buried under the name María Maggis (00:53:48–00:54:20) before being relocated to its permanent resting place in La Recoleta Cemetery in Buenos Aires, housed in a concrete vault eight metres below the surface, and secured by a steel tombstone (00:58:00–8).

The second narrative thread that Seoane recounts through the vehicle of her fictional narrator develops in a chronological fashion, beginning with Eva's move at the age of fifteen to Buenos Aires, where she would struggle to earn a living as a radio host and actress, model, and film actress (00:07:21–00:13:15). The focus of Rodolfo's account, however, is on Eva's later years in the capital city, where she would meet and marry Juan Perón and in so doing become one of Peronism's central players. We see in the on-screen transformation of her animated figure into a well-dressed blonde, as well as in the portrayal of Eva's flourishing relationship with Juan and in her move from among the masses to the stage – or balcony, rather – of Argentina's political scene that "Evita's story," as Sarah M. Misemer aptly notes, "was a Cinderella story come true."[8]

The use of animation to reconstruct these events surrounding the death and life of Eva Perón has resulted in the film being repeatedly pronounced as fiction with "touches" of documentary (i.e., the archival materials) by the handful of national news media sources that acknowledged its release in 2011. At this same moment in time, however, Seoane made a statement about the film's creation that opposes the perpetuated dichotomization of animation/fiction and archival/documentary. In an interview for the daily news source *Página 12*, the novice film-maker and established journalist ascertained that "no hay datos falsos. Soy rigurosa con los hechos que cuento, aunque sea en dibujo animado" (there is no false information. I am rigorous with the facts that I tell, even if through animation).[9]

As we discovered in the previous chapter, aesthetic decisions involving certain animation styles and techniques can cause a film to be underappreciated, or even misunderstood. If this was visible in the poor popular and critical reception of Colombian-made *Little Voices*, this is perceptible to an even greater extent in the (lack of) attention towards *Eva from Argentina*. Theatre attendance for the film totalled a mere 4,381 spectators, less than a fraction of a single per cent of ticket sales from the year 2011, which topped forty million for forty national films.[10] From the national box-office statistics for that year, we can conclude that the source of inattention to the Argentine animated film is not a lack of interest in the topic, as, that same year, Paula de Luque's live-action drama *Juan y Eva / Juan and Eva* saw 90 per cent more spectators than did Seoane's *Eva from Argentina*.

What it seems to boil down to is disapprobation for the use of animation in general and Seoane's "animated comic" style in particular, as well as a widespread lack of awareness of animation's narrative potential. In a rather callous review for *La nación*, film critic Gustavo Noriega labels the film as "pobre estéticamente" (aesthetically poor), writing that the result of the flat, largely immobile figures, to which is added, in his opinion, more interesting archival materials, is an aesthetic that "es estático y fatigoso, sin brillo y caricatural" (is static and tiring, dull and caricaturesque).[11] Noriega's reaction to *Eva from Argentina's* visual aesthetic can be seen as an expression of a widely felt sentiment, which is somewhat surprising for a nation with such a rich history of animation and comics art.

Noriega's strongest critique, however, is that the limitations of the film, namely a simplification of history due to its animated aesthetic, is laid bare on screen. This piece of criticism is problematic for a number of reasons. First, it suggests that animation need be visually alluring, as something synonymous to "enjoyment" and "entertainment" and a means of capturing and maintaining the viewer's attention so that they might engage in a storyline that is being told around – but not through – a film's visual aesthetic. In other words, this is a view of animation that sees the art form as itself devoid of any narrative potential. Noriega's statement also suggests a conceptual link between animation and simplification, while in the case of Seoane's film as we soon shall see, animation is not only a powerful meaning-making tool, but one that allows for multilayered meanings to be communicated.

We can at least find solace in the knowledge that the tool of animation is addressed in the scholarly criticism that *Eva from Argentina* has received, even if specifics regarding style or technique are overlooked. Attention to Seoane's most recent film is scant, very unlike the criticism that continues to surround her co-authored work of investigative non-fiction, *La noche de los lápices / Night of the Pencils* (1986),[12] one of the dozen historical books that the recently named "Ciudadana Ilustre" (Illustrious Citizen) has penned to date.[13] In fact, *Eva from Argentina* has been analysed by only a single author in a pair of recent articles: Jimena Cecilia Trombetta's "El lenguaje de animación como herramienta poética para mitificar la historia de Eva Perón" / "The Language of Animation as a Poetic Tool for Mythologizing the Story of Eva Perón,"[14] and "La ficción y su función de memoria: A propósito de Eva Perón" / "Fiction and Its Memory Function: On Eva Perón."[15] Trombetta's main objective in her earlier article, which she summarizes and cites in the second, is to interrogate how testimony and archive in *Eva from Argentina* are used to fictionalize historical fact, while what she calls the "poetics of animation" function allegorically in a present-day reading of the protagonist as symbolic of *el pueblo* (the people).

In dialoguing with Trombetta's recent and singular interpretation of Seoane's film, the aim of this second chapter is to explore two additional ways in which animation fosters a political gaze when taken up as an aesthetic tool in documentary film: on the one hand, as backwards-looking historical revisionism, as Trombetta has begun to show, and, on the other, as a forward-thinking medium through which sociopolitical ideologies of the past can be drawn (both literally and figuratively) into the present. When it comes to the former, that is, to painting a specific picture of history, I highlight how the animation-archival dynamics in *Eva from Argentina* work together to illustrate what sociologist Juan José Sebreli would call Seoane's *peronismo imaginario* (personal myth of Peronism).[16] Sebreli means this to be the way in which Peronism can change in the mind of its individual adherents, where the invented and the real are conflated in one's imaginary. This tendency should not come as a surprise, as Peronism has been classified as a "hodgepodge" that not only allows for but also favours all sorts of interpretations,[17] as a movement that "has proven successful in adapting itself to changing circumstances,"[18] and as something ambiguous. Hispanist Jon Beasley-Murray writes,

> As to whether Peronism was a movement of the left or of the right: it was both. (And it was neither.) Peronism's ambiguity was further accentuated by the fact that the figure of Evita was always available as a second pole for identification: from the guerrilla version of Evita as rebellious incarnation of the Peronist left, as in the chant "If Evita lived, she would be a Montonero!" to her right-wing portrayal as the image of fidelity and subservience to patriarchy.[19]

Key to the Argentine director's personal myth of Peronism is the figure of Eva Perón, not unlike Sebreli, for whom Evita served as the "ingrediente decisivo" (decisive ingredient).[20] Seoane's Eva, as will be explored, symbolizes a romantic, populist, and leftist Peronism. Meanwhile, building on Trombetta's study, I problematize the idea that Seoane's political gaze solely arises from the integration of archival segments and materials into an otherwise fully animated aesthetic. In drawing attention to the animation's direct association with Argentina's comics scene, that which is thought to have had its golden age during the first period of Peronism in the mid twentieth century,[21] I will argue that the aesthetic serves a political project in and of itself. Of particular interest are critical debates surrounding *The Eternaut*, whose iconography has served as a symbol of popular resistance against Argentina's dictatorships and military power for nearly four decades now.[22]

In this regard, and when it comes to animation as a forward-thinking medium, particular attention is paid to the way in which Seoane simultaneously draws and draws on the period known as "classical" Peronism (1945–55), specifically the birth of the movement in the Plaza de Mayo on 17 October 1945, to illustrate the present-day potential of an "Argentina más armónica"(more harmonic Argentina), in which there is "reconocimiento de derechos sociales y políticos, especialmente para las mujeres"(recognition of social and political rights, especially for women).[23] These ideals rooted in Peronism, according to the director, are very present in Kirchnerism, which recuperates Peronism as one of the great moments in Argentine history.

As the attentive analysis of this scene will show, Seoane harnesses the creative control of animation to weave together through a quick succession of shots a highly politicized take on the birth of Peronism, in which Eva Perón is granted a fundamental role, with a poetic picture of its (and Eva's) continuation in, decades later, the figure of Cristina Fernández de Kirchner. In this regard, I will examine animation's boundlessness in the representation of time. By this I mean its unfettered ability to not only reconstruct the events of different eras across time, but to also bridge two different sociopolitical moments within a single image and a single frame, one that at once functions mimetically – that is, to create a visual link with the bodies of the historical figures they are depicting with the ultimate goal of validating history[24] – and evocatively – to reveal or explore subjective things that cannot be seen.[25]

These objectives will be carried out through a more nuanced reading of how the comics-related animation and the archival operate both poetically and politically in Seoane's filmic narrative, necessarily from the perspective of animated documentary studies, but also by paying attention to comics studies. Central to this analysis will be Annabelle Honess Roe's recently developed notion of the relationship of animation to the archival in commercial or mainstream live-action documentary, where it serves to make "connections" with the archival veneer (i.e., to stand-in for lacking archival footage) or "disruptively interject" the archival veneer (i.e., carry the potential to make a critical and/or political impact by way of disrupting the flow of the otherwise archival imagery).[26] I argue that, in the case of animated documentary, this can also function in reverse. While it is hard to conceive of the archival in terms of "connective tissue" within an animated narrative, as animation's increasingly limitless capabilities leave little to no room for a lack of reconstructed footage, it is easy to see how the archival might function as a "disruptive interjection" in an otherwise animated narrative, where it is meant "to highlight and hammer home" the film's political project with perhaps extra oomph and power due to the still pervasive conceptions of the truth claim of a recorded image, which gains even greater weight through its sparing and highly strategic use.

Poetics, Politics, and Personal Myths of Peronism

For its primary use of animation, *Eva from Argentina* stands out from traditional live-action biopics and seems to be on the forefront of a new way of dramatizing the life of historical figures.[27] Yet Seoane's film diverges from both traditional live-action and fully animated biographical films for its heavy incorporation of audiovisual archival materials. Straddling the genres of documentary and biographical film, then, *Eva from Argentina* could be classified as what Cristina Formenti calls "the sincerest form of docudrama," given that the film features particular aesthetics and codes conventionally accepted as markers of the documentary genre, yet it employs the "grammar of fiction film-making" and features "a cinematic technique, such as animation, that is considered the fictive technique par excellence."[28]

Today, however, nearly a decade after Formenti wrote these words, animation's capacity to accurately – and at times even more aptly – represent the past now stands undisputed and well theorized, although it should be said that perhaps there remains room in the cultural realm for its emergence as a stand-alone category in awards shows from the Goyas to the Oscars. Of equal importance, live-action film-making has time and time again been used for fictive purposes in the mockumentary genre and beyond, paving the way for the problematization of automatically equating live action with veracity in the documentary genre and subgenres. Not to mention that, in these "times of hybridization," as Patricia Serrano Abarca notes in a study on memory and reality in docudramas and animated documentaries, "muchas de las formas de 'documentar' una realidad vienen borrando las fronteras con la ficción y el arte, expandiendo la representación a otros lenguajes, más allá del registro audiovisual directo de los acontecimientos, que marcó durante años la esencia retórica de la no ficción" (many of the forms of "documenting" a reality blur the borders between fiction and art, expanding its representation to other languages, beyond the audiovisual record of events, which for years marked the rhetorical essence of non-fiction).[29]

Beyond a consideration of formal properties, if we recall Honess Roe's definition of animated documentary as that which creatively represents the world in which we live, rather than a world imagined by the filmmaker, then an indisputable case for *Eva from Argentina* as an animated documentary can be made, not to mention that this is, in fact, how the film has largely been received by news media critics and film scholars alike. Honess Roe's definition of animated documentary does not rely on a set quantity of archival materials as a yardstick for classification, but rather the understanding that animation and live-action elements are integrated to the extent that the meaning of the film would become incoherent were the animation to be removed.[30] This is arguably the case for *Eva from Argentina,* whose audiovisual archival elements run consistently throughout the film, inextricably linked to the animated elements, and vice versa.

Although the mimetic animation style employed in *Eva from Argentina* is not in its most extreme form of photorealism, the drawings aim to create a strong visual link with the bodies of the historical figures they depict. This can be seen in figure 2.1, a screen capture featuring a medium close-up from an early scene in the film that recreates the pair's initial encounter on 22 January 1944 at a charity gala held at Buenos Aires's Luna Park Stadium to benefit victims of the earthquake that devastated San Juan. Eva, whose shoulders sit squarely in the centre of the left side of the frame, sports her bleach-blonde hair swept up and fashioned at the nape of her neck, that which is noticeably slender and delicate next to the thick neck and frame of her new love interest, whose eyes she gazes into with her own (exaggeratedly) large brown eyes framed by dark, arched brows.

The representational mimesis even extends to the detail of Eva's meticulous make-up, coiffed hair, and fine jewellery; a woman well known to strategically create "the image of a princess with her elegant clothing and dyed blonde hair piled high on top of her head," as a means of, at a time characterized by relative economic stability, bolstering "popular faith in the Peronist rhetoric that promised equality and prosperity to the most disenfranchised of the population."[31] Likewise, the dark-haired Juan is faithfully depicted in his smart military dress. The former general's athletic frame is emphasized by the fact that his broad shoulders extend beyond the cinematic frame. And, although the slight grin he displays in this scene does not creatively capture Perón's iconic smile, the side profiling allows for the representation of the former political leader's unmistakable strong features and square jawline.

In light of this early scene, and through a series of segments that follow, we begin to detect how archival materials disruptively interject the animated narrative to help promote Seoane's personal myth

Figure 2.1. Mimetic animation in *Eva from Argentina* (00:14:30)

of Peronism, the foundation of which is a love story; a not uncommon sentimental interpretation of Peronism that provides, in the words of Amarantha Wright, more than "just the singular satisfaction of Fatherland or Mother-country. Evita and Juan offered a full Parent-nation."[32] This suspicion is visually confirmed not a minute later in a scene that features historic photographs superimposed onto the animated backdrop of an album-like scrapbook, created by, we are to believe, Rodolfo, who at times enters the frame as his hands manipulate the photographs on its open pages (00:15:08–36).

The subjective camera, imitating Rodolfo's gaze, moves across the open-faced album pausing briefly on both formal and informal photographs of Juan and Eva Perón, who are at times pictured together and in other moments separately, but in all cases transmit togetherness and an unfettered happiness (see figure 2.2). As the camera pans over the black-and-white snapshots, the blurred edges of the frame highlight each photograph as the object of Rodolfo's gaze, while the individual, archival images serve as connective tissue linking the (re)animated moment of the couple's encounter to a larger history of a very public relationship, many moments of which are reconstructed in scenes that follow. That is, on one very basic level, the superimposed photographs along with their hand-written captions function to visually "explain, clarify and illustrate" the blossoming of the Peróns' relationship that is otherwise being reconstructed through animation.[33]

Figure 2.2. Archival interjections: Curating the Peronism love story as "reality" and "past" (00:13:57)

These archival images also carry heavy critical potential, as they are inserted into the animated narrative to communicate a point of view that Seoane would later explicitly speak to during an interview to mark the release of a new edition of her book *Eva Perón: Esa mujer / Eva Perón: That Woman*, co-authored with Victor Santa María, which coincided with the one hundredth anniversary of Eva Perón's birth.[34] Seoane elucidates that her purpose was

> contar la historia de amor de Eva, pero no solo con Perón. Esa historia del peronismo protagonizada por Perón y por Eva es una gran historia de amor, tanto de una pareja, como una gran historia de amor política. La política sin amor, es como una constitución sin pueblo, es como una aventura sin alma.
>
> (to tell Eva's love story, but not only with Perón. The story of Peronism protagonized by Perón and Eva is a great love story; it is as much about a couple as it is a political love story. Politics without love is a constitution without the people, an adventure without soul.)[35]

The manner in which the filmic narrative progresses from this early encounter scene leaves little room for doubt that Seoane's objective for her animated film, about which she has said relatively little, mirrors that which she describes of her recent literary project. And, the strategic use of archival photographs carefully curated by Rodolfo's hand, and by extension that of Seoane, in which Eva and Juan Perón's bodies appear ontologically distinct from their animated counterparts, functions as a disruptive interjection through which the director can "highlight and hammer home" her vision of Peronism as a political love story. This is especially understandable if we consider Roland Barthes's argument that photography renders it impossible to "deny that *the thing has been there*. There is a superimposition here: of reality and the past."[36] Equally significant is André Bazin's assertion in "The Ontology of the Photographic Image" that a photograph's viewer is "forced to accept as real the existence of the object reproduced, actually re-presented" as a result of a "transference of reality from the thing to its reproduction."[37]

Due to the strategic interjection of these archival photographs into the narration of Eva's rags-to-riches romance, this impression of an undeniable reality, or transference of reality, of this love story from the past, extends in the mind of the viewer to what they next see in the animated reconstructions, which mimetically build on the moments pictured in the collection of images. Here, a fade-to-black transition advances the narrative from the mid-seventies moment in which Rodolfo gazes upon the pages of the scrapbook, while the subsequent fade-in brings the viewer back in time in a scene that reconstructs the events surrounding a photo of the pair in formal dress – Eva Perón donning a white ball gown and Juan Perón, who stands to her left, sporting corresponding white military garb – as they attend a performance at Buenos Aires's Teatro Colón (Columbus Theatre; 00:15:37–00:16:43).

Overall, the opera scene serves to illustrate a quick shift in the couple's relationship, notably a lateral one, in which Eva takes her place beside the general in their balcony seats, from where they become an object of both curious and disbelieving stares. The highlighting of the couple's physical position above the crowd gains significance, especially when read against the illustration of their encounter among the people (albeit an imaginably elite group) seen in figure 2.1, and when read against later balcony shots recreating the couple's appearances outside Argentina's Presidential Palace, the Casa Rosada (literally, "Pink House"), as the nation's president and first lady. What is more, Seoane employs animation to mimic the archival by concluding this scene with a bright flash, which, we quickly realize, emanates from a camera, as what follows the sharp burst of light is the on-screen materialization of a drawn photograph, which fills the shot and features the couple standing on the same balcony (see figure 2.3).

In the final seconds of the opera scene, the pair of animated figures is rendered black and white; Eva frozen in the initial act of greeting the crowd

Figure 2.3. Animating an archive (00:15:15)

with a timid wave and Juan gazing lovingly down at her. The drawing of the black-and-white photograph blurs an otherwise clear ontological distinction between the previously seen archival photographs and the animated reconstructions that precede and follow it, allowing the animation to effortlessly draw on the photograph-as-veritable-reality conceptual link that was purposefully erected in the scrapbook scene. Seoane's subversive use of both the archive and animation allows for the viewer to imagine the black-and-white image of the new couple as likewise belonging to Rodolfo's scrapbook, and, accordingly, compels them to picture Eva's – and Peronism's – irrefutable rise in power within the bounds of an unlikely (in the sense that anything is possible) romantic relationship.

Fifteen minutes later, and exactly halfway through the film, we witness the same employment of archive as a myth-shaping, home-hitting interjection between two poetic animated segments that reconstruct Eva Perón's philanthropic and political work through the Eva Perón Foundation (00:31:31–00:34:11). Here, however, these archival interjections comprised largely of audiovisual newsreels function to frame Eva, who at this point in the narrative wields political power as Perón's wife and the nation's first lady, as compassionate champion of the poor and women's suffrage; the very image of *Santa Evita* (Saint Evita) to use the moniker popularized in 1995 by prominent Argentine writer Tomás Eloy Martínez in the title of his book.[38] Meanwhile, the animation works symbolically to construct this image of Eva, "aquella en donde el traje sastre y el rodete eran los característicos" (one in which a tailored suit and a chignon were characteristic) during what has been classified as the second stage of her political career.[39] Alicia Dujovne Ortiz notes in her biography of Eva Perón that "in order to observe Peronism, it was enough to look at Eva. In the period starting in 1948 and ending shortly before her death in 1952, authoritarianism would go hand in hand with her severe hairstyle."[40]

This sequence begins with a long shot of Buenos Aires's legislative building, the Concejo Deliberante (Deliberative Council) at the time, in which the tall colonial-style structure appears cloaked in darkness save for a beam of light cast by the full moon radiating from the top right corner of the frame and a single, lit window on the building's façade visible in the bottom left quadrant. A quick camera jump to outside this window brings a medium shot that cleverly frames the shadowed figure of Eva inside a dimly lit room, from where she gazes down at a letter in her hand, with myriad others visible on the surface of the desk where she sits. The complete creative control that animation allows for paints a picture of Eva working tirelessly to personally read and respond to the letters penned by impoverished children from around the nation that, we learn in the shots that follow, petition for toys, construction materials, educational necessities, and bicycles. A number of these young authors are represented in still photographic portraits that form the backdrop of the scene, as well as by a sequence of youthful voice-offs that narrate the contents of a number of featured letters. Meanwhile, the historical photographs, here a tool for verisimilitude, as Trombetta has rightly noted,[41] slide across the shot from right to left in a pattern that matches Eva's eye movement as she reads the letters in her hand, from where she is drawn into the foreground of the medium close-up shot.

This scene presents an interesting case of the trend specific to Latin American film that was introduced in chapter 1: what María Soledad Paz-Mackay and Omar Rodríguez call "the image of children as politics" in Latin American cinema.[42] Although neither this scene nor the film in general is protagonized by children, this animated segment employs their photographs and childlike voices to promulgate an adult's politicized historical reconstruction. Through a series of shots we understand that the archival photographs of young, impoverished children along with their family members on the visual level, together with the faux archival voice-offs on the verbal level are under the artistic control of the adult creators to proffer the director's own view point as opposed to that of the children. Specifically, the images (and voices) of real children are employed for the purpose of constructing Seoane's image of Eva Perón as that of *Santa Evita*, very unlike the employment of Colombian children's voices and representational drawings that allowed for the articulation of their view of the armed conflict, as well as their role in it, that we saw in the previous chapter's analysis of *Little Voices*.

The ideological use of the portraits and voices of young Argentine children becomes particularly apparent as the filmic narrative progresses. Seconds later, another fully animated scene employs a forward-facing shot to capture Eva squarely behind her desk, this time the singular subject of the shot, wearing a warm smile and a white dress shirt as her figure sits directly between two lamps that cast a glow around her figure, seemingly emanating from her. Here again the entire *mise en scène* paints the definite picture of a saint-like woman, symbolically drawn as a light in the darkness, as a multitude of letters rains down in the foreground of the shot, signifying their pouring in, and Eva's smile shines even brighter. We learn in the following series of animated shots that Eva's response to these letters results in the manufacturing, packaging, and shipping of the requested items, chief among these toys, off to places like Neuquen, Chubut, La Pampa, Misiones, and Jujuy. That is, to all corners of the nation.

While critics of Peronism denounce the Eva Perón Foundation's work of annually distributing toys as an engagement in populism and patronage to win votes from the poor, it is undeniable that these toys, some of which were recently put on display in Buenos Aires's Museo Evita (Evita Museum) to commemorate the one hundredth anniversary of her birth on 7 May 1919, "played a vital role in the rise of Peronism in Argentina."[43] They also play a role, as we discover in this scene, in the director's personal myth of Peronism. Daniela Pelegrinelli outlines the function of children's toys in the politics of Peronism in the context of Juan Perón's first presidency, noting that manufactured playthings, which exploded as an industry in the mid-1940s, were previously not a part of the social imaginary and accordingly not present in the daily lives of the nation's youngest citizens.[44] Through their mass distribution by the Foundation, toys functioned as part of children's politics during Peronism, by incorporating the young recipients in Argentina's political scene; the state-provided toys, Pelegrinelli concludes, represented both a right and a duty for the child recipients, who were not so subtly regarded as the "political vanguard" of Argentina's future.[45]

What we see in these scenes from *Eva from Argentina*, however, is not a criticism of these mass distributions, but rather its glorification; one that is bolstered by archival footage beginning from 1947, the year before the Foundation's official establishment. Eva Perón smiles and waves as she distributes packages to the hands of eager recipients from what appears to be the open window of a slow-moving train car. This brief clip commences a montage of newsreels dated up to 1951 that portrays the first lady's interactions with the nation's young children and women, as well as the deliverance of many official speeches. These celebrate, for example, the vote for women under Argentina's Law 13,010, enacted in 1947, which established equality of political rights between men and women and universal suffrage in Argentina, and communicate hope for social justice for all under the recently created Secretaría de Trabajo y Previsión (Secretariat of Labour and Social Welfare), a post first held by Juan Perón in the two years leading up to his first presidency.

The succession of newsreels are unified by a bold white date marker in the bottom left corner of the shot, the constant changing of which reiterates the notion of Eva's tirelessness. A continuous audio recording also ties the string of brief clips together, the voice of Eva Perón delivering the opening words from her speech on 23 September 1947 following the sanction of Law 13,010. Eva Perón's off-screen voice resounds from seemingly nowhere and everywhere as the montage of video footage begins to play. The double dose of archival material here, simultaneously playing on their respective visual/verbal registers, can be read as a doubly disruptive interjection. The newsreels, on the one hand, being a different register than the animated reconstruction of Eva in the opening of this Foundation scene, create the type of visual disruptive interjection theorized by Honess Roe. On the other hand, we can also argue that the additional archival recording against which the videos play functions as an audio disruptive interjection within Rodolfo's narration to help emphasize Eva's philanthropic work.

An extra layer is added to this myth-building sequence when the narrator himself momentarily interrupts the grainy audio soundtrack to clearly transmit from his present moment in time the words of one of the former first lady's most celebrated sayings: "Esa mujer decia, 'donde hay una necesidad nace un derecho'" (That woman would say, "Where there is a need, a right is born"). Rodolfo's narrational interjection – and Seoane's, by extension – echoes the mounting sentiment of Eva's altruism, primarily underway through the scaffolding of shots featuring poetic animation and the resignified archive. On this visual level, it should be added, the uncharacteristic pace of one-to-two-second shots creates an energetic tone, first in the archival clips of Eva Perón's charitable work, and immediately following in the animated segment that depicts labourers erecting brick by brick the building that was to become home to the Eva Perón Foundation. The scene nears its conclusion with a prolonged long shot of the completed building, in front of which a large crowd gathers.

This scene ends with a medium-wide shot depicting a mighty-looking Eva, majestic even, raising a fist in a triumphant pose against a backdrop of a bright and stormy sky as she proclaims that "la justicia social se cumplirá, cueste lo que cueste y caiga quien caiga" (social justice will be fulfilled, whatever the cost and whoever may fall) to an audience, we are led to believe, of citizens who gather to form a large crowd outside the doors of the now-finished Foundation building. This scene does not coincide with historical accounts that state that the first lady, whose health in 1951 was fast failing, would not witness first-hand the building's inauguration.[46] Nevertheless, the (re)animation of this historical event suggestively sutures Eva into the course of action, effectively creating the illusion of the two events – inauguration and public speech – occurring in the same locale and on the same occasion despite the fact that Eva Perón gave this speech on 1 May 1950, being the nation's *Día del trabajador* (Workers' Day).

The fast pace of the scene fosters an assumption in the viewer's mind that Eva Perón played an integral role in the inauguration of the Foundation's intended headquarters and in Peronism's growing populism and power by extension, as the rapid cinematic transitions leave little time for questioning or scrutiny. What is more, this segment evinces animation's boundlessness in the representation of time; its ability to effortlessly, and almost imperceptibly portray a number of different historical moments within the same scene. This midway scene becomes the culminating point in the recounting of the centrality of Eva Perón to Peronism's rise to power, before the narrative transitions to the recounting of the first lady's rapid demise and untimely death. It gains significance when read in relation to the earlier reconstruction of what has been called "Peronism's primal scene."[47]

Here, perhaps more than anywhere in the film, the resignification of the archival is perceptible within the reconstruction of events that led up to a revolution in the Plaza de Mayo on 17 October 1945 to liberate then Colonel Juan Perón (00:15:44–00:19:19). The spinning newspaper trope that opens the scene relays the impact and immediacy of Perón's arrest at the hands of military forces. As the black-and-white copy of *El diario* (The Diary) halts its rotation to fill the screen with a shot of the front page, the all-caps headline announces the action that is to take place in the scene that follows: "HUELGA GENERAL DE LOS TRABAJADORES POR LA LIBERTAD DE PERÓN"(WORKERS' GENERAL STRIKE FOR PERÓN'S FREEDOM). The foreshadowing of this scene by means of a reconstructed newspaper, although kitschy, is strategic as it appeals to the archive as a means of positing that what unfolds in the animated segment that follows is a reconstruction of events straight from the pages of history – and the front page of history at that.

Yet the ensuing scene makes clear that it is a specific version of history that is being retold: the birth of Peronism, figuratively speaking, which memorializes Eva as the movement's symbolic mother. As a result,

Seoane's take on the events leading up to Peronism's primal scene goes against that of her contemporaries, as journalists and historians alike have come to the conclusion that, although the official story grants Eva Perón a decisive role on 17 October 1945, she was not only not an integral part of the movement, but was likely not even present in the streets or in the plaza.[48] Historian José María Rosa, who also speculates on Eva Perón's likely absence from the scene, wrote of that day:

> La tradición ha dado a Eva Duarte una actividad legendaria en el 17 de octubre. Sin mengua de la extraordinaria figura que fue Eva Perón como esposa y colaboradora del general no corresponde atribuirle una función decisiva en el levantamiento popular. Que no fue solamente levantamiento de obreros organizados, sino de todo un pueblo. Es cierto que *Eva Duarte* conocía a los dirigentes obreros que visitaban a Perón en la calle Posadas, pero no tenía la difusión ni el poder en los medios obreros que alcanzó más tarde cuando fue *Eva Perón* ... Nadie preparó el 17 de octubre, nadie lo ordenó, nadie lo "planificó" (para usar una palabra grata a los que no creen en las conmociones sociales, sin planes cuidadosamente estudiados). Fue espontáneo.[49]

> (Tradition has given Eva Duarte a legendary activity on 17 October. Without diminishing the extraordinary figure that was Eva Perón as the wife and collaborator of the general, it is not appropriate to attribute to her a decisive function in the popular uprising. It was not only the uprising of organized workers, but of an entire people. It is true that *Eva Duarte* knew the labour leaders who visited Perón on Posadas street, but she did not have the diffusion or power in the working-class media that she later reached when she was *Eva Perón* ... Nobody prepared October 17, nobody ordered it, nobody "planned" it [to use a word gratifying to those that do not believe in social commotions without carefully studied plans]. It was spontaneous.)

Not only does Rosa signal Eva Perón's lack of direct involvement that day, and disassociate the origin of Peronism from her figure, but from the outset the historian also denies the former first lady the very name adopted by the movement. In purposefully referring to her as "Duarte," Rosa points to Eva Perón's illegitimacy with regard to a role that history has come to give her in this story, and the author likewise signals her role of illegitimacy to the future president at this moment in history as his mere mistress. Unlike this strand of thought, Seoane grants Eva a very official role, transforming her into the *Pasionaria* of the revolution and Juan's one true love.[50]

These dynamics are evident from the opening of the revolution scene, which begins, we see, not in the plaza but within Eva's home, notably in the intimate space of a dressing room, where a framed photograph of Juan Perón is placed on the surface of a large vanity, in front of which sits Eva. The significance of the image of Eva tying a white scarf over her loose blonde hair is twofold. On the one hand, the free-flowing hair links her to the symbolic image of Eva Montonera, and thus late, left-wing Peronism of the 1960s and 1970s; that is, decades after this general strike would take place. Ortiz, in her biography of Eva Perón, refers to this image construction as the "red myth": a left-wing Peronist army of some forty thousand men looking to radicalize Peronism, who referred to themselves as Montoneros, using Evita as their flag.[51] On the other hand, the white fabric ties Eva to another later movement that also began a ritualistic congregation in the Plaza de Mayo facing the Casa Rosada: that of the *Madres de la Plaza de Mayo* (Mothers of the Plaza de Mayo), and fittingly evokes a "white myth" that depicted Evita as "a virgin in the flesh, as maternal tenderness, the very meaning of sacrifice."[52]

These visual cues, coupled with Eva's determined gaze captured in the reflection of her vanity mirror by a subjective camera cleverly poised behind her figure, set a tone of anticipation as the viewer likewise becomes an observer as they follow in the footsteps of Eva, who is on the verge of heading towards the plaza. As the young Argentine sets out in her motor car, the distinctive white headscarf serves as a symbol of public struggle for Eva, just as it would symbolize the public struggle for the mothers who sought justice for their "disappeared" children from the late 1970s onwards. The implication then is that the liberation of then Coronel Juan Perón, on what would later become the *Día de la lealtad* (Loyalty Day), becomes Eva's own public struggle. In other words, by swathing her protagonist in the symbolic white fabric, Seoane adopts the Peronist regime's own tactic, noted by Beasley-Murray to be the rewriting of Peronism's narrative through the ritual re-enactment of the scene in the plaza in 1945 "by constructing Evita as its central organizing principle."[53]

It is in this scene that the Argentine director's personal myth of Peronism, in which the figure of Evita plays a starring role, is most clearly articulated. Still clad in her white headscarf, Eva sets out about the town knocking on doors of union and government officials to rally support for the liberation of Juan. As Trombetta has accurately stated of this scene, the clever superimposition of archival footage onto the window panes of the vehicle that carries Eva on this journey to the plaza results in the impression that Eva witnesses the success of her purported individual efforts as she gazes out upon the mobilizing masses (see figure 2.4).[54]

Figure 2.4. Re-signification of the archival in the "revolution scene" (00:17:38)

That Rodolfo echoes the words of Raúl Scalabrini Ortiz's 1947 "El subsuelo de la patria sublevado" as this happens,[55] to recount that the labourers "venían hermandos en el mismo grito y en la misma fe" (came united in the same cry and the same faith), is one instance in which we can gauge that the resignification of the archival runs deeper than the visual register.[56] Moreover, it communicates the director's perspective that, from the birth of its movement, Peronism had adherents in both the working class and the intellectual. This increasingly common perspective was only just gaining critical ground around the time of *Eva from Argentina*'s release, with foundational texts such as the edited collection *Intervenciones intelectuales en el contexto del peronismo clásico / Intellectual Interventions in the Context of Classical Peronism*.[57] In other words, we see in *Eva from Argentina* echoes of a critical debate germinating in scholarship at this same moment, which challenge the predominant view of classical Peronism as an "anti-intellectual" movement, one in which the intellectual played no role – whether through writing history or acting in it – and one that upholds an ideological schism between the intellectual sphere and that of the masses.

But the role of the intellectual is only one of many details that emerges in regards to Seoane's perspective on the birth of Peronism in this scene. Also to be considered is what the animated and archival elements say about the role of Eva Perón. For Trombetta, the purpose of having Eva view (and hear, I would add) the results of "her" actions in this fictional scene is to construct a heroic image, be it that of *Santa Evita* or *Eva-Militante*. While accepting this, I would argue that the foremost image being constructed of Eva here is not one that evokes her immortalized image of saint or revolutionary activist posthumously by later generations, but rather one that speaks to her very human life's work during this stage of classical Peronism of 1945–55. As a result, the image that is being constructed is rather that of Eva as, to quote the closing lyrics of the song *Santa Evita* from Rice and Lloyd Webber's musical, "madre de todos los niños / De los tiranizados, de los descamisados / De los trabajadores, de la Argentina" (mother of all children / Of the tyrannized, of the shirtless ones / of the workers, of Argentina).

What we are presented with is the image of a revolutionary mother figure, birthing a movement so to speak, because of her love for the people as much as her desire for Juan. This purposefully constructed image draws a picture of a sociopolitical movement that, from the moment of its conception, offers a full-parent nation through the figures of Eva and Juan Perón. Pinpointing the illustration of a full-parent nation is crucial to understanding the poetic action that unfolds as the revolution scene progresses, an essential matter as this vital scene has been largely misunderstood by the handful of film critics and scholars that have turned their attention towards the film. For it is also within this scene that the Argentine director articulates the role that Peronism plays in her present-day political ideology, skilfully through the art of animation, drawing connections between politics of past and present, from the classical Peronism of the 1940s and 1950s to the Kirchnerism of the 2010s.

The action continues as the masses of *descamisados* (shirtless ones) arrive at the Plaza de Mayo, and along with them Eva, who is now on foot. Immediately upon her arrival, the maternal, justice-seeking symbol of the white headscarf is taken to another level, literally and figuratively, as the piece of white fabric is swept up in a gust of wind, brushing by a rallying labourer perched atop a streetlamp with a hand-painted picket sign to his right that reads "¡Liberen a Perón!" (Free Perón!). No doubt one should expect to encounter this image within Seoane's reconstruction of the original 17 October, as the drawing of a streetlamp protestor is, as Trombetta notes, a historic image employed on many occasions to represent loyalty and social struggle.[58] Perhaps because of its pervasiveness, however, the potential for a poetic resignification of this image as it appears in *Eva from Argentina* continues to go unnoticed.

Upon closer inspection, we discover from the striking resemblance he bears to a young Néstor Kirchner that this is no archetypal protestor. Were this (animated) cameo appearance, so to speak, to take place in any other segment of the film this would come off as blatantly anachronistic. Nevertheless, we quickly become attuned to the fact that the action that ensues is anything but a factual reconstruction of a specific historic moment. That is, at least not of a single historic moment. Within the retelling of Peronism's primal moment, Seoane visually digresses for a few brief seconds to illustrate a continuation of Peronism in Argentina of the 2010s through the figures of the late president Néstor Kirchner and first lady turned president Cristina Fernández de Kirchner.

The gaze of the protestor from his vantage point of the streetlamp is transfixed on the (representation of the) allegorical statue of Liberty that tops the city's Pirámide de mayo (May Pyramid). In the blink of an eye, that of the Néstor protestor but also that of the cinematic spectator, the stone statue becomes animate, gaining movement in its limbs and colour across its form. No doubt the Liberty statue's long free-flowing hair, now a subtle shade of blonde and swaying in the wind, initially evokes the image of Eva Montonera. There is also no doubt that, as the arm of the female figure reaches out towards the protestor, who reciprocates this gesture, Seoane visually plays on Michelangelo's *The Creation of Adam* and Eugene Delacroix's *Liberty Leading the People* to show, as Trombetta skilfully notes, that Eva "es la creadora del obrero y es su libertarian" (is the creator of the worker and is their libertarian).[59]

And yet a much deeper meaning, one central to the film's political project, can be found in the careful composition of this animated segment. As I have already suggested, the young man pictured is no archetypal protestor. Or, conceivably, his figure is imbued with a dual symbolism, as he represents both the loyalty and the social struggle of the mid-twentieth-century masses, as well as the individual person of the future leader, who would carry on these values under the banner of Kirchnerism over fifty-five years later. What this politicized play on the image of the streetlamp protestor ultimately symbolizes is the former president's death, which occurred the year prior to the release of *Eva from Argentina*.

We do not know if this visual digression was a late addition to the film, or had its place on the storyboard from the early planning stages. What we do know, however, is that in a very recent editorial for a special number of the cultural magazine *Caras y Caretas* (Faces and Masks), formulated to pay homage to Néstor Kirchner ten years after his passing, Seoane, who pens the number's short editorial, describes the moving experience of witnessing a distraught young man clinging to a plaza streetlamp on the occasion of Kirchner's death on 27 October 2010. For the Argentine director and writer, this memorable image stands as the most powerful symbol to describe "la pasión, la desolación, el dolor multitudinario y la incredulidad por la muerte maldita y temprana de Néstor Kirchner" (the passion, the desolation, the massive pain and the incredulity for the early and ill-fated death of Néstor Kirchner).[60] Accordingly, it can be argued that under Seoane's direction the drawing of the Plaza de Mayo streetlamp protestor is not merely a historically based image. At the very same time, and in the very same shot, it also becomes an illustration of Argentina's present political landscape, and this rings even truer as the action continues to unfold.

While Michelangelo's *The Creation of Adam* depicts the fingers of God and man in a perpetual state of reach, those of the now-mobile feminine statue make contact with that of the Néstor lookalike. The flash of light that emanates around this point of contact can be read as a means of symbolically communicating the 2007 transfer of power from the nation's fiftieth president to his wife and successor Cristina. To emphasize this further, at the same moment we see the spark of light, the hair of the statue turns a deep shade of brown to match the first lady turned president's iconic appearance. And, as a means of quelling any doubt that might remain in the mind of the spectator, the statue's garments assume the bright sky blue of the Argentine flag, adding to the notion of Liberty through the nation's former female leader a sense of a new mother of the nation (see figure 2.5).

The resulting symbolism from this poetic segment as a whole is that of a new full-parent nation in the figures of Néstor and Cristina Fernández de Kirchner. While the left-wing Peronists of the 1960s and 1970s used Evita as their flag, as Ortiz noted, this sequence of shots clearly illustrates that Seoane does the same with Cristina Fernández de Kirchner for today's Kirchnerism that is rooted in yesterday's Peronism. Classical Peronism's reach, we see, is poetically illustrated with the passing of the mantle (made literal through the soaring white headscarf) from Eva to Néstor, and, subsequently, a transfer of power to Cristina. That the Liberty statue, sprung to life, at first loosely resembles Eva Montonera with its subtly shaded long blonde hair, only to transform into a figure with darker, fuller locks shortly thereafter can itself be read as an assertion that, to quote a recent headline from a *New York Times* opinion piece following the 2019 re-election of Cristina Fernández de Kirchner as vice-president, "A New Evita Rises in Argentina."[61]

It is here that animation's boundlessness in the representation of time becomes most apparent. Earlier in the analysis of the Foundation scene we explored how the creative control inherent to the animated *mise en scène* allows for the seamless suturing of one historical moment to another, to suggestively rewrite history in a series of shots within a single segment. Alternatively, the revolution scene illustrates the capacity for

Figure 2.5. Illustrating Peronism's continuation in Néstor Kirchner and Cristina Fernández de Kirchner (00:18:30)

animators to frame both past and present within a single shot, thereby spatializing time for the viewer. That is, time becomes a fourth dimension of otherwise 3D cinematic space in which we sense the length, width, and depth of a scene captured within the frame. As is often the case of animated film and is *always* the case of live-action film, time remains separate from space. The movement of time, whether chronological progression, flashbacks to the past, its repetition or ellipsis, is portrayed through a succession of individual shots. However, *Eva from Argentina* evidences the fact that the tool of animation affords the option to illustrate time as a fourth dimension of space, that is, for time to play out within the space of a single shot.

This poetic segment, which is certainly the revolution scene's culminating moment, presents the notion that Peronism's reach has endured the test of time, carried on and embodied by its leaders from its mid-twentieth-century origins with Eva and Juan Perón to its early twenty-first-century transformations in the Kirchnerist movement through the late Néstor and then president Cristina Fernández de Kirchner. Returning to the idea that Seoane illustrates the transfer of power between these two leaders, within the single frame figured above we see the depiction of a definitive historical moment, the 2007 transfer of presidential power in the light emanating from the very centre of the frame, as well as of the broader timeframe of the Kirchners' rule from Néstor's 2003 inauguration to the ongoing presidency of Cristina at the moment of the film's release as we extend our gaze to the borders of the frame.

In this fantastic scene (in all senses of the word) the series of shots that turn our attention from Eva to the Néstor protestor to the symbolic statue also stand as a prime example of why animation has become known as the "inclusive art."[62] The segment partially captured in figure 2.5 clearly displays "animation's capacity to embrace all of the other arts within its production process ... as a radical tool in the reinvention, re-engagement or reinterpretation of social, cultural and historical materials."[63] Here we see a confluence of painting, drawing, sculpture, and even comics art in Seoane's re-engagement with the past.

The function of embracing the latter cannot be ignored in the film that the director herself refers to, as we have already stated, as an "animated comic." It is no secret that the production of *Eva from Argentina* in the years leading up to 2011 occurred in a context in which national comics art was being appropriated for political use. One key occurrence of this phenomenon is that Peronism, in the words of Cristian Palacios, "became the political and ideological framework for an Argentine president turned superhero."[64] Palacios is referring to a fast-spreading image appearing on banners, placards and T-shirts that was quickly dubbed the "Eternestor" or "Nestornaut" by the communications media: a black-and-white image of Néstor Kirchner sporting the Eternaut's iconic scuba suit and helmet, through which is visible a superimposition of Juan Perón's face and trademark smile.[65]

A number of recent studies have examined the transformation of the Eternaut from cultural icon to political symbol in the creation of the Nestornaut.[66] The image was first conceived as a visual gimmick in an advertising campaign for the rally of the Peronist Youth at Luna Park stadium on 14 August 2010, but following Kirchner's death, only a few short months later, it would transform into "a veritable emblem of the Kirchnerist movement, not only as one of the most representative images used by vast crowds that attended the leader's funeral, but also as an icon of the political struggles that were to follow."[67]

Although Seoane's film does not directly employ the image of the Nestornaut, which was seen in 2010 as "a symbol of resistance to powers which did not see eye to eye with the State, a power which the then head of state, Cristina Fernández de Kirchner, widow of the Nestornaut, was having to confront,"[68] the *Eternaut*-related visual aesthetic can be said to play a key role in the political project that underpins the film. The animated comic style, inspired by Argentina's iconic illustrator Solano López, "embraces" comics art, to use Wells's preferred term,[69] in order to, I would argue, position itself as an additional symbol of resistance in favour of then president Cristina Fernández de Kirchner.

Nevertheless, the comics-related aesthetic remains one of the film's most underappreciated qualities. Bearing in mind what has been argued about Seoane's personal myth of Peronism, and knowing as we do that "*El Eternauta* is one of the Argentine cultural texts that has been promoted, so to speak, by the Kirchner/Fernández de Kirchner governments,"[70] the overall animated comic aesthetic that characterizes *Eva from Argentina* should not be devalued, but rather recognized as integral to a cutting-edge cultural product that features a mode of discourse indicative of Peronism in power.

With this symbolic illustration of the continuation of Peronism in mind, one can also see how animation continues to function both mimetically and evocatively as this scene draws to a close. After the fingers of the Kirchner figures touch, a fade-in transitions to an animated reconstruction of Juan Perón's liberation that very evening, backed by an archival recording of Juan Perón's infamous freedom speech from the balcony of the Casa Rosada. The animation in this segment no doubt functions mimetically to recreate these events, as a shot-reverse-shot technique presents Juan on the balcony victoriously addressing a crowded plaza of protestors below. The cinematography surrounding this animated scene mimics what Beasley-Murray calls populism's "balcony effect": a cinematic device of shot and reverse shot to capture the public spectacle. The alternating shots guarantee that Juan and multitude are not represented together, but rather a division is maintained between the expansive multitude in the plaza and the political leader addressing them from the balcony.[71] The balcony effect, according to Beasley-Murray, "insinuates a limit between multitude and state, substituting a social contract for the social *contact* that the multitude desires and threatens, and thus recomposes the multitude as the people."[72] In short, the brief but triumphant segment illustrates that it is in the plaza, where the people congregated under the balcony of a liberated Juan, that Peronism is born.

Yet the fact that this historical reconstruction takes place directly following the poetic shot of the Néstor protestor together with the Cristina/Liberty statue allows for an additional, symbolic reading as the re-liberation (or rebirth) of classical Peronism under Kirchnerism. This is captured in the title of Uğur Tekiner's very recent article: "Back-to-Roots Again? Kirchnerismo as a Reclaiming of Classical Peronism."[73] Tekiner's assertion that "Kirchnerism, with its center-left agenda, has attempted to reclaim traditional Peronism by highlighting its focus on political sovereignty, economic independence and social justice,"[74] echoes Seoane's own statement in her 2020 editorial that Néstor Kirchner "fue el reconstructor del peronismo, que pudo volver al poder con su esencia de justicia social, soberanía política e independencia económica treinta años después de la muerte de su líder, Juan Perón" (was the reconstructor of Peronism, which was able to return to power with its essence of social justice, political sovereignty and economic independence thirty years after the death of its leader, Juan Perón).[75]

The conclusion of the revolution scene returns to a certain representation of the birth of Peronism by means of an animated segment that depicts the marriage of Eva and Juan under the light of the full and bright moon. Rodolfo, who is pictured in the foreground of the shot, extradiegetically, we are to understand, appears to look back on the intimate moment between Juan and Eva as the liberated leader slips a ring onto Eva's finger, and she on to his, before they begin a two-second tango, and finally embrace. Rodolfo's commentary that what he is seeing is "un final felíz en la conmoción de la noche … ese diecisiete de octubre de 1945 cuando en verdad comenzó todo" (a happy ending in the commotion of the evening … that seventeenth of October 1945 when everything truly began) erroneously portrays the date on which Juan and Eva were married, as well as the place (00:20:19–27).[76]

However, in light of the revolution scene, one could argue that Eva's animated figure functions non-mimetically, or allegorically, for the national project of Peronism, and thus in this concluding segment becomes indicative of a different kind of marriage: one between Perón and the people; a love story between a leader and the people who rallied to show him their support on that historic day. Here again, animation suggestively sutures two different historical moments together to attribute the founding of Peronism with the marriage of Juan and Eva, precisely Wright's assertion that Peronism offers a full-parent nation.

Accordingly, while the revolution scene constructs the birth of Peronism around the figure of Eva Perón, and her union with the president as the fulfilment of a mother/father national project, it also shows its lineage and continuation in Néstor Kirchner and Cristina Fernández de Kirchner, the former Argentina's fiftieth president (2003–7) and the latter, as mentioned, succeeding in the role from 2007 to 2015, a time in which Seoane's film was being produced and released. Kirchnerism, we are to believe, is a contemporary full-parent nation sociopolitical love story, equally marred by an untimely death, but, in this case, not of the central figure but rather of her spouse. Cristina lives on as the nation's current vice-president, serving under the nation's leader, President Alberto Fernández (2019–).

But it remains to be asked what implications the comics-related (and, moreover, *Eternaut*-related) aesthetic has for the two primary historical moments being reconstructed in Seoane's film: Peronism's rise and fall in the mid twentieth century and Peronist resistance and revolt at the dawn of the Dirty War in 1976, which respectively unfolded just prior to the publication of *The Eternaut*'s first season and simultaneous to the publication of the second. If, as Oesterheld pronounces in the prologue to the first season, *The Eternaut* is a story that upholds as its hero "a collective hero, a group of humans,"[77] and accepting as true what Joanna Page writes in a new reading of the Oesterheld/Solano López collaborations, that the reflexive and performative text is "overwhelmingly concerned not with the experience of the popular sectors of society, but with the role of the intellectual and political leader,"[78] then we can see the way in which the film draws on this tale to itself reflect on the committed role of the intellectual in relation to popular revolution; that is, not always but overall working together with the "men of action," to quote Page,[79] both integral to the notion of the Peronist revolution's collective hero, who marches under the banner of its leader, Evita.

Given that, as has been my aim to show, *Eva from Argentina* artfully establishes from early on that what is being drawn might at once be a picture resembling politics of the past as well as a poetic image of the very same in the present, the director's final word in the concluding scene can be read under the same dual lens. A pair of related segments serve as fictional bookends to the historical reconstruction of the life and death of Eva Perón narrated by Rodolfo (00:02:06–30 and 00:57:23–00:58:25, respectively). The focalization of this two-part nightmare-esque scene is, as Trombetta rightly states, under the director's own view from the present rather than the gaze of the film's fictional narrator.[80] I have already showed how this directorial gaze appears in the visual digression that occurs during the revolution scene, in order to draw a picture of Peronism's continuation in Argentina of the 2010s.

It is this same vision that we see reiterated in the film's conclusion. In the recurring nightmare scene, a young Eva flees her father's funeral after his legitimate family and the oligarchy in attendance supernaturally transform into a threatening flock of ravens. For Trombetta, these signify the oligarchy, the military, and the church, although Seoane herself has stated that they signify a more general darkness that looms from the tragedies that mark Argentina's history: intolerance, discrimination, and political violence against the popular sectors.[81] As Eva escapes along the railroad tracks in the countryside of her home province, a shot-reverse-shot technique reveals that she is running towards a train that remains just out of arms reach. At least, that is, until the arm of an adult figure enters a close-up shot from, we are to believe, the train's caboose that remains just off screen and the young girl manages to grab hold of the helping hand. We find out in the concluding segment, which re-enacts a portion of this frantic pursuit, that it is the helping hand of Evita that rescues the young girl.

As Trombetta notes, the animation in this scene synthesizes what Eva meant for the people, as it "logra plantear simbólicamente que la representación de Eva siempre se vinculó al pueblo, es decir, a ella misma" (manages to symbolically suggest that the representation of Eva was always linked to the people, that is, to her own self).[82] While this is right and true, this hand-in-hand moment is not the end of the filmic narrative, and deeper symbolic meaning in this scene can be found. The shot of the clasped hands transitions through a sharp frame-filling burst of light, visually echoing what takes place as the two fingers make contact in the highly symbolic segment from the revolution scene. Importantly here there occurs a momentary shift to a subjective camera from the caboose of the train as it advances along a now bright and serene countryside. The shift in perspective, which leaves the viewer looking back at the landscape in which the young Eva once stood, is a not-so-subtle indication that the final shots are to be viewed from the present moment in time.

In this regard, the two side-by-side figures of Evita and the young, brunette girl gazing contentedly back at the countryside symbolize the director's own contented gaze looking back on the reconstruction of the country's past (see figure 2.6). From this present standpoint, in which exists the ideological adhering of comics to Kirchnerism, the horizon towards which the duo travels becomes highly symbolic of Argentina's rose-tinted future, just as the train – a reconstruction of Juan Perón's *El descamisado,* as we learn earlier in the film – signifies a carrying on of classical Peronism into this hopeful future. In this shot, where landscape can be read as political landscape and transportation as transporting ideologies, the figure of Evita remains her iconic, immortalized self. The young girl, on the other hand, on whose head Evita's right hand rests in a posture of maternal guidance, beyond mimetically representing a young Eva Duarte, can also be read metaphorically as next-generation – and, in this case, next-millennium – Peronism, a movement in the firm grasp of a young brunette who stands under the banner of Evita and is powered by classical Peronism.

Eva from Argentina's final shot provides unyielding proof for the argument made here that, beyond its unique capacities for historical reconstruction, animation also serves as a forward-thinking medium through which sociopolitical ideologies of the past can be almost effortlessly drawn (both literally and figuratively) into the present, with future politics in mind. It was further argued that often times both backwards- and forwards-looking functions play out at the same time

Figure 2.6. Illustrating the (political) landscape of Argentina's past, present, and future (00:58:11)

and within the animated frame. This chapter has explored this idea by highlighting how Argentine director María Seoane employs a national comics-related aesthetic in her biographical film to promote her personal myth of Peronism, a *peronismio imaginario*, to use sociologist Juan José Sebreli's term, at the centre of which stands Evita. I explored how Seoane's strategical use of archival photographs, newsreels, sound recordings, and newspaper reconstructions within a decidedly controllable animated *mise en scène* allows for the rewriting of a highly specific version of Peronism, despite its accepted and acknowledged ambiguity.

A nuanced reading of key scenes depicting, for example, the 1945 encounter of the soon-to-be president and first lady, the latter's political and philanthropic work through the Eva Perón Foundation, as well as the inaugural Loyalty Day, revealed in the film a Peronism characterized by a left-wing, populist love story whose central organizing player – mother figure, even – is Eva Perón, and which culminates in a real marriage that symbolized a fulfilled love story between a leader and his people and signified a full-parent nation. My analysis of such scenes in this underappreciated film also emphasized that the current journalist, author, and film director's personal myth of Peronism readable in the film has as much to do with Argentina's current political landscape as it does with the past. By reading the filmic text against a number of the award-winning journalist's current journalistic texts, I outlined how Seoane illustrates a continuation of classical Peronism in the late Néstor Kirchner, and especially so his wife and presidential successor Cristina Fernández de Kirchner. The latter, I argue, is poetically depicted as the nation's "new" Evita, and as a new flag for Peronism in twenty-first-century Argentina, or at the very least for Kirchnerism rooted in classical Peronism.

Central to this argument was the fact that, while animation itself is an ideological tool (and, in this case, the resignified archival materials are as well), it is the animation's loose cultural connection to the long-running national comics saga *The Eternaut*, as well as its direct association with celebrated illustrator Francisco Solano López, who collaborated on the film's character design, that endows the film with a particular political power. While numerous studies throughout the last decade have sought to explore the transformation of the cultural icon, the Eternaut, into a political symbol with the emergence of the Nestornaut in 2010, it seems that there exist other mutations of this comics-Kirchnersim discursive practice from within Argentina's cultural realm that, through warranted critical attention can add to this emerging discourse. Seoane's *Eva from Argentina* is one prime example, and this second chapter has aimed to do just that.

The following chapter will forge ahead with an even deeper look at animation's ability to embrace comics art – and animators' readiness to do so – in the name of a national project, in this case historical memory in Spain's first so-called "graphic novel documentary": Manuel H. Martín's *30 años de oscuridad / 30 Years of Darkness* (2012). In a reading of this pioneering feature-length animated documentary from Spain, released on the heels of Seoane's *Eva from Argentina* just over a decade ago, I will continue to examine animation's strategic inclusion of the comics medium as a vehicle for historical reconstruction at a time when the critical potential of animation itself was not recognized in Spain as in Latin America. And yet, I will ask how the contemporary medium, characterized by character staticity and narrational voids, becomes the most appropriate choice for the recounting of the decades-long physical immobility and societal invisibility experienced by those who found themselves on the losing side of the Spanish Civil War.

3 Animating Autobiography: Historical Memory and Catharsis in Manuel H. Martín's Graphic Novel Documentary *30 años de oscuridad / 30 Years of Darkness* (2012)

The year 2012 saw the release of Manuel H. Martín's *30 años de oscuridad / 30 Years of Darkness* in Spain.[1] The Goya-nominated, eighty-five-minute film blends a graphic novel aesthetic, archival materials, and talking-head interviews to recount the story of the Iberian nation's so-called post-war "moles" that, fearing assassination or incarceration at the close of the Spanish Civil War (1936–9), were forced into hiding for the duration of the decades-long Franco dictatorship that ensued (1939–75).[2] Making its debut at the fifteenth edition of Málaga's Film Festival in one of Spain's southernmost regions, Martín's documentary provides a very local account of the civil war and Franco era that, for decades, held the entire nation in its grip. As Joan Roman Resina so aptly writes, "Dark, or depressingly gray, was the Spain of Franco. Except, perhaps, for its beneficiaries."[3]

Echoing this sentiment from its very title, *30 Years of Darkness* illustrates the atmosphere of terror, death, and uncertainty that enveloped all those on the losing side of the Spanish Civil War. The conflict, which lasted just shy of three full years, erupted when a group of Nationalist generals led a military revolt against the Second Spanish Republic (1931–9). At its close, members of the losing side were not only those who identified as pro-Republicans, but rather anyone who was seen as politically opposed to Franco and the Nationalists. These ill-fated citizens were relegated, as Spanish cultural studies scholar Jo Labanyi writes, "to the ghostly status of 'the disappeared' – consigned to physical or cultural death."[4] Martín's animated documentary draws on this collective experience of "disappearance" from a private perspective, centring on the real testimony of Manuel Cortés Quero (1906–91). A barber by trade, on 3 March 1936 Cortés would become Málaga's last Republican mayor in the issuing of a public appointment that ultimately condemned him to a life of extreme privacy.

30 Years of Darkness illustrates how, unable to escape Spain after the Republicans surrendered Madrid, an event that brought an official end to the fighting, Cortés made the covert retreat to Málaga. There, with the help of his wife, Juliana, the exiled politician created a hiding place within the walls of a family member's home, unaware at the time that he would inhabit this and other small hiding spaces within his own home for the next three decades. This information is presented to us in the first-person "yo" (I), although the voice that resonates from off screen does not belong to the historical figure. Cortés's reconstructed testimony is voiced by popular Sevillan actor Juan Diego, the implications of which will be discussed shortly. Meanwhile, the narration at times shifts to the third person, as the live-action interview segments feature expert historians and family witnesses, who corroborate Cortés's story and likewise provide accounts of other so-called "moles."

Meanwhile, on the formal level, the graphic novel aesthetic does the work of, in the words of the film's director, "animando los hechos" (animating the facts).[5] The *mise en scène* that comprises Cortés's auto/biographical segments is constructed to resemble the 2D comics page, a single shot often demarcates a single panel, and almost all on-screen movement is created by the camera as it pans across and zooms in towards and out from the largely static characters and action being depicted, much in the same way that the eye of the comics reader would scan the page. Thus, through its pioneering animation comics-technique, *30 Years of Darkness* mirrors the way in which comics are "at once static and animate."[6] Martín himself describes his chosen aesthetic as "una novela gráfica en movimiento" (a graphic novel in motion).[7]

If, as we explored in the previous chapter, Argentine director María Seoane's *Eva from Argentina* features markers of the comics medium (2D characters whose on-screen movements are minimal and whose vocalizations occur through a separate, i.e., off-screen, line of narration), these features can be identified to an even greater extent in the Spanish production *30 Years of Darkness*. Thus, the timing of the release of Martín's documentary film can be seen as significant when we recall that it was just prior to this, in 2011 and on Latin American soil that Seoane conceived of *Eva from Argentina* as an animated comic. When we consider this pair of films together, it becomes apparent that animated documentarians from the Hispanic world began positively exploiting what has been noted as "the rise of graphic narrative as documentary, history, and journalism" in the development of a film's political project right around the time that contemporary, feature-length productions of this type were being released on a global scale.[8]

In fact, Martín's film was widely received by Spain's news media as "una novela gráfica documental" (a graphic novel documentary), a classification that Martín himself adopts and promotes in a special version of the film's trailer made in preparation for the 2012 edition of the Goya Awards.[9] But Martín's media-mixing, genre-bending documentary is so much more. The cutting-edge film signifies the marrying of Spanish comics and cinema, and, more importantly, the divorcing of current cinematic civil war representations from a more realistic documentary or *costumbrista* (local, everyday life) style that has predominated since the 1990s.[10] Furthermore, *30 Years of Darkness* demonstrates a creative coming together of documentary with other genres common to the history of comics and cinema internationally.

On the one hand, Martín's film heavily relies on tropes from the autobiographical comics genre, a form of life writing whose proponents have displayed a particularly profound commitment to creating testimonies of war and conflict. As was noted in the introduction to this book, this class of graphic narratives has been central to the cultural and institutional legitimization of the comics medium. In Japan there was Keiji Nakazawa's manga *I Saw It: The Atomic Bombing of Hiroshima* (1972), while on American soil in the 1990s there appeared Art Spiegelman's Holocaust survivor's tale *Maus* (1991) and the beginnings of Joe Sacco's portfolio of comics journalism with *Palestine* (1993). Prior to this even, in the Spanish context, Carlos Giménez's autobiographical series *Paracuellos*, which chronicles his upbringing in the orphanages of Franco's Spain, began appearing in the comics magazine *Muchas Gracias* (Thank You Very Much) from 1975. This was notably the year of Franco's death and the start of the nation's bumpy but successful transition to democracy, a period known as *La Transición* (the Transition), which is widely thought to have been achieved in 1983.

What started as an alternative – otherwise called independent – comics movement during the mid to late twentieth century has only gained momentum as comics artists continue to acknowledge autobiography as a useful tool for, in the words of one author, "analysing society, reflecting on politics and chronicling the experiences of whole generations."[11] Since Giménez put into panels the trauma he endured as a child living under the roof of the titular orphanage as part of Spain's social assistance program, Spain's *historietistas* (comics artists) have churned out a great number of autobiographical comics as well as graphic narratives based on family testimony, inscribing private memories onto the visual-verbal page in an effort to both broaden and challenge the public discourse of events. These textual constructs have been viewed as part of a process described by one author as "the democratization of history and memory on the Peninsula."[12]

In the 1990s, long-time comics artist Miguel Gallardo (1955–2022) collaborated with his father, Francisco, to turn the latter's long-withheld testimony into the aptly titled comic *Un largo silencio / A Long Silence* (1997, re-edited in 2012). Just over one decade later, comics author Antonio Altarriba and illustrator Kim co-created the National Prize–winning comic *El arte de volar / The Art of Flying* (2009), which, in a similar fashion, provides an account of Altarriba's father's wartime experience. Following this, publications of auto/biographical Spanish Civil War comics snowballed and diversified, notably culminating in Ana Penyas's *Estamos todas bien / We Are All Well* (2017), a female-centred reconstruction of life during the dictatorship and the early years of Spain's democracy, created on the basis of stories told by the author's maternal and paternal grandmothers.

In a roundabout way, *30 Years of Darkness* participates in this predominant comics trend, as the film plainly positions itself as a screening of Manuel's autobiographical comic, in which Martín assumes the reduced (but certainly not passive) role of reader and the camera the position of the film-maker's eye. But beyond participating in Spain's comics memory project, *30 Years of Darkness* claims new cultural territory for this trend beyond the bounds of print-based publications. Ultimately, Martín's hybrid comics-documentary project is evidence of animation's capacity as "the inclusive art," as Paul Wells argues in his animation manifesto, to "embrace all of the other arts within its production process,"[13] just as it is tangible proof of what Frederick Luis Aldama describes as "the exciting ways that comics have permeated other media forms such as literature and film."[14]

Beyond this, *30 Years of Darkness* invokes the thriller genre, evidencing the fact that, as some have begun to show, "popular" genres like fantasy and terror are capable of addressing profound social, political, cultural, and even religious issues – often with even greater insight than realistic productions.[15] Martín's film re-employs the trope of haunting, an element that brings cohesion to the alternating animated and live-action segments, a device common in the highly allusive representations of Spain's turbulent past released prior to the 1990s, but one that waned with what Labanyi has repeatedly called a "memory boom."[16] By this, Labanyi refers to a cultural discourse on Spain's twentieth-century war and dictatorship that first emerged in the years surrounding the nation's political transition to democracy, largely through the vehicles of cinema, television, and literature during the late 1970s and 1980s. And although in the early years of the twenty-first century the flood of civil and post-war texts has been said to have abated, especially in the case of the Spanish novel,[17] we have seen a new surge, as mentioned, in the graphic novel format, what has proven to be "a formidable ground" for the historical memory debates taking place in contemporary Spain.[18] These image/text narratives of Spain's civil war and its aftermath participate in what Leah Thamassian has aptly called "Spain's memory cultures," which accounts for the boom in cultural production of which Labanyi speaks, as well as social and political debates on historical memory in the form of legislation, court cases, and the exhumation of bodies from mass and unmarked graves.[19]

According to Thamassian, the documentation of these graphic accounts is motivated by an anxiety that these stories be transmitted "before the first and even second-hand testimonies slip irretrievably into oblivion."[20] The power that such testimonial graphic narratives hold in Spain and beyond is the capacity to, as Thamassian notes, "bear witness, presenting visual evidence through drawn marks on a page,"[21] a sentiment that recalls the words of Hillary Chute in *Disaster Drawn*, where she writes that this class of comics "materially retrace inscriptional effacement; they repeat and reconstruct in order to counteract."[22] However, beyond bearing witness and a counter-inscription of prevailing discourses on the past, what Daniel Ausente describes as the necessary work "de dar voz a las sombras" (of giving voice to the shadows),[23] historical memory in Spanish comics exhibits a cathartic function for present generations. This is precisely what comics historian Antonio Martín, in his invited prologue to *The Art of Flying*, has suggested of the comic's author, Antonio Altarriba.[24] Antonio Martín's assertion echoes the broader understanding of the healing powers of storytelling, a notion expounded by Irish philosopher Richard Kearney, who has continually theorized the ways in which narrative retelling and remembering might provide cathartic release for sufferers of trauma.[25] Antonio Martín's comment can be read as an ushering in of this idea into the realm of Spanish comics, and likewise an attempt to further the Kearneysian notion of narrative catharsis, which largely recognizes the cathartic power of storytelling "to review *one's own* insufferable pain."[26]

What the seasoned comics historian seems to suggest is that, through narrative recounting, catharsis can also occur for later generations, who, despite not having lived the traumatic past being depicted, still identify in so many ways with the experience. Walthier Bernecker writes that "el pasado de la Guerra Civil siempre estuvo presente en España, hoy más que nunca" (the Civil War past was always present in Spain, today more than ever).[27] For Bernecker, the Spanish Civil War, a touchstone of political and ideological loyalties, continues to condition the consciousness of later generations.[28] Thus, in Antonio Martín's assertion (and Bernecker's, for that matter) can also be found echoes of Marianne Hirsch's concept of postmemory, a frequently cited term introduced in the early 1990s, notably through her encounter with Spiegelman's *Maus* book series.[29] Hirsch herself continues to define and redefine the term that at its core suggests the transgenerational transmission of trauma: "Postmemory most specifically describes the relationship of children of survivors of cultural or collective trauma to the experiences of their parents, experiences that they 'remember' only as the narratives and images with which they grew up, but that are so powerful, so monumental, as to constitute memories in their own right."[30]

Given this definition, and knowing as we do that second-generation remembrance is a key characteristic of historical memory in Spanish comics, not to mention a "necessary process," as Thamassian writes, "through which personal testimony becomes cultural and historical memory, in order for societies to remember,"[31] it should not come as a surprise that postmemory has recently become a key critical lens through which *The Art of Flying* and other civil war comics have been read.[32] In his prologue, Antonio Martín makes specific reference to Altarriba, who published his comic in the wake of his father's suicide at the age of ninety. Yet resonances of the comics historian's notion of the cathartic function of Spanish comics for broader and later generations can be found in much recent scholarly work,[33] which asserts that the testimonial value of these graphic narratives transcends personal memory to become representative of collective memory, a painful remembering not only for the sake of generations past, but likewise for "the later generations, who haven't lived this traumatic past but who still feel it as its own."[34]

And, given this understanding of the pervasive historical memory debate playing out in the pages of Spanish comics, it should not come as a surprise that the Andalusian documentarian turned to the comics medium as an aesthetic vehicle for shedding light on a story of the decades-long repression experienced by Spain's "post-war moles." Although in different ways, animated films and comics converge in requiring viewer engagement with the meaning-making potential of a narrative's visual aesthetic. However, this is more readily accepted and put into practice in comics scholarship, a field of study that has, as Aldama further notes, recently "arrived,"[35] while there remains a lack of recognition and attention to animation as a form. As we have already seen, Wells laments a general recognition of story over style when it comes to celebrating animated films.[36]

Yet we have further seen that over the last decade, there have been a notable number of attempts to analyse how animation functions in the animated documentary genre, largely stemming from Annabelle Honess Roe's *Animated Documentary*.[37] Central to Honess Roe's book, which analyses documentaries that make use of myriad animation techniques from CG animation, to Rotoshop, to traditional hand-drawn animation, is the question of how animation functions as a representational strategy in documentary. This question becomes increasingly relevant for *30 Years of Darkness*, which, as has already been made clear, employs a non-conventional animation technique. But an analysis of the function of the graphic novel aesthetic in Martín's film must likewise take into account that there has been much recent dialogue in comics studies regarding the documentation of history through drawing. A key issue explored in Chute's *Disaster Drawn*, for example, is to what end, aesthetically and politically, the now numerous comics about world-historical conflict visualize testimony.[38]

Keeping in mind these trends in cultural production and the resulting debates in the academic realm, the purpose of this chapter is to directly engage with the graphic novel aesthetic that characterizes *30 Years of Darkness*. In its analysis of Martín's film, chapter 3 offers a chronological progression and geographical expansion of this study, while remaining within the territory of the feature-length animated documentary to continue building on the theme of past and present politics on the big screen. This third chapter seeks to, on the one hand, explore the ways that the comics medium bears on the reconstruction of the past in *30 Years of Darkness*, and, on the other hand, explore the cathartic function, following comics historian Antonio Martín, that the graphic novel documentary has for present-day Spain.

30 Years of Darkness: From Historical Memory to Hauntology

If what Thierry Groensteen says in *The System of Comics* is true (and indeed he begins, "In truth"), that "in an image-based story, as in film or comics, each element, whether it is visual, linguistic, or aural, participates fully in the narration,"[39] then we are faced with many factors for consideration in the interpretation of Martín's comics-based animated documentary thriller. *30 Years of Darkness* combines a dark colour palette of black, grey, and blue tones with a suspenseful soundtrack, and uncanny fluctuations between abrupt character movements (the turn of a head, the blink of an eye, and the brusque movement of a limb) and the complete staticity that one would expect from figures within a (print) comics panel.

While *30 Years of Darkness*'s graphic novel veneer explicitly echoes the notion that, during the bleak years of the Franco dictatorship, comics were "el mejor sitio para irse a vivir" (the best place to go live),[40] the elements that make up the *mise en scène* fittingly invoke the theme of terror that infiltrated comics in Spain beginning in the post-war period and that proliferated during these so-called thirty years of darkness. The jarring concurrence of movement and staticity that the added motion lends to the comics aesthetic heightens the mood of suspense and terror built within the documentary narrative. We see this from early on in, for example, the scene depicting Manuel's attempt to flee Málaga at the outbreak of the war. En route by foot to the Republican zone in the seaside city of Almería, a medium shot situates the protagonist among a crowd of roving exiles. These are collectively drawn in the act of walking, yet appear on screen completely immobile, save for the sudden turn of Manuel's head as he spots warships approaching. The ships, depicted in the following shot, almost imperceptibly bob in the water as their flashing lights amid the foggy seascape constitute the majority of the on-screen movement, and also a serve as a stark sign of warning for Manuel and spectator alike.

This motion should not be perceived as cinematic animation, which, within a comics panel, would result in competing temporalities, but rather can be classified as short animation loops that "can be used within the [comics] panel without overly distorting the temporal map or impeding the reader as they move their attention across space" and, accordingly, do not change the role of the reader to that of a viewer.[41] In a study on the communicative potential of animated elements within digital comics, Joshua Gowdy notes that, when short animation loops are inserted into a comic's panel, the primary mode of narrative progression remains spatial, as "the loop in isolation does not progress either temporally or through space … as it operates at the rate of the reader's attendance."[42] A loop, according to Gowdy, "continually plays whether the reader is looking at it or not, it is only an active element of the fictive world while the reader attends to it; through attention to the preceding and subsequent panels, the reader is able to intuit duration in the same way they would with static panels."[43]

For Gowdy, these movements have purpose. While they provide the reader with an "immersive experience" of a real-world environment, they should not be seen as a superfluous addition (as Groensteen himself has claimed of motion added to digital comics), but rather as one of many elements of signification – that is, with communicative potential – cooperating within the comics page.[44] Gowdy continues that "motion can also be employed to represent specific acts or emphasize ideas that are latent within the still image,"[45] as a means of "provid[ing] additional layers of signification to panels, contributing connotative meaning to mostly denotational images."[46]

A quick jump to a close-up of Manuel reveals his shocked expression, eyes wide and mouth agape, as Diego's voice-over narrates, "De pronto comenzaron a disparar contra nosotros. Fue terrible" (Suddenly they started shooting at us. It was terrible; 00:15:35). Emphasizing this, one ship fires a missile into the crowd of again stationary onlookers, their dark motionless silhouettes lifting unnaturally into the air before being enveloped by a cloud of black smoke and flames. In a subsequent shot, an extreme close-up features the ships' guns as they fire once more and another quick jump to an extreme long shot of the seaside reveals the guns' target as the camera ever so slightly pans across the crowd of exiles along the seaside escape route. Here, the majority of the motion is reserved for the exploding artillery, billowing smoke, and angry rising flames. On the one hand, these largely atmospheric injections of motion, which can be read as Martín's directorial touch in Cortés's autobiographic narrative, introduce to the film's comics aesthetic "a general sense of liveliness, and arguably a means to achieve immersion."[47] Amid the carnage, the depiction of the citizens as motionless black dots together with the restrained movement of the camera reflects the notion of paralysis from fear, and likewise the vulnerable and diminutive position the exiles hold facing the attacking war ships.

In a subsequent shot, which features a total juxtaposition of mobility and stasis, the camera rapidly zooms in on Manuel's motionless figure and face, his frozen look of terror rendered even more powerful by animation's creative control, as the sparks and ash that fly around his expressive but static face serve as minute on-screen indications of the full-scale horror that is being taken in by his terror-stricken eyes (see figure 3.1). With a swift shift to a subjective shot, the viewer now watches from Manuel's perspective the massacre of dozens of civilians, women and children included, in what has become known, as the film narrates, as "el Guernica andaluz" (the Andalusian Guernica; 00:16:50).

And while in early scenes, such as the reconstruction of the Andalusian Guernica, the animated *mise en scène*, together with creative control of motion and stasis, are used to communicate the suspense or terror the protagonist feels as a political refugee during the civil war, the same techniques further along in the film, along with character creation processes, are employed to move beyond suspense and terror to build an aesthetics of haunting that symbolizes Manuel's experience in hiding for decades and likewise the phenomenon described by Patricia Keller in *Ghostly Landscapes* as "feeling the past in the present,"[48] as will be

Figure 3.1. The "Andalusian Guernica" (00:15:53)

discussed in the pages that follow. Keller's assertion that "ghosts are everywhere in contemporary Spain and hold a pervasive and profoundly palpable place in the country's cultural landscape" reflects a predominant psychological interpretation of historical memory that has prevailed in Spanish cultural studies.[49]

While Labanyi is credited with having inspired the pervasive application of a Derridean hauntology to Spanish cultural texts, asserting by 2007, for example, that habitually silenced testimonies re-emerge in an "aesthetics of haunting,"[50] many other notable critics of Spanish literary and cultural studies have since alluded to the notion of a *haunting* within contemporary Spanish society. In his contributing chapter to *Consequential Art*, titled "Drawing (on) Spanish History," Samuel Amago writes from a very recent standpoint that "the country's authoritarian past still reverberates through its cultural present."[51] Through a slightly more violent metaphor, Ulrich Winter speaks to the "irruption" of the lost past, which rematerializes in the present,[52] a notion echoed more than one decade later by Resina in *The Ghost of the Constitution*, where he states that "the Civil War's and the dictatorship's effects erupt in contemporary Spanish society."[53] And although Resina leaves the question of what the "ghost of the constitution" may be an open-ended one, Keller, in her review of the book, aptly writes that "it may very well be historical memory itself, operating as the necessary force that keeps the door to that unbearable breach open, relentlessly working to make us – and future generations – aware that the past remains here, with us, always."[54]

In accordance with this notion of a *ghostly* haunting specifically, José Colmeiro cites the "spectral nature" of Spain's past, which contains stories that have been "silenced and erased, leaving only their ghostly traces."[55] Likewise, social anthropologist Francisco Ferrándiz speaks of the "recent rapid emergence of the ghosts of the Spanish Civil War" in his article that documents the exhumation process of mass graves in the first decade of twenty-first-century Spain.[56] The final two sections of this chapter develop the argument that Martín's graphic novel documentary dialogues with the Derridean concept of hauntology to reflect this cited "spectral nature" of Spain's past, and likewise plays with the idea of the ghost through, in the words of sociologist Avery Gordon, "the merging of the visible and the invisible, the dead and the living, the past and the present."[57] *30 Years of Darkness* becomes an exceptional case, then, for not only employing the trope of haunting, but for doing so to directly refer to a traumatic past, and likewise by employing a modern aesthetic that does not reinforce the "pastness of the past," and thus symptomatically create a disconnect between the narrative and the present-day audience,[58] but rather does the work, in the words of Chute, of offering the "absorptive intimacy" inherent to comics narratives, while "defamiliarizing received images of history … to communicate, [and] to circulate in the realms of the popular."[59]

Specifically, the following sections examine how the reconstruction of Cortés's body, carefully constructed from photographs and voice-overs of contemporary actor Juan Diego, results in a ghostly imbrication of past and present. I will suggest that *30 Years of Darkness* becomes a filmic space to symbolically, as Derrida says, "speak *to the* specter, to speak with it, therefore, especially *to make or to let* a spirit *speak*."[60] Discussion then turns to how the film, largely through camera work and elements of the *mise en scène*, plays with the motif of the haunted house, to not only reflect Spain's spectral past, but likewise the notion that it still lingers within the borders of contemporary Spain. Lastly, I read the shift from animated to archival bodies in the film's final scene as a moment of catharsis, a symbolic exhumation of these Franco-era spectres, and an emblematic unsuturing of the past from the present.

To understand how the trope of haunting that guides *30 Years of Darkness* lends itself to the nature of the "moles" post-war experience, one has only to look as far as the live interview segments that guide the narrative. As Jesús Torbado, author of *Los Topos / The Moles* (1977),[61] states, "Aunque físicamente Manuel Cortés estaba vivo, moralmente estaba ya muerto" (Although Manuel Cortés was physically alive, he was already morally dead; 01:04:56). Torbado's revelation is soon after reiterated by Cortés's granddaughter, María de la Peña, who admits,

"Lo que percibo ahora es que era una fantasma dentro de su casa" (What I perceive now is that he was a ghost within his home; 01:05:26). Torbado's statement coupled with Peña's remark suggests an inversion of the typical ghost, however: these men were physically alive yet morally dead, and their presence in society and family life was reduced to an onlooker lurking and imprisoned in the darkness of their hiding spaces. In perpetuating this notion of imprisonment and invisibility, *30 Years of Darkness* questions the very term *post-war* for the Republican and other moles that lived in the shadows for three long decades, as the title suggests.[62]

Although free to emerge from hiding following the Franco regime's official pardon in 1969, Spain's 1977 Amnesty Law, with the aim of forgetting the civil war and moving forwards with a clean slate in newly democratic Spain, resulted in the silencing of the moles' testimonies and those of their families for another thirty years, until the enactment of a subsequent law that directly opposed the Amnesty Law's narrative of "forgetting" the past. Spain's Historical Memory Law, enacted under José Luis Rodríguez Zapatero's Socialist government in 2007,[63] did not seek to point the finger of guilt at either side, but rather encourage open dialogue at long last about historical memory. This changing political atmosphere, together with a growing social movement aimed at recuperating historical memory, meant both a metaphorical digging up of testimony and a literal excavation of mass graves containing thousands of unidentified war victims, with the first scientific exhumation taking place in the year 2000.[64]

The irony of recuperating the memory of Spain's post-war moles through the documentary genre is that these citizens attempted to live for decades without a trace. Juliana recounts how she destroyed most photographs of Manuel in the hopes that it would help him avoid recognition from neighbours and authorities (00:23:37). Her confession highlights the scarcity of any archival materials with which to reconstruct this particular story. Luckily, the merits of a graphic novel–esque reconstruction need not be debated, as cultural studies has reached the point where it readily accepts "the power of *drawing to tell*,"[65] and likewise recognizes that animation is not only a legitimate substitution for the archival, but moreover, that its capabilities to represent certain aspects of life can in fact go beyond that of live-action film-making.[66]

Yet to the spectator familiarized with Spanish cinema, and likewise with the predominant realism within civil war portrayals and the documentary genre alike, *30 Years of Darkness* raises questions, not just for the fact that it lacks any indexical sign that points to the real Manuel Cortés, but, moreover, for the fact that it displays a *double*-indexicality that points to an altogether different person, from an altogether

Figure 3.2. Rotoscoped image of actor Juan Diego for Manuel Cortés Quero (00:03:31)

different era: contemporary Spain in the voice and face of Juan Diego. In the documentary, Manuel both sounds and looks like someone other than himself, save for one brief archival clip at the film's conclusion, the implications of which will be discussed below. Yet the creative element of Diego's vocal and visual inspiration behind Cortés's figure (and that of fellow Sevillan actress Ana Fernández behind his wife Juliana's character) is one immediate way that the film introduces the trope of haunting. Not only does the colour palette and *mise en scène* evoke a spectral past, as mentioned, but the specific character animation technique likewise evokes the concept of this past haunting the present.

As Honess Roe has argued, in animated documentary indexical connections to real subjects can result in an "uncanny sense of reality haunting the animated image."[67] This sense becomes heightened in Martín's film, as Manuel's body seems not real enough, or not archival enough, and yet appears too real, and too indicative of the present. The word *behind* is not coincidentally used here, as the actors' likenesses appears to exist just behind the layer of animation (see figure 3.2). Using a process similar to Rotoshop, which uses computer software to achieve a hand-drawn yet photorealistic appearance, the production team captured Diego and Fernández's emotions over 400 times in photographic form to assure the final drawing of their protagonists were conceivably lifelike. Although, as noted above, comics narratives that document war and trauma have the purposeful effect of "defamiliarizing received images of history,"[68] Diego, being a very recognizable face in Spanish cinema, gives Manuel an uncanny aspect of familiarity and reality. He is at once graphic and photographic, present and absent, himself and yet "Other." Likewise, it renders the real Cortés virtually invisible in the documentation of his own testimony, tacitly re-emphasizing the invisibility he faced during his decades in hiding. Ultimately, we can view Martín's deliberate process of character creation as proof of the fact that, as Amago writes, "sensitively rendered drawings of human beings in distress form the aesthetic core of contemporary Spanish 'postmemory' comics."[69]

Fittingly, Derrida's notion of hauntology directly relates to what Freud calls "the most striking" example of something uncanny: the return of the dead, and spirits and ghosts.[70] In depicting Manuel's narrative through Diego's likeness, the dichotomies of past/present, presence/absence, and history/story become uncannily blurred. The animated aesthetic of Manuel's testimony acts as a border, but one that is permeable, between Cortés's memory and the communicating body, Diego, and likewise as Cortés's uncanny double in the Freudian sense. The psychoanalyst mentions the *interchanging* of the self that gives rise to the double. This occurs when "the subject identifies himself with someone else, so that he is in doubt as to which his self is, or substitutes the extraneous self for his own."[71]

This first appearance of Diego on screen, as he identifies as Manuel, likewise suggests the apparitional debut of the latter's ghost as he speaks: "Mi nombre es Manuel Cortés Quero, y fui uno de esos hombres que pasaron toda una vida entre las sombras"(My name is Manuel Cortés Quero, and I was one of those men who spent an entire lifetime within the shadows; 00:03:24). The shot mimics that of a traditional talking-head interview, and the result is that the Spanish actor appears not to be re-enacting, but rather to be transmitting a testimony, apparently possessing the knowledge, feelings and experiences of the historical figure known as the "mole of Mijas." In this sense, the fact that Diego is never actually portrayed as speaking (his mouth remains closed as Manuel's voice reverberates from off screen), can be read as an additional suggestion that the action on screen is not an objective re-enactment, but rather a subjective remembering.

Photorealism in animated documentary has largely been said to function as what Honess Roe has called "mimetic substitution"; in the absence of archival footage striving to "create a visual link with reality" by closely resembling it, or, one step further, to "create an illusion of a filmed image."[72] For Martín's film, however, the double-indexical link to Diego suggests that, rather, the animation serves an "evocative" function: the portrayal of certain concepts, feelings, emotions, and states of mind that live-action imagery has difficulty representing – regardless of whether or not live-action footage exists.[73]

The graphic novel aesthetic in *30 Years of Darkness*, then, can be said to exhibit Honess Roe's function of evocation, ironically through a style that is highly mimetic, rather than the more common abstract or symbolic style that usually characterizes evocative animation.[74] The distinctive animation technique stands out as even more remarkable considering that by "activating the past on the page, comics materializes the physically absent. It inscribes and concretizes, through the embodied labour of drawing, 'the spatial charge of a presence,' the tactile presence of a line, the body of the medium. The desire is to make the absent appear."[75] Rather than capitalizing on the medium's ability to make the absent appear, the photorealism of Martín's graphic novel aesthetic renders Manuel as absent, or only spectrally present, while likewise sketching Diego's contemporary figure into the historical past. And, rather than concretizing either presence, the animated yet highly realistic anachronism becomes an apt means of evoking the spectral quality of ghosts, which, in the words of Colmeiro, are "nor [*sic*] here nor there."[76] Or as Keller has pointed out, following Derrida, the understanding "that ghosts exemplify not only a non-presence (the presence of an absence) but also the condition of non-contemporaneity."[77] In short, the aesthetic should not be seen as a means of suggesting fiction, but rather of suggesting friction, precisely the *merging* of the visible and the invisible, the dead and the living, and the past and the present of which Gordon writes.

It does not seem casual that Martín employed Diego to act as the communicating body for the Franco-era spectre, as the actor's previous work in notable cinematic productions portraying the Franco dictatorship makes the conflation of his figure with the post-war spectre an easy one in the spectator's mind. Diego has both symbolically and directly embodied Franco, through his role as señorito Iván in Mario Camus's filmic adaptation of *Los Santos Inocentes / The Holy Innocents* (Spain, 1984), and his portrayal of the former dictator in Jaime Camino's *Drágon Rapide / Dragon Rapide* (Spain, 1986), a career-defining performance that led to the first of his nine Goya Award nominations. Throughout his career, the Sevillan actor has also participated in other Spanish productions that allude in various ways to Francoist Spain, such as José Luis García Sánchez's *La Corte del Faraón / Court of the Pharaoh* (Spain, 1985).

However, his more recent participation in Azucena Rodríguez's nameless short documentary is notable, as the film published in 2010 on Spanish media sites such as RTVE.es and ElPais.com, among global social media sites such as YouTube, similarly appears to dialogue with a Derridean model of hauntology. Rodríguez's film, part of the larger project *Cultura contra la impunidad del franquismo* (Culture against Francoism's Impunity), features fifteen personalities from the Spanish arts scene who embody civil war victims that were summarily executed. In less than ten minutes, the recognizable faces of nine men and six women alternate on screen to deliver brief but compelling first-person testimonies that similarly conclude with the words "Mi familia sigue buscándome. ¿Hasta cuándo?" (My family continues searching for me. Until when?), after which the sound of gunshots ring out as the subject fades from view in a phantasmagorical fashion; the dimly lit backdrop remains on screen throughout while each talking head in turn fades out, dissolving from view as the next subject fades in directly in its place.[78] The direct and (often unblinking) identification of the artist as victim unquestionably evokes the paradoxical "return" and apparitional debut of a ghost theorized by Derrida, while the repetition of the closing statement, "Until when?," emphasizes the lingering of the past in the present that is currently alluded to by proponents of Spanish literary and cultural studies.

It is to an even greater extent, however, that *30 Years of Darkness* plays with the return/apparition of the post-war spectre. Derrida reasons that the apparition of the ghost cannot be controlled: "Each time is the event itself, a first time is the last time. Altogether other. Staging for the end of history. Let us call it *hauntology*."[79] Unlike Rodríguez's documentary, which relies solely on the concept of a communicating body, Martín's own film evokes a first apparition as a purely auditory phenomenon. Manuel's first line delivered in the film, set against a black screen, appears as "an echo without a communicating body."[80] Manuel recounts, "Recuerdo como si fuera ayer, la boda de mi hija" (I remember my daughter's wedding as if it were yesterday; 00:01:30). Following this statement, shots of the festivities materialize on screen as the off-camera voice – seemingly everywhere and yet nowhere – carries on speaking, describing how at his daughter's wedding, for the first time in a long time, the house was filled with music, dancing, and laughter, save for from his wife and daughter, who were on high alert due to the risk that he might be discovered. Not unironically, then, the first apparition as a purely auditory event mimics Cortés's experience as a mere haunting presence at his daughter's wedding, his memory limited to the sounds of the festivities.

As the scene unfolds, the suggestion is that, as Manuel's ghost is given the opportunity to tell this memory, to speak, his presence becomes more tangible. The second apparition provides a partial view of

Manuel as the camera follows a curious young guest into the house and up the stairs. The change of music as the young girl enters the house to a soundtrack of chilling string instruments and pluckish piano notes, together with the creaking floorboards and echo of footsteps, suggests the magnitude of the discovery that is about to take place as she reaches the door behind which Manuel hides, until the tension and eerie silence are shattered with Juliana's sharp command "No entrés ahí"(Don't go in there; 00:02:39). Following this, an extreme close-up features an eye centre screen, captured in the act of peering through a brass key hole belonging to this door. As the camera holds still, the eye momentarily wavers in the key hole before vanishing from sight. In contrast to the jovial celebration taking place outside on the terrace, this early scene works to introduce the Cortés's home as a haunted house, a metaphor that the film continues to employ from these opening moments onwards. After establishing this motif in the opening scenes, the narrative introduces a third apparition of the ghost, this time by means of the communicating body pictured in figure 3.2.

From this third apparition onwards, Diego seemingly becomes the vehicle through which the spectre communicates, although many subsequent shots similarly restrict the view to a single eye, symbolically reflecting the way in which the moles' identity was reduced during their confinement. In many scenes, the camera becomes the eye, framing the action through a small hole in a wall or foundation, attributing to these men the quality of haunting observer. The eye becomes a synecdoche *pars par toto* for the figure of the mole, accurately rendering them nothing more than a watchful eye.[81] This cinematic tactic reflects how their other human senses diminished, sometimes purposefully, as the role of sight increased. Manuel recounts how he tried not to move, became accustomed to not speaking, and even willed himself not to fall ill (00:29:03). Limited to this subsistence, Manuel's own home becomes what Freud calls an *unheimliche Haus*.[82] Rather than security, his house, and his relationship to it becomes characterized by surveillance.

Surveillance is a control tactic seen in many regimes, and Franco's was no exception. The largely inanimate representation of Manuel's character also speaks to the limits of his experience within his own home under the regime's surveillance. In this vein, it does not seem casual that Cortés's animated yet largely inanimate figure juxtaposes Franco's archival figure, depicted in a newsreel clip of his victory parade (00:24:53–00:25:21). The former dictator appears very much animate, visible, and present; three attributes emphasized by subsequent long shots that capture him high on his podium as he surveys the parade in the streets of Madrid. While this segment reinforces the mood

Figure 3.3. The film studio and the haunted house motif (00:13:22)

of surveillance and Franco's omnipresence, the narration of Manuel's testimony in sequential, panel-like shots, rather than fluid animation or newsreels, metaphorically speaks to "a fragmentary, discontinuous, spectral past,"[83] just as it does his desire to escape notice, or, metaphorically speaking, slip through the cracks. As Chute explains, while "comics is a form about presence, it is also stippled with erasure – in the interruption provided by the ambiguous spaces of the gutter."[84]

Aside from the animated and the archival, the film studio can be read as a third space that substantiates the motif of the haunted house. The live interviews recorded against a solid black backdrop are offset by beige partitions, onto which dull beams of light are cast (see figure 3.3). The dim spotlights aimed at these partitions, rather than at the interviewees' bodies, results in the casting of shadows over their figures. In this space, the camera likewise creates the majority of the movement, creeping around the expert and family witnesses. The camera bobs, draws near to, and sways around the subjects, but rarely provides a direct, head-on shot, as if the interviewees are unaware of this looming presence and are in fact addressing an unseen audience.

As the haunted house motif from the animated segments crosses into the shots of the film studio, the metaphor extends itself both forwards and backwards temporally. The spectator understands that, just as Manuel's life was reduced to a haunting presence within the walls of his own home, so too this spectral past lingers within the borders of twenty-first-century Spain. This notion of a multi-temporal haunting emerges through the relationship between the archival, live-action, and animated spaces in yet another way. The setting of the film studio is evidently a space of the present, notable in on- and off-screen cues such as language, clothing, and furnishings, as well as the production clarity and techniques. Conversely, the numerous archival scenes clearly indicate a space of the past: grainy shots depict agrarian culture in the western region of Andalusia, battlefield scenes from the civil war, Franco's troops occupying Málaga, and the 1939 Victory Parade. However, a third temporal space – the comics realm of Cortés's first-person testimony – is not so easily defined. On the surface, mid-twentieth-century Spain as reconstructed by the graphic novel animation style also appears to be a space of the past, yet closer attention to this space, especially when juxtaposed with the indisputable spaces of past and present depicted through live-action and archival footage, reveals that it is actually a space in which both the past and the present are in flux. The aesthetic reveals a spatiotemporal nonsynchronism: the image of the past has been reconstructed using modern tools and has a modern façade, and while the narrative recounts the traumatic happenings of mid-twentieth-century Spain, the voice and face of the story point to the present. Ultimately, the aesthetic mirrors, in the words of Keller, the fact that a haunting occurs "at a disjuncture in time," which is to say that "time can be (and can be *made* to be) out of sync with itself."[85]

In other words, Martín's chosen aesthetic for transmitting Manuel's testimony does the opposite of reinforce the "pastness of the past," which, as Colmeiro suggests, is the effect of realistic and *costumbrista* depictions.[86] Instead, it depicts the imbrication of past and present; a (de)familiar grey area emphasized by the grey tones on screen. In short, the comics realm is the medium through which the spectre of the past is (re)animated: cinematically drawing them on screen, and likewise drawing on the notion of its return. In this regard, there is an important juxtaposition between the animated sphere and the film studio, one that has to do with the notion of letting the ghost speak. Derrida theorizes that when it comes to letting the ghost speak, a scholar "believes that looking is sufficient," and is therefore "not always in the most competent position to do what is necessary: speak to the specter."[87] While the film studio is a place in which the ghost is *spoken of* by intellectuals and scholars, the animated narrative is a place in which, as the film suggests, the ghost *speaks*. Cortés's testimony is voiced by popular culture, aptly through a popular culture medium.

Derrida suggests that we talk to ghosts out of a need "to exorcize not in order to chase away the ghosts, but this time to grant them the right … to a hospitable memory … out of a concern for justice."[88] Derrida's suggestion is that ghosts of the past feel anything but hospitable memory, which is something Manuel remarks early on in the film: "A veces lo único que nos queda en la vida son los recuerdos, aunque para nosotros estos no son más que pesadillas" (Sometimes the only thing we have left in life are our memories, although for us these are nothing more than nightmares; 00:02:45). Following Derrida, in order to move from nightmare to hospitable memory, Manuel's ghost must speak. Performing this, Martín's film becomes what Ferrándiz calls the "resonating chambers" that voices like Manuel Cortés lacked for over sixty years.[89] Moreover, the film's conclusion suggests that through recounting its testimony, Manuel's ghost becomes exorcized.

A Cathartic Release: When Spectral Memory Becomes Historical Memory

The film's concluding scene visually suggests a separation of Manuel's ghost from its communicating body. This scene can be said to contain the first appearance of Manuel's archival body, and likewise the last apparition of his ghost. The tone of the accompanying music changes from the eerie tune that dominates the film to a peaceful piano melody that parallels the calm that Manuel, now an old man, feels as he experiences his first few steps as a free man in his home. A brighter turn in the colour palette, at times iridescent white, also suggests that his home has returned to a *heimlich* place once again, and likewise accentuates the cathartic moment being depicted. As Manuel makes his way slowly throughout his home and towards the front door, the camera adopts his view. This time, however, the subjective lens is not restricted to a hole-in-the-wall perspective, but rather, offers a full view of his surroundings. The mood is no longer one of threatening surveillance, but rather the bright colour palette and wide-angle shot suggest the freedom to both see and be seen.

Through the subjective lens, the spectator experiences the walk towards freedom, descending together with Manuel the staircase from his second-story hiding place, pausing with the old man to consider the family portraits on the living room wall, as Manuel's reflection in the glass frames emphasizes his spectral presence within his family and likewise his absence within the photos, and finally approaching the front door, through which he is about to traverse. As Manuel opens the door, the subjective shot abruptly changes to an objective one. The camera draws backwards as the spectator is left gazing at the back of the animated Diego-figure standing at the threshold. The scene suggests an exorcism of Cortés's ghost, and the audible and prolonged exhale that we hear emphasizes this moment of release. The action puts into pictures what Resina describes in words: "At best, the past can be laid to rest, like a corpse or an exhausted body. Forgotten does not mean 'gone.' It merely means 'out of mind.'"[90]

The following scene reiterates the notion of a separation of the ghosts of the past from the consciousness of the present. Now outside the Cortés's home in the streets of Málaga, the camera rests in front of Manuel and Juliana. No doubt this scene makes us recall the words of Keller on historical memory, being "the necessary force that keeps the door to that unbearable breach open."[91] As the camera crosses the threshold with a definitive cut to an outdoor scene, there is the implication of a door closing. Although for a brief moment the duo is depicted in their animated bodies, the camera again draws backwards as the animated bodies simultaneously shift into the archival figures of the Manuel and Juliana. The distancing of the camera from the archival bodies communicates a distancing of the past, and, with the turn to verisimilitude in the film's final moments, there is a positive connotation to the pastness of the past. The film's singular archival photograph of Cortés confirms what the scene at the threshold suggested: a moment of catharsis in which there is a release of a spectre of the past from the present (social) body. The trope of haunting ceases to exist in the narrative at the moment this archival scene appears, as it is at this point that the exhumation has apparently taken place and the imbrication of the past and present ceases.

The turn to the archival at the film's conclusion is a characteristic that *30 Years of Darkness* shares with the aforementioned acclaimed documentary *Waltz with Bashir*. Honess Roe has noted of Folman's documentary that "concluding the film with live-action footage suggests narrative resolution."[92] Honess Roe ponders, however, whether or not the sudden switch from a consistent animation style throughout to live-action material undermines the potential of the animation that came before, especially at this moment of narrative resolution. This is also an appropriate question for Martín's film, but one to which there is a definitive answer. Here, the turn to archival in the conclusion of a film that employs the trope of haunting is a reinforcement of the exhumation of the ghost, of the departure of the past from the present, and of the perceived end of the haunting through the long-awaited speaking to the past. This cinematic move at the film's end accurately reflects the nature of the ghost, which, as Gordon writes, are "haunting reminders of lingering troubles."[93] However, as Gordon continues, "Once the conditions that call them up and keep them alive have been removed, their reason for being and their power to haunt are severely restricted."[94] Moreover, Gordon elaborates on the photograph's relationship to haunting and to the ghost story, noting that "when photographs appear in contexts of haunting, they become part of the contest between familiarity and strangeness, between hurting and healing, that the ghost is registering."[95]

In this case, the spectator understands upon viewing the archival image that it is familiarity and healing that wins out. With the archival turn, Cortés's story is relegated firmly to the past, or, better yet, to the realm of historical memory. This visually communicates the same notion echoed by Torbado in the final minutes of the film. As Torbado narrates, in all the uproar that has risen about historical memory, no one has remembered those people who were the most victimized of all (1:19:24–34). What is more, Juliana's wide smile and Manuel's slight grin in the archival image communicate Derrida's notion of the past becoming a "hospitable memory."[96] In this sense, *30 Years of Darkness* performs the work of unsuturing the past from the present. Although this separation is not yet so definitive on the level of society, the film's conclusion is indicative of the ongoing work of relegating the spectres through the political, social, and cultural recovery movements taking place. *30 Years of Darkness* stands as an example to other film-makers of how to go about (re)animating the past through innovative methods, emerging as proof that comics are entering in relationship with other media forms, and as evidence that, as Chute notes, the visual-verbal form is expanding the reach, range, and depth of documentary.[97]

30 Years of Darkness blurs the boundaries between animated documentary and the comics medium to a greater extent than we have seen from other cartoonists and film-makers from the Spanish-speaking world to date. Furthermore, it aims to establish additional grounds for the argument that the marriage of comics and animation – two undoubtedly ideological tools – plays a decisive role in shaping the political project that underlies these novel and still limited number of (increasingly) intermedial documentary products from the Hispanic world. That is, comics have come to be conventionally understood as "characterized by an intermedial structure" and even "*per se* intermedial phenomena."[98] *30 Years of Darkness* evidences comics' increasing intermedial capabilities. Martín's so-called "graphic novel documentary" stands as recent proof that an inherently hybrid medium is becoming ever more intermingled with other forms of media, such as literature and film. In the case of the pioneering project from Spain's cultural realm, this is a matter of integrating a genuine comics visual aesthetic into animated documentary while injecting it with motion.

This burgeoning relationship between comics and animated documentary that is unfolding on Spanish soil is explored further in chapter 4's analysis of Aleix Saló's intermedial *Españistán / Spainistan* (2011) project. Here, this study's discussion of the politics of (the very recent) past and present exits the realm of feature-length productions aimed at the big screen and moves into the territory of Spain's digital public sphere. Likewise, the context in question moves from twentieth-century Spain to the twenty-first century, and from the Spanish Civil War to the Spanish financial crisis of 2008 and post-crisis Spain. In chapter 4, I will ask how Saló's six-minute, forty-five-second viral video *Españistán: de la Burbuja Inmobiliaria a la Crisis / Spainistan: From the Real-Estate Bubble to the Crisis* (Spain, 2011) functions as a "disruptive interjection," to borrow Honess Roe's term, within a sea of crisis-related, live-action news and media reports from Spain's official public sphere. By approaching *Spainistan* as a piece of animated journalism, I explore how Saló relies on an editorial cartoon style to artfully synthesize many of the pervasive media debates with its own unique grammar for millions of viewers, while also furthering a number of these most recent debates.

4 Simply A-musing: Aleix Saló's *Españistan / Spainistan* (2011) as Animated Journalism in Spain's Comic Public Sphere

Aleix Saló's six-minute, forty-five-second animated short *Españistán: de la Burbuja Inmobiliaria a la Crisis / Spainistan: From the Real-Estate Bubble to the Crisis* (Spain, 2011) is a to-the-point video that illustrates key events in the ten years leading up to Spain's 2008 real-estate market collapse through a style that oscillates between didactic animation and what can best be described as motion-injected political cartoons.[1] The iconic online short, which appeared in Spain's digital public sphere in the midst of the Spanish financial crisis that erupted in 2008 along with the nation's housing bubble has been widely viewed and has been labelled many things. To the co-editors of *Consequential Art*, Saló's *Spainistan* has been deemed "a definitive shorthand narrative of the crisis for millions of viewers."[2] According to its most-liked comment on YouTube, *Spainistan* is an "obra maestra" (masterpiece), a sentiment echoed by the nearly three million hits the viral video received during its initial three weeks of circulation online.[3]

To Spain's economists and economic journalists, whose specialized knowledge has led to both critical and celebratory estimation of the short film, Saló's *Spainistan* is seen as, for example, a "columna de opinión, pero dibujada y animada" (opinion column, only drawn and animated).[4] Meanwhile, national news and entertainment media discuss the piece more generally, and refer to the film in broader terms: "cortometraje animado" (short animated film); "vídeo ilustrativo" (illustrative video); or even, more simply still, "vídeo" (video).[5]

Back over in the academic realm, in his own contributing chapter to *Consequential Art* Spanish film and comics scholar Matthew J. Marr notes that *Spainistan* "is – from a certain perspective – an animated documentary film short,"[6] though this author later concludes that the "free internet video … begs certain questions with respect to genre" and is "perhaps more descriptively classifiable as a 'book trailer.'"[7] In fact, it is this term (although spelled "booktrailer") that is used by the young Catalan cartoonist himself in the categorization of his pioneering promotional video.[8] None, however, have thought to read Saló's short film as a piece of animated journalism, though if we accept as true what Nea Ehrlich says of this form of animated non-fiction, that it is "a close cousin of the animated documentary,"[9] the pages of this book offer fertile ground for developing a more nuanced understanding of the viral video as well as the ways in which animated journalism converges and diverges from its "cousin" form.

The reason for this critical oversight can first be attributed to the fact that animated journalism had not yet gained traction in the cultural realm at the time that Saló was scheming up *Spainistan*. On this very topic, Rachel Porter, a UK-based journalist and freelance writer and director of London's visual thinking agency Scriberia, writes in a colloquial vernacular that "the landscape in which journalists operate has changed and continues to change so dramatically, that to cling to the belief that news – or indeed any other information, like academic research, or an annual report – should be presented in a certain way seems pointlessly blinkered."[10] Porter highlights how, within the last half decade, animation has been embraced as a form of journalism, and its place in the news realized by established national news papers such as *The Guardian*, and its increased use recommended by the BBC in their 2015 Future of News Report as one method of reinventing the news to engage younger audiences as animation is well suited to appear in-stream on a variety of social media platforms.

As proof that the journalistic animation of factual events "is gaining a foothold everywhere," Porter also provides examples of Bloomberg's infographic-style explainer on the European debt crisis and the "completely bonkers" work of *TomoNews*, an English-language branch of Taiwan's broadcasting channel Next Media Animation, in animating the UK's Labour leadership election. In fact, Ehrlich offers as one case study (among others mentioned by Porter, such as the *Guardian*) *TomoNews*, which daily produces upwards of thirty breaking news stories from around the globe, along with what they themselves consider "the craziest, weirdest, most unexpected stories" through animation and a tone that favours both snark and satire.[11] Perhaps we can credit the equally satirical and in its own way "bonkers" *Spainistan* with paving the way in the Spanish imaginary for the positive reception of the two-and-a-half-minute *TomoNews* report, hailed by Spain's news media as a "cómico" (comical), "resumida y divertida" (simplified and entertaining) take on the Spanish state of affairs, which in 2012 included the ongoing crisis and its side effects such as financial cutbacks, tax hikes, and popular protests, as well as concurrent political (re)actions such as the Catalan separatist movement.[12]

To Porter and Ehrlich's findings we can add that, around the same time, and overseas on US soil, the Berkely Graduate School in Journalism Advanced Media Institute offered a two-day workshop on storytelling through animation for, among others, journalists, editors, media professionals, and educators. All of this points to the fact that, as Ehrlich writes from 2018, "the use of animation in factual reporting is now clearly an increasing journalistic norm."[13] Of secondary importance is the fact that, as a natural consequence, scholarship on animated journalism is only a recent development and a developing discourse.

Ehrlich appears as a lone voice in the anglophone tradition; unless we consider Wibke Weber and Hans-Martin Rall's conflation (although perhaps not consciously) of animated documentary and comics journalism in their assertion that both forms of non-fiction storytelling "bring a fresh and surprising tone into journalism."[14] Although these authors do not explicitly consider the possibility of animated journalism as itself a form of documenting reality, the proposed taxonomy of ten authentication strategies that they outline in their article (five for each genre) are, according to their concluding words, "well suited to examine continued convergence and assimilation between both genres."[15] Given that their intent is prophetic, it is somewhat ironic that nearly one full decade earlier, Saló's *Spainistan* evidenced this convergence, as an assimilation between comics journalism and animated documentary, as the majority of its shots, as was already said and as we shall soon see, can be classified as motion-injected political cartoons.

Meanwhile, in Spanish-language scholarship we can find preliminary musings from animated documentary scholar-practitioner Emilio Martí López, who sees attention to journalism as a missing component of Honess Roe's otherwise "fantástico" (fantastic) book on animated documentary.[16] Maker of *MAKUN (No llores): Dibujos en un C.I.E. / MAKUN (Don't Cry): Drawings in an Immigrant Detention Center* (Spain, 2019), a thirty-minute animated documentary that illustrates some of the many injustices and human rights violations that occur within the walls of Spain's Immigration Detention Centres, Martí López interchangeably refers, from the very title of his article, to his own filmic production as a work of "animated journalism" and animated documentary. And while throughout his own metatextual musings the film-maker of experimental animation does not explicitly classify *MAKUN (Don't Cry)* as one form of animated non-fiction or the other, in the conclusion to his article Martí López does suggest that factors related to distribution and denouncement can provide a starting point for classifying an animated non-fiction film as animated journalism.

In terms of distribution, this means possibly skirting a slow and costly animation technique for something more quick and cost-effective if the theme is urgent. It also means opting out of the traditional and beneficial (in terms of merit and money) route of release in festival circuits and cinemas for open, online, and immediate distribution. Beyond thematic urgency, Martí López notes that animation can act as a "contrapeso, como cuarto poder, a gobiernos, jueces y congresos – y añadiría, medios de masas –, que también usan la emoción para trasladarnos sus verdades" (counterweight, as a fourth power, to governments, judges, and congresses – and, I would add, mass media – who also use emotion to convey their truths to us).[17]

That both of these ring true for the distribution of and denouncement within *Spainistan* solidifies its case as a piece of animated journalism. What makes *Spainistan* an interesting case for study, then, is precisely the relationship of the short film to the Spanish media coverage of the crisis in the moment of its appearance. In the pages that follow I will argue that Saló's animated documentary stands as an important "animated interjection," following Honess Roe,[18] arising from Spain's digital public sphere, which, around the very time of *Spainistan*'s release, evolved into a platform for alternative or counter-hegemonic discourses to those of the official public sphere.[19] That it does so through the vehicle of satire also makes it a signifier of what Caron has very recently called the "comic public sphere"; a parodic counterpart to Habermas's public sphere that is a product of the creative union between satire and the public sphere.[20]

As an animated interjection, *Spainistan* intentionally disrupts the steady stream of live-action crisis-related media coverage permeating Spain's newspaper pages and broadcast news, in short – and through a short – aiming "to highlight and hammer home," to borrow Honess Roe's alliterative idiom,[21] the causes of the crisis. Specifically, by means of its own unique grammar, laden with visual metaphors, *Spainistan* both succinctly and satirically interjects into the stream of five widespread media debates "that to some extent explain scenes of [Spain's] particular 'narrative' or 'story' of the crisis."[22] Chronologically speaking, these are "Is There a 'Real-Estate Bubble'?" (2003–7), "The 'Champions League' Economy, or, An Economy in Crisis" (2008), "Green Shoots" (2009), "Spain Is Not Greece" (2010), and "Maybe the Banking Industry Isn't Such a Model" (2011).[23]

These debates were critically taken up within Spain's business and economic journalism both leading up to and during the crisis, while public authorities as well as the most influential businessmen, as Ángel Arrese concludes, "tried to minimize the seriousness of the situation."[24] As will be concluded later in this chapter, Saló's short piece of animated journalism stands as a critical expression that, on the one hand, interjects into these debates and, on the other hand, also stretches these debates – effectively functioning, we could say, as an interjection with interventionist aims. This will in fact be argued of Saló's narration of the most recent pair of debates that gained traction during the production and publication of the *Spainistan* project, in which government and media alike patriotically adopted and promulgated the slogan that "Spain is not Greece," and the media's "blindness" or quasi-deferential attitude towards the strength of Spain's national banking system.

From a definition standpoint, understanding *Spainistan*'s role as one of "intervening" in Spain's popular consciousness implies that the film was made with a political project in mind that would seek to prevent or alter an already established way of thinking. This already stands as a change from the official media and popular masses alike, who have decried the documentary's pro-socialist slant.[25] Alternatively, Marr, for whom the iconic YouTube video "represents an unexpectedly meaningful and memorable intervention" in Spain's popular consciousness,[26] employs this term to show that *Spainistan* is "a comics-based exercise in public pedagogy that ... subversively 'uses and abuses' certain elements of 'the very structures and values it takes to task.'"[27] And, while both of these understandings of intervention imply a distinct political project that underpins Saló's film, I wish to reveal a different political project, one intrinsic to its animated aesthetic. Viewing *Spainistan* as a piece of animated journalism that intentionally *interjects* more aptly captures the film's main goal of interrupting an already occurring dialogue to provide a unique expression or exclamation through an unrelated grammar. The six-minute journalistic short seeks the same audience as Spain's communications media, yet makes a memorable statement with its own unique grammar and intervenes in the most current crisis-related debates.

Spainistan and the Satire Two-Step of A-musement

In *Spainistan*'s cold open, a scene set within the year 2011, as indicated by a time stamp in the top left corner of the frame, the viewer encounters a personified Spain, appositely drawn as a mere outline of itself (00:00:10; see figure 4.1). Having just woken up, Spain sits upright in bed, visibly suffering from a hangover, as suggested by the character's audible groans as well as the emanate: here, small bubbles and stars that originate

Figure 4.1. Spain's economic hangover (00:00:26)

from Spain's head, floating upwards before bursting near the top of the shot. This is quickly confirmed by the narrational voice-off, which explains that the country, the real (social) body in question, is "jodamente jodido" (royally fucked) from its decade-long "fiesta de padre" (mother of all parties) – in other words, the rampant consumerism of which Marr speaks. It is here that the filmic narrative's alternative title is introduced in a Quijotesque fashion by the off-camera narrator – "A esta historia la llamo 'De aquellos barros, estos lodos'" (I am calling this story "From that mud, this sludge") – following which the film moves to the opening scene, which transports the spectator backwards in time to 1998.

On screen, a small, black-and-white caricature representing Prime Minister José María Aznar is struck by the notion of neoliberalism, literally, in this case, as his character is humorously yet violently jolted by a lightning bolt representing his illumination to the neoliberal policy that promoted the liberalization of land to boost the construction sector and a widespread facilitation of access to credit (00:00:45). This satirical scene parodies the Old Testament story of Moses and the Ten Commandments, as Aznar, here stylized as the biblical prophet, is for a second time literally struck by his neoliberal policy, this time flattened into the earth by a stone tablet that falls from the sky and fittingly reads, "Ley de Suelo" (Land Law; see figure 4.2). The biblical parody is apt, perhaps above all for the fact that the decree law enacted by Aznar greatly benefitted the Spanish Catholic Church, which saw its ability

Figure 4.2. Prime Minister Aznar struck by neoliberal policies (00:00:48)

to register property in its name extended to places of worship such as cemeteries, smallholdings, chapels, and cathedrals. This start not only foreshadows the parodic nature of the film's source text highlighted by Marr, but also sets the tone for the satirical short.

In fact, Saló's use of humorous satire is one of the main reasons why Marr chooses to classify *Spainistan* as a documentary film, despite the fact that satire counters the predominant solemn tone within social documentary cinema. Marr draws parallels to the work of American director Michael Moore and "the ways in which both artists, when confronted with social circumstances of disaster, harness the power of dark humor in their respective projects of satirical public pedagogy."[28] While I prefer to classify the *Spainistan* book trailer as a work of animated journalism, I find great value in Marr's reasoning that satire should not be conceptualized as antonymous to documentary in general, and to animated documentary in particular, as this argument rings true for other forms of animated non-fiction such as animated journalism. Here, satire appears to counter the anticipated authenticity, which, in forms such as news reports and journalistic articles "is closely linked to accuracy, credibility, trustworthiness, and truthfulness."[29] However, taking what Caron says as true, that satire, "no matter how aggressive its laughter-provoking presentation" implicitly advocates for the "values of reasoned debate, facts and evidence, accountability, and transparency that characterize Habermas's concept of the public sphere," we can see how *Spainistan* as

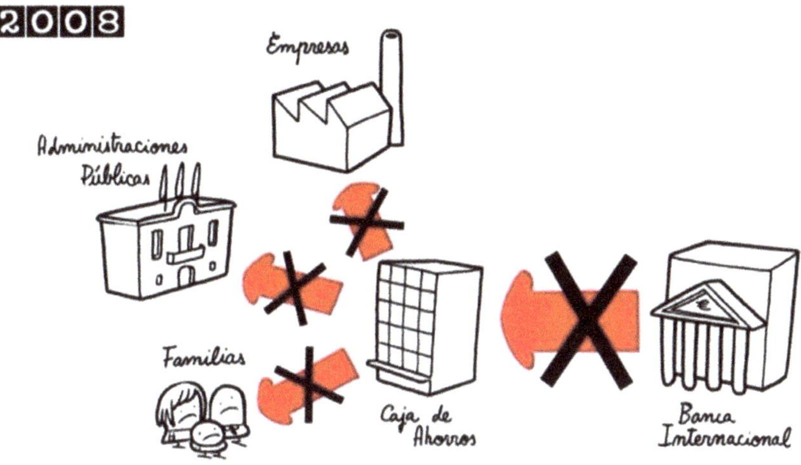

Figure 4.3. *Spainistan*, the animated documentary: crisis foregrounded (00:06:03)

a piece of animated journalism should be read as an authentic voice in the crisis debates circulating in Spain's public sphere.

The idea for *Spainistan* came about when, at the start of his career, Saló sought an effective way to promote his first Spanish-language graphic novel, the semi-homonymous *Españistán: Este país se va a la mierda / Spainistan: This Country Is Going to Hell* (2011), which appeared the same year as its video counterpart.[30] First released on Saló's personal website on 25 March 2011, the video was then posted to YouTube two months later, where it went viral. The intent behind the online offshoot of *Spainistan* was to promote the print text, as mentioned, but more importantly to contextualize, essentially functioning as a factual prologue to the more colourful and narratively complex fictional comic.[31] The author-artist himself has commented that "el cómic es una mirada cínica a nuestro futuro, mientras que el vídeo es una mirada crítica a nuestro pasado" (the comic is a cynical look at our future, while the video is a critical look at our past).[32]

In just over six minutes, *Spainistan* sets the stage for the comic's potential reader by reporting on the real social, political, and economic factors and events that contributed both to the growth of Spain's real-estate bubble at the turn of the twenty-first century and to its burst; the latter event generally understood to be the "epicentre" of Spain's 2008 Spanish economic and financial crisis.[33] As figures 4.3 and 4.4 show, the cover of the print comic aptly captures how this same (f)actual crisis that is at the

Figure 4.4. The cover of *Spainistan*, the comic: crisis as factual context in a fictional tale

fore of the animated film serves as the background for the fictional tale, which centres on the quotidian exploits of a *nini* (slacker) named Fredo.

The print comic, which was swiftly adapted into a digital (e-book) version, offers a parodic tale that unfolds within what has been called Spain's "temporality of crisis (2008–2013)":[34] the handful of years following Spain's 2008 financial and economic crisis, which coincided with a global economic recession. *Spainistan: This Country Is Going to*

Hell tells of Fredo's misadventures as a twenty-five-year-old average citizen navigating a life suddenly marred by a never-ending mortgage and harsh unemployment. In the shaping of Fredo's tale, Saló's graphic narrative notably parodies J.R.R. Tolkien's *The Lord of the Rings*, though it also plays with many other classic and popular cultural texts from within and beyond Spain's borders.[35]

Meanwhile, the animated pretext offers an admittedly simplified vision of the decade leading up to the 2008 financial crisis, making clear, as Saló himself felt called to explain in the international weekly newspaper *El economista* (The Economist), that the disaster was not only an avoidable one, but one in which all of Spain's social sectors collectively played a fundamental role in creating.[36] Despite its secondary – or supporting – role, it is well known that the release of the *Spainistan* video, rather than the publication of the *Spainistan* comic, launched the cartoonist's career, and that within a few short years, the comics artist from Catalonia became a successful author-artist of what has been called a "narrative universe."[37] This creative cosmos centring on social criticism begins with a work in Catalan published by Glénat Spain, *Fills dels 80: La generació bombolla / Children of the '80s: The Bubble Generation* (2009), and includes the transmedial *Spainistan* project along with what have been commonly classified as two other "graphic essays," each one slightly preceded by a respective promotional video: *Simiocracia: Crónica de la gran resaca económica / Apeocracy: Chronicle of the Great Economic Backwash* (2012), and, two years later, *Europesadilla: Alguien se ha comido a la clase media / Euronightmare: Someone Devoured the Middle Class* (2014), both published by Random House Mondadori.[38]

In short, the reach of Saló's comics-based corpus of cultural products rapidly grew from the regional level to that of the national to the international, and from a local language to a national tongue and subsequent translations into many international languages. And, while the Catalan cartoonist effectively vanished from the limelight of Spanish media and culture following this four-year concentrated period of creativity, he suddenly re-emerged on 16 April 2020. How this happened was in habitual fashion, with the posting of another book trailer to YouTube, the seven-and-a-half-minute *Todos nazis / All Nazis* (Spain, 2020). Unlike *Spainistan*, I would without hesitation classify this short video as an animated documentary. *All Nazis* blends animation and archival materials, notably a heavy dose of early twentieth-century editorial cartoons and black-and-white photographs. The digital short also creates a dialogue with history rather than with debates surrounding current events, though no doubt Saló has an essayistic intent here too, as he illustrates how history is repeating itself with the rise of the ultraright within and beyond Spain's borders.

The film, which at one point received tens of thousands of hits on YouTube, is seemingly no longer available. During its brief run, however, it no doubt served the purpose of promoting Saló's latest comic, *Todos nazis: Cómo España se llenó de "fascistas" hasta que llegaron los fascistas / All Nazis: How Spain Filled Up with "Fascists" until Fascists Arrived* (2020), which was released one month following the animated documentary, this time under the banner of Reservoir Books. One subscriber to Saló's YouTube channel, making a pointedly apt comics-related commented on one of his videos, writes that "Aleix es batman, aparece en tiempo de crisis y luego no se le vuelve a ver por aquí en años" (Aleix is Batman; he appears in times of crisis and then you don't see him again around here for years).[39] This is true to a certain extent of the innovative illustrator, whose costume and cape would be the oft-sported graphic tee and zip-up hoodie, although it should be noted that the low-profile cartoonist explicitly rejects any attempt by the media to place him in a hero-type role, which was an initial and immediate reaction to the release of *Spainistan*. In one interview given in the wake of the publication of *Euronightmare*, the budding cartoonist admitted that he once read of himself that he was the "dibujante de la revolución" (cartoonist of the revolution),[40] while more than a handful of news articles declared that, without trying to or wanting to, Saló became the "portavoz" (spokesperson) of an entire generation.[41] For the young cartoonist, this is a tactic of the media, who "van locos por encontrar un referente" (go crazy looking for a referent) from the younger generation of Spaniards.[42]

As Marr argues, the significant public attention garnered by Saló's *Spainistan* video can be understood in the context of the 15-M Movement or *Indignados* (Outraged) Movement,[43] an anti-austerity movement arising publicly on 15 May 2011, as the name indicates, with mass mobilizations in many of Spain's popular *plazas* (squares), although connectivity and collaboration were initially generated online through various social media platforms. These demonstrations sought a regeneration of Spain's political landscape, long characterized by a two-party political system. The protests, carried out by millions of mostly younger Spaniards, were fuelled by Spain's lingering financial and economic crisis, the results of which left this particular demographic calling for basic rights related to housing, work, political participation, culture, health, and education. However, the Catalan-born comics artist has stated outright that the goal of his many media appearances is not to incite rebellion, but rather simply to sell books,[44] and in relation to the crisis it would be more accurate to speak of Saló as reporter rather than revolutionary.

This does not mean that Saló's satirical, well-researched *Spainistan* video is devoid of political commitment. Even though it does so within a mere six and a half minutes, *Spainistan*, as has been said, critiques "both Spanish governmental economic policy and a societal shift towards rampant consumerism,"[45] and, I would add, leaves no room for doubt about its status as animated journalism that features a distinctive angle. What the author-artist sought to bring to his compatriots was a rigorously researched, but admittedly simplistic "visión de calle. La de alguien que explica las cosas tal y como lo haría con un amigo, en una sobremesa o en una tertulia de bar" (street view. That of someone who explains things just as he would with a friend, in an after-dinner conversation or in a social gathering at a bar).[46]

In fact, news headlines have repeatedly highlighted the satirical video's fresh take on the crisis surrounding Spain's real-estate bubble: "'Españistán,' un divertido vídeo de YouTube explica la burbuja inmobiliaria" ("Spainistan," a Fun YouTube Video Explains the Real-Estate Bubble); "Dibujos para entender la crisis" (Drawings to Understand the Crisis).[47] Saló, in accordance with these, headlines his personal website "Important Problems Explained through Comics & Comedy," and a subtitle further explains, "We try to cover problems that matter in a fun and visual way."[48] When asked by *La Vanguardia* (The Vanguard) to comment on citizens' ability to understand the messages systematically delivered by Spain's communications media, Saló admits that he himself was the first to falter in his understanding of the crisis, as otherwise comprehensible figures and denominated political movements were often delivered in pieces devoid of a general context: "La principal barrera para entender este mundo socio-político y económico no es una falta de formación, sino una falta de tiempo. Uno tiene que dedicarle muchas horas a la actualidad para entenderla. No todo el mundo dispone de esa hora al día"(The principal barrier in understanding this sociopolitical and economic world is not a lack of training, but rather a lack of time. One has to dedicate many hours to the present in order to understand it. Not everyone has that time in a day).[49]

Spainistan's greatest strength is that it declutters Spain's early twenty-first-century sociopolitical and economic climate for its viewer, with its own precise and concise grammar that is far from simplistic. For its present-day treatment of the economic crisis, *Spainistan* appeals to one of the oldest forms of comics making in Spain, just as in the whole of the Western world: the political cartoon, a form commonly characterized by a language that is both satirical and metaphorical. Saló's *Spainistan*, in other words, performs what Caron calls the "satire two-step of a-musement": that is, it provides "a pleasurable reflection on the civic issue at hand."[50] As Caron continues, satire engenders a comic laughter that "entails two steps for the audience: be entertained but then be thoughtful about the critique embedded in the satire." It is for its aim to simplify, noted by Saló and the Spanish press, as well as its performance of the satire two-step of a-musement that in the title to this chapter I have labelled the short film as "simply a-musing." And though the aim of Caron's seminal book is to highlight "satire's robust presence in contemporary American culture,"[51] the same – or even more, for that matter – has been said of Spain, where satire has been a present force throughout the nation's history, "configurándose en una suerte de correa de transmisión, de vehículo informativo y comunicacional" (configuring itself as a type of driving force, for an informative and communicative vehicle).[52]

For both of these scholars, the ubiquity of satire in contemporary Spanish and American culture is due in large part to Web 2.0, as a place to both produce and share political satire, and for Caron specifically, YouTube as the "progeny" of the Internet, is for this purpose "a video world unto itself."[53]

It is from this realm of social media that Saló's direct and unapologetic take on the causes of Spain's financial and economic crisis dialogues with the crisis debates, largely taking the same "no illusions" approach that is noted to have been characteristic of the Spanish media.[54] From its very title, *Españistán: de la Burbuja Inmobiliaria a la Crisis* dialogues with an institutional refusal dating back to 2003 "to recognize the existence of a bubble, and thus not speak about the perverse consequences of a potential burst."[55] Just as this institutional avoidance of the topic did not hinder "the media from using that concept and having regular discussions about it," *Spainistan* draws on Spain's real-estate bubble and its "perverse consequences" (read: *Crisis* with a capital C), and, meanwhile, the short video also draws immediate attention to these two previously taboo topics with the same treatment of "Burbuja Inmobilaria." With this stylistic move, not seen in the titles of his other works, the Catalan cartoonist further emphasizes the use of these recently controversial terms by unconventionally capitalizing them despite that they are not the first word in the video's title – thus breaking with Spanish-language capitalization conventions that are respected by the press.

In this and in other more important ways yet to be seen, Saló's journalistic short surpasses the function of the Spanish press, which "has been the one-eyed in the land of the blind, or at least in a country where many didn't want to see at all."[56] To suggest that *Spainistan* takes the same "no illusions" approach as the communications media in the claims that it makes about Spain's sociopolitical and economic actuality during the decade leading up to the crisis does not imply a simplicity or minimalism of language in either context – whether verbal or visual. In fact, in trying to reflect Spain's true state of affairs during the financial and economic crisis, the Spanish press has been noted to employ "the power of the conceptual metaphors to create shared frames of interpretation for current events."[57] This, despite the ideological and editorial diversity of the many Spanish newspapers, which has ultimately led to criticism of "the extent to which the media coverage of economic issues tends to produce uniform thinking, interpretations dominated by technical arguments, and institutional and elitist explanations of current events,"[58] resulting in, as Arrese and Alfonso Vara-Miguel argue, a situation in which "the media have not been able to distance themselves from the specialized frameworks of analysis used by experts and economic agents."[59]

While the varied Spanish communications media have been said to frame the national and continental crisis in a rather homogenous way, "produc[ing] uniform thinking, interpretations dominated by technical arguments, and institutional and elitist explanations of current events,"[60] Saló's *Spainistan* can be said to reframe Spain's 2008 financial and economic crisis for its viewer in a way that is remarkable. On the one hand, it does so by employing its unique visual-verbal grammar, as already noted, and, as will further be discussed, by notably reframing the financial and economic crisis through a medium that is economical and one that historically favours synthesis: highly didactic animation and motion-injected political cartoons. In short, rather than relying on the power of conceptual metaphors to say things with a bit more colour, so to speak, *Spainistan* employs what Chute calls "the power of *drawing to tell*,"[61] presenting the facts through simple, black-and-white images, often layering visual metaphors on top of the common conceptual metaphors and other narrations in the voice-off. Furthermore, in turning to ink and pen, and subsequently to motion in order to dialogue with many of the media's rhetorical debates through visual metaphors, Saló's short recognizes "the witnessing power of drawing in the age of the camera."[62]

This is visible in a sequence of shots that playfully draw attention to the second media debate, chronologically speaking, *The "Champions League" Economy, or, An Economy in Crisis* (2008). This year-long debate, which addresses the bleak outlook for Spain's economy, resulted from a comment made by then Prime Minister José Luis Rodríguez Zapatero on 11 September 2007, when the Socialist Workers' Party leader optimistically affirmed that, "haciendo uso de un símil futbolístico, se podría decir que la economía española ha entrado en la *Champions League* de la economía mundial" (to use a soccer simile, it could be said that Spain has entered into the Champions League of the world economy). It was not so much Zapatero's affirmation that sparked the debate, but rather the political leader's prolonged negation of the crisis that ensued.[63] In this case, the use of the conceptual metaphor "'Champions League' economy" adopted by the media is a direct denouncement of Zapatero's own choice words, a public figure who, it has been said, was no stranger to employing metaphors as a form of obscuring a grim reality or indirectly answering a question in his political-economic discourse.[64]

Saló retrospectively adds a layer of satire to this particular public economic debate, playing with visual metaphors to dialogue with the conceptual metaphor of the "'Champions League' economy." Midway through the video is a midshot of Zapatero, caricaturized as wall-eyed, giving a toothy grin and raising his trademark eyebrows in excitement as a speech balloon that rivals his figure in size relays in a tone of equal excitement, "¡¡Estamos en la Champions Lij!!" (We are in the Champions Lij [*sic*] !!; 00:03:17). The focal point, however, is the upside-down funnel atop Zapatero's head, evoking the well-known Hispanic phrase *ley del embudo*, a refrain inspired by the funnel's conical shape that often goes "Lo ancho para mí, lo estrecho para ti" (roughly translated as "The wide part for me, the narrow for you"), and sometimes "Lo estrecho para otros, lo ancho para uno" (roughly translated as "The narrow part for many, the wide for one"; see figure 4.5). The dunce-like funnel, visually antonymous of a crown, becomes a satirical jab at the political figure, who appears more like a court fool than a king of champions.

The asynchronous image, framed within a shot that features a 2005 time stamp in the upper left corner while the famous utterance parodied in the speech balloon on the right occurred in 2007, can be understood not as erroneous, but rather as a way of extending this attitude of inequality that the *ley del embudo* exemplifies to near the start of Zapatero's two-term presidency, which ran from mid-2004 until the end of the calendar year 2011. The notable absence of the word "crisis" within this scene echoes Zapatero's own tactics of negation, while the makeshift dunce cap appears as a clear denouncement that signals the former prime minister's failure to properly execute his duties. Thus, the visual metaphor works towards denouncing on two levels: on the one hand, it criticizes the notion of a "Champions League" economy, and, on the other, it calls attention to a foolish head (a clear metonym here for head of state just as the personified map of Spain initially appears as metonymous for the social body) that conceived of this notion.

Figure 4.5. *Ley del embudo* / funnel law (00:03:17)

In fact, as Arrese reminds us, this idealistic vision of Spain's economy and banking system was still promoted well into the fall of 2008, when Zapatero, despite finally acknowledging that the crisis was a reality, "reunió a los principales editores de medios para pedirles moderación, para que evitaran dar una visión catastrofista de la situación – como la que, en opinión del gobierno, estaban dando –. Al mismo tiempo, se debía comunicar a la ciudadanía la fortaleza del sistema bancario español – a diferencia del de otros países –, y la capacidad de respuesta de la economía española ante la crisis" (got together the chief media editors to ask for their moderation, in order to avoid giving a catastrophic vision of the situation – like that which, in the government's opinion, they were giving. At the same time, they should communicate to Spanish citizens the strength of the Spanish banking system – unlike that of other countries – and the Spanish economy's response capacity facing the crisis).[65] The successful promulgation of this false vision culminated and quickly crumbled when some now-famous choice words were spoken in May 2009 by finance minister Elena Salgado, who publicly announced, "Esperemos unas semanas y se verán los brotes verdes" (Let's wait a few weeks and the green shoots will be seen).[66] From this widely criticized comment, the "green shoots" debate began to unfold, in which field experts, politicians from opposing sides, and national and international media alike challenged the idea of such early and rapid recuperation. It would not be until 2015, in fact, when a legitimate, although not unproblematic and certainly not uncontested, narrative of recuperation would emerge.[67]

Accordingly, at the time in which *Spainistan* appeared, the general consensus of the debate was still, in the words of an editorial from *The Economist*, that "Spain's decade of growth has come to a painful end. In contrast to much of Europe, which is home to a few green shoots, Spain's economy still looks as arid as the meseta."[68] It is around this sentiment, it seems, that Saló draws his own conclusions – pun intended – on the "green shoots" debate. The final series of shots in the short documentary dialogue explicitly with the notion of an arid economy and a lack of green shoots in the same characteristic way of, as already mentioned, layering original visual metaphor upon common conceptual metaphors.

For starters, the narrational voice-off simultaneous to the representation of an exploding atomic mushroom cloud tells us that in 2008, the financial crisis exploded in the United States, after which, in Spain, as the narration goes, "de la noche a la mañana, los bancos dejaron a prestar dinero" (overnight, the banks stopped lending money; 00:05:54). Meanwhile, the visual narration depicts a large cactus seated in a plush arm chair behind a desk, occupying the place of a banker, next to a sign that reads, "Caja Morcillo: Habla mucho que no te escucho" (Morcillo Savings Bank: You can talk but I'm not listening). The succulent plant, native to arid regions, is a clear metaphor for Spain's economy: dry, inhospitable, and even thorny. And, rather than draw this scene into the aforementioned central territory of the meseta, Saló chooses to emphasize the desolateness by placing the action at the "caja de Morcillo"; a savings bank within a remote municipality of the nation's westernmost and borderland province, Cáceres, Extremadura.

The visual metaphors that add to this debate do not stop here. Moments later, as Saló's narrational voice-off goes on to say that "el consumo se desplomó, se contrajo la economía, las empresas empezaron a hacer despedidos en masa"(consumerism plummeted, the economy contracted, and businesses began making mass-layoffs), a literal green streak runs across the screen at midlevel, entering a personified Spain through its midsection, into which it momentarily disappears. A split second later, the streak, now red and representing the nation's gross domestic product, can be seen to emanate from this same region, this time running towards the right side of the frame as a means for Saló to graphically depict the collapse of national consumption yet also symbolically communicate a bleeding out of Spain's economic lifeline. The shot that follows features a line of a different sort: a snaking procession of bodies waiting at the doors of the Instituto Nacional de Empleo de España (National

Figure 4.6. The Spanish dream or gummy-bear land? (00:01:26)

Employment Institute of Spain), a scene strictly portrayed in black and white, communicating the unequivocal, or absolute truth of this reality.

These scenes, which, I argue, dialogue with the "green shoots" debate, become especially poignant when read against a highly memorable scene from earlier in the film; the most colourful and fanciful scene in the short animated documentary by far. Bright red hearts, colourful rainbows, flying unicorns, and smiling hills, clouds, and meadow flowers frame a young couple, mid-embrace, positioned under the slogan "Spanish Dream," scripted in a soft marshmallow font (00:01:26; see figure 4.6). The scene is rounded off with a rendition of Bob Marley's *One Love*, as the lyrics "Let's get together and feel all right" work to frame the happy couple in an additional way. However, the Spanish dream is just that: an illusory image not actually unfolding on Spanish soil but rather in "el país de la gominola" (literally, "gummy-bear land") as we are told by the narrational voice-over.

It is understandable that the notion of "green shoots" of recovery did not sit well when, only a decade earlier, the so-called Spanish dream was rooted in the illusion of fertility and abundance – that is, the notion that, as is aptly illustrated in one scene, Spain had long been sitting on a pile of money (00:05:14) – and when, in the current context, the realization that the nation's economic growth was caused by deep seeded debt was an unavoidable one. In short, when the illustration of the cactus in the later scene is read against the anticipation of economic prosperity in the earlier scene, it once again becomes evident that Saló has taken the "no illusions" approach as the news media on this particular debate, just as he does by openly naming from the get-go the real-estate bubble as well as the crisis, criticizing the notion of a "Champions League economy" prior to 2008 and, in the year that follows, the notion of economic "green shoots." Yet as I have aimed to show, the cartoonist deepens these debates, offering an even more transparent stance through the use of visual metaphors coupled with the conceptual metaphors reiterated by the news media.

On the other hand, the Catalan cartoonist uses the same tactic in an effort to reframe the crisis by offering a contrastive perspective on a number of the debates highlighted by Arrese. Specifically, *Spainistan* can be seen as an animated interjection with interventionist aims into two of the more recent debates taking place during the creation and distribution of *Spainistan*: "Spain Is Not Greece" (2010) and "Maybe the Banking Industry Isn't Such a Model" (2011). An analysis of *Spainistan*'s position on the 2010 debate brings us to the conclusion of the short film. The final exclamation point of what is understood here as Saló's animated interjection into media and cultural narratives of the crisis reveals another visual metaphor: the bull, which is generally considered an icon or symbol of national identity, or Spanishness par excellence, albeit one that is not associated with politics.

Here, however, the symbol bears heavy political underpinnings when it is read as part of a dialogue inherent to other cultural representations of the crisis (from graffiti and slogans to cooking television shows and horror movies) that use gastronomy – the social circulation of food images – as one decisive symbol for the landscape of the crisis.[69] In *Spainistan*'s final moments, the drawing of the emaciated bull emphasizes the biopolitical links between nutrition, economy, and society that underpin Spain in its current state. That is, with a singular black-and-white drawing, or rather, through the on-screen substitution of one illustration to a related yet dissimilar one, Saló concisely relates the multifaceted effects that the crisis has had on Spain's socioeconomic body (00:06:24–9).

Further, when read in comparison to the image of Spain in the cold open as a personified map, the spectator is made aware that the price to pay for consumerist "gluttony" and all of Spain's other "sins" is not merely a temporary hangover, but rather an enduring malnourishment. The shift from the fancy-scripted word "España" to a wobbly written "Españistán" accompanies the cut from the centred shot of a solid-coloured and proud-standing black bull to that of an emaciated and foolish-looking bull. That the bull is unwell and only a mere outline of itself, much like the symbol of Spain in the cold open, emphasizes the politicization of the image of the bull.

As is well said by Rodríguez Bartolomé in *El economista*, although in reference to the short film in its entirety, "Lo que hace bien el video … es explicar en escasos siete minutos el proceso de empobrecimiento que ha seguido España hasta convertirse en Españistán, en clara referencia a la mala situación económica que se vive en las repúblicas del Asia Central que acaban en 'istán'" (What the video does well … is explain en scarcely seven minutes the impoverishment process that Spain has followed to become Spainistan, in clear reference to the poor economic situation that is being lived in the republics of Central Asia and those that end in "istan").[70] Along the same lines, Muñoz-Basols and Massaguer Comes say of this final sequence that "a skinny cow appears to the sound of Middle Eastern background music, thereby reaffirming the humour evoked by the drawings through the effect of 'anchoring' the viewer-listener in this imaginary *Españistán*, where poverty and political chaos are the norm."[71] While these authors are correct in the assertion that image of the malnourished bull, together with the appearance of the film's title on screen, evokes a poverty and political chaos that imaginatively links Spain to the Middle East, they appear misguided in their reading of the background music as a reaffirmation of this conceptual link (as are many of the social media users that commented on the YouTube video in search of the origins of this song, which has remained shrouded in mystery and assumptions).

Closer attention to the soundtrack, which has a Middle Eastern ring to it, reveals that the closing song is actually the Macedonian-Roma song *Usti Usti Baba*, translated into English as "Wake Up, Wake Up, Father." The song is meant to celebrate the moment during a wedding ceremony when the bride's dowry, the *cheiz*, is brought out of her house. As the song plays in the background during the final moments of *Spainistan*, a second and simultaneous conceptual tie is formed, linking Spain to the likewise crisis-laden Greece. What the country is on the threshold of, however, is not a marriage but rather a bailout from the European Union, and what is at stake is not a dowry but rather a larger debt. Furthermore, the lyrics "Wake up, wake up, father" in the final seconds of the video create a conceptual link back to the cold open, where Spain becomes awake – here literally and figuratively – to the reality of the crisis.

Given this understanding, the video's final scene, and, accordingly, the conclusion to the piece of animated journalism, is punctuated by uncertainty. While the image of the sickly bull stands as an exclamation point in Saló's animated interjection, the musical link to Greece also renders the image a big fat (while alarmingly skinny) question mark as the scene dialogues with the narratives constructed around the Greek crisis by the Spanish elite press. The media debate, "Spain isn't Greece," revolves around "a new slogan [that] emerged, which actually was approved by everybody – including government, media, and other institutions – that reads 'Spain is not Greece.'"[72] The debate, which was not really a debate but rather an assertion in the form of a slogan, gained traction in May 2010 alongside the first international bailout package of Greece and extended well into the second half of the decade.[73] To the viewer-listener in tune with the then budding news media insistence that "Spain is not Greece," Saló's final scene poses the lingering question "… or is it?" and thus effectively emerges as one voice that gives the so-called "debate" credence to this name.

The image of the emaciated bull further challenges this slogan by dialoguing with a fear of "'contagion' from the Greek 'terminal' financial situation";[74] a key point in the discussion as, from the span of 2010 to mid-2012, the spotlight was on both Greece and Spain together, as the two nations similarly suffered problems with sovereign and banking debt. This fear of metaphorical contagion, as Arrese and Vara-Miguel remind us, was echoed in news media coverage, while Saló's final visual statement of the sickly looking bull, set against music native to the Macedonian territory as mentioned above, suggests that this is not a possibility to be feared, but rather a fact to be faced, and that, when it comes down to it, Spain is not that different from Greece. Furthermore, when viewed from the cultural realm, and especially from the specific niche of short animated non-fiction digital productions, Saló's *Spainistan* can be seen to dialogue with Christos Lefakis and Yannis Konstantinidis's animated trilogy *The Greek Crisis Explained* (Greece/UK, 2010).[75] Whether Saló drew his inspiration from the prior production is untold, but in hindsight his own crisis-explaining animated short from the following year, as well as an implicit dialogue with the "Spain is not Greece" debate, leaves room for sound speculation that there is a creative link between the two cultural products from the pair of crisis-laden countries.

But, this is not, as mentioned, the only debate that Saló artfully expands. *Spainistan* similarly can be said to go further beyond the consensus within Spanish news media during the early years of the crisis on what Arrese calls the "Maybe the Banking Industry Isn't Such a Model" debate, entering the debate as an interventionist interjection. The strength of the banking system is, as Arrese notes, "the aspect of the Spanish economic and financial crisis about which the media was blindest."[76] The traditionally kept deferential attitude to the industry was fostered largely by attitudes and official statements of strength and solvency from high up within the Spanish banking system, government officials, and even field experts.[77] The sharp turn in perspective did not occur, it has recently been concluded, until late December 2011, around the time of the formation of Mariano Rajoy's government,[78] while others pinpoint the shift to the time shortly following the European Union–wide banking stress tests of 2010.[79]

If the former were true, it could certainly be said that Saló's *Spainistan* diverges from the media consensus of the time, being released already in the spring of 2011. But either way, *Spainistan* interjects into the debate with a direct and unrelenting criticism, rather than perpetuating a veneer of untouchability surrounding the industry and a "quasireverential and too respectful attitude" to Spain's national banking system.[80] This is evident largely in a string of scenes around the two-thirds mark of the film. Here begins a didactic segment in which Saló uses charts and graphs to show the skyrocketing cost of housing per square metre, the falling unemployment rates, the fact that housing prices more than doubled from 1998 to 2005 while salaries "se habían quedado más congelados que Walt Disney" (stayed more frozen than Walt Disney), and finally Spain's poorly performing average salary (read: "sueldo de mierda" [shit salary]) compared to that in other European Union nations like Germany, Belgium, the UK, and France in the year 2005 (00:03:35–00:04:05).

Following this, an unspecified character, serving as an on-screen sounding board for the off-screen narrator, appears in the centre of an otherwise blank shot to ask why people keep buying houses if housing prices keep rising and salaries stay the same. In response, Saló narrates that this is where "TU AMIGO EL BANCO" appears, in what is perhaps the boldest statement the short film makes in more ways than one (00:04:05–15). On a formal level, the solid black bubble font that slides into the shot from the top of the frame and comes to rest in front of the character fills the width of the screen, shielding the figure from sight while symbolically covering up the suspicion raised by his voice. On a deeper level, the bold statement can be read as sardonic criticism of the trustworthiness of Spanish banks as well as a widespread (like the font) naivety of its patrons that would come to be echoed by economic experts in years following, notably by economist Santiago Niño-Becerra, who repeatedly put out warnings from 2012 onwards stating, "¿Engañado? El fallo fue pensar que el banco era nuestro amigo" (Tricked? The fault was thinking that the bank was our friend), and "El señor del banco nunca es tu amigo" (The banker is never your friend).[81]

Saló's early criticism of the industry continues with a cut to a similar banker's scene; only here it is a smiling, waving clown that occupies the banker's chair, seated behind a desk with a red carpet leading up to it from the bottom of the frame (00:04:18). The numerous visual metaphors here are obvious, and as pointed as the large sign shaped like an arrow to the clown's right, replete with flashing lights, in which shines the message "Caja de Morcillo: Créditos a porrillo" (poorly translated as "Morcillo Savings Bank: Credit in abundance"). The confluence onscreen of the clown, circus lights, and red-carpet welcome evokes the singular image of a fun house, while the viewer's screen serves as a mirror that provides a distorted reflection of the risk of entering into a relationship with the bank under relaxed credit requirements. Meanwhile, in the words of Niño-Becerra, "La realidad era que cuantos más créditos se concedieran, mejor: más consumo y más comisiones para el banco; y cuanto más aumentase la deuda, más mejor: más crecimiento para esa entidad financiera; y cuantas más preferentes se vendieran super mejor: más personas felices por poder obtener un cacho de las ganancias financieras" (In reality, the more loans were granted, the better: more consumption and more commissions for the bank; and the more debt increases, the better: more growth for that financial institution; and the more *preferentes* sold, even better still: more people happy for being able to get a piece of the financial profits).[82]

Fast-forward two minutes in the film, which also brings us to 2008, and the banker is illustrated in a much more distant, and official light. So distant, in fact, that only his arm is visible on screen, reaching in from the right side of the frame as he hands an unhappy family their eviction notice for their failure, we are told, to make payments on their mortgage (00:06:09). Here, rather than fun and games, the bank is portrayed as all business; the featured arm is clad in a black suit and white dress shirt, and the hand holding the eviction notice approaches the frowning trio in a downturned and dismissive posture, which is a sharp contrast to the two-handed, welcoming wave given by the clown.

It is from here that Saló's fast-paced piece of animated journalism speeds towards its conclusion, illustrating the extent of Spain's debt problem with money "stolen" from the future, as well as the fact that the nation, which was poor all along, was no longer Spain but rather Spainistan. The critical work that Saló achieves in only six minutes, on both a verbal and a visual level, is extraordinary, as is his ability to not only interject into a number of key crisis-related debates occurring within Spain's news media coverage, highlighting and hammering home for a news-saturated viewer, for example, the institutional refusal to call the real-estate bubble what it was, the Zapatero government's false vision of a "Champions League" economy, and the notion of rapid recovery in the form of "green shoots."

What is more, the Catalan cartoonist's "a-musing" animated report, to recall Caron's term, does more than interject in these debates. As we saw, Saló's *Spainistan* also intervenes in a number of the most recent crisis debates, effectively challenging the notion the "Spain is not Greece" and drawing heavy-handed criticism of the banking industry from early on. The comics and digital content creator does so, as has been shown, by adding his own unique visual metaphors to the common conceptual metaphors used within the Spanish press and broadcast news of that time, while also dialoguing with a tendency from the cultural realm to represent the crisis by means of gastronomy to illustrate Spain's "malnourished" state.

This visual-verbal criticism seems exceptionally extraordinary when one considers that the opposite has been said about the very industry with which Saló enters into a dialogue: as Arrese concludes in his early article, "It's hard to say that the Spanish press, particularly the country's economic and business journalism, delivered extraordinary critical work, alerting and condemning in an exemplary fashion, before and during the current financial and economic crisis. The very immaturity of the industry probably made that task impossible."[83] Interestingly, the relative immaturity of economic journalism in Spain, which dates back to the late 1970s during the Transition era, taking off and gaining relevancy following Spain's 1986 entrance into the European Union,[84] does not even compare to the fact that "the Spanish comics industry has emerged, ironically, with the crisis."[85] Moreover, as we have already noted in the introduction to this book, a mix of old and new generations of comics artists in Spain found inspiration in the hardship created by the nation's financial and economic crisis, turning this in to one of the main themes in the graphic novel publishing boom of the 2010s, no doubt the backbone of the recently (re)emerged industry.

Saló is one of these new generation artists, and his book version of *Spainistan* is a critical cultural text that displays, to recall Marr's words, an "activist spirit of satire,"[86] and thus, I would add, is a comic that signifies Spain's comic public sphere, just as does its digital, animated counterpart. Though the six-minute viral video has been read largely through the lens of comics studies, as a hard-to-classify cultural text that seemingly skirts the borders of Spain's recently reborn comics industry as well as its growing animated documentary sector, this chapter has sought to locate it firmly within the emergent territory of animated journalism, while showing that its connections to comics creation run much deeper than its status as a promotional tool for its graphic novel source text. I have aimed to show the significance of the fact that Saló draws on the long-standing tradition of the editorial cartoon, shaping many a scene around what I call motion-injected political cartoons, fittingly using these as a vehicle for entering into dialogue and debate with Spain's news media from the digital public sphere.

By reading *Spainistan* as a piece of animated journalism, this chapter has responded to a recent call for proponents of animated documentary studies to pay more critical attention to other forms of animated non-fiction. In the same way, the following chapter also pushes the bounds of scholarship on animated documentary. There, we will see how Germany-based Mexican animator Victor Orozco Ramírez composes *Reality 2.0* (Germany/Mexico, 2012) as a highly personal animated essay through which he compares and contrasts for the viewer what I call his "two Mexicos": one that is based on a utopic vision of traditional culture, and another where narcoculture has become a "hellish" new daily reality.

5 Tracing Cultural Continuities: Rotoscope, Archons, and Archive 2.0 in Victor Orozco's Essayistic *Reality 2.0* (2012)

Victor Orozco Ramírez's eleven-minute animated documentary *Reality 2.0* (Germany/Mexico, 2012) was the highlight of the young Mexican film-maker's career at the Hamburg University of Fine Arts.[1] Despite being the product of a novice director, Orozco's short film has garnered an impressively long list of awards (twenty) and an extensive record of film festival participation (over 150) in the years since its release.[2] For the Mexican-born animator, who emigrated to Germany in 2003 as a late twenty-something from his native city of Guadalajara, one difficult part of the project was deciding in which direction to take the film.

An initial idea, he says in an interview with *Singulares* (Outstanding), was that *Reality 2.0* would offer an essayistic comparison of Orozco's host country with his home.[3] This is still perceptible in the film's title sequence and opening segment: as a starting point for comparison, and a metaphorical opening to the film, Orozco draws a muted and altogether underwhelming sun, veiled in smog-like animation. The film-maker, who serves as the film's off-screen narrator, all but says in an opening line that the German sun does not compare to "el sol de México" (the Mexican sun; 00:00:47). The pale yellow orb, which rests in the upper right-hand corner of the shot but does not come close to filling it, is the focal point of a backdrop over which the film's title is cast, across the bottom left-hand corner in a hand-drawn retro-style pixel font.

Overpowering both image and title is the increasingly loud sound of a plane in rapid descent. The realistically drawn aircraft enters the shot from the very top of the frame, seemingly having passed over the spectator's head – an almost 4D-viewing experience due to the intensity of the sound and the direction from which the plane arrives on screen into a rotoscoped runway scene. In the action that ensues, we are made aware that this sun-and-cloudy-skies backdrop is captured from Germany, current home to Victor, the director's protagonist- and narrator-self.

Orozco's off-camera narration tells us that he has just arrived here, leading us to imagine, in retrospect, that what brought him was this very plane, although this seems impossible given that the aircraft combusts into a ball of fire after a drawn-out bumpy and skiddish landing.

The fiery explosion, radiating outwards to fill the frame of the wide-angle shot, offers an abrupt transition to a medium shot of the director's protagonist-self on a city bus. Victor, it seems, has been transported from the crash site to his seat on the bus, as he comes into view through a cloud of jet-black smoke that quickly dissipates over his head. The bus scene is constructed around rotoscoped footage of the director and the bus driver, who appears to be the only other person on the vehicle. Rubbing his eyes and visibly shaken, what seems to preoccupy Victor more than his inexplicable near-death experience is the fact that the driver is more focused on an open copy of a German tabloid than on the road in front of him, an element that is drawn in to the scene, as is the cloud of smoke that links the bus scene to the plane crash in the prior arrival scene. Nevertheless, Victor's apprehension then turns to a look of amazement as his gaze shifts in the opposite direction, out the window to the German landscape.

It is through this opening scene that the film-maker discloses his longing for Mexico (specifically, and in this order, for his family, his friends, the food, and finally the sun), while we also hear him marvel at the things that one seemingly does not find in Germany (streets lined with dogs, rats, and children). The streets of Germany offer for Orozco a visual-verbal starting point for developing this country comparison. Speaking through synecdoche and in a statement laden with metaphors, in which the street becomes a microcosm of both German and Mexican society, Orozco marvels at the fact that "aquí, en este país exótico, y gracias a los avances en la ciencia, habían transformado las ratas en conejos callejeros" (here, in this exotic country, and thanks to scientific advances, they have transformed the rats into stray rabbits; 00:01:02). Though we see through Victor's eyes – thanks to a quick jump to a subjective camera – a colony of rabbits roving the forested landscape along the tree-lined roads, it takes little effort to realize that the "stray rabbits" (literally, "street rabbits") of which Orozco speaks are actually fleets of Volkswagen vehicles, another *pars pro toto*, as the metaphor refers to the compact car that debuted in Europe in 1974 as the "Golf" but quickly earned the "Rabbit" moniker following its import to North America. This Volkswagen allusion offers yet another synecdoche, this time for the German automotive industry, which, together with the manufacturing and export of machines and chemicals, contributed to Germany's post-war economic success and its socio-cultural transformation following the 1945 fall of Nazi Germany,[4] and along with it, the nation's anti-Semitic ideology, alluded to by Orozco with the mention of rats.

It is at this early moment, and through his reflection on Germany's history of war, "rats," and "rabbits," that the film's focus shifts, following Orozco's directorial gaze towards his home country, even though he wants, as he narrates, "distanciarme un poco de México" (to distance myself a little from Mexico; 00:01:23). Yet the comparative framework persists even with this narrowed focus, around which the remainder of the documentary film is organized. Only, what the Mexican film-maker ultimately juxtaposes for his audience in *Reality 2.0* is two different Mexicos. These are not the "two Mexicos" depicted by global business and economic journalists and political scientists over the last few years – one highly productive, characterized by modernization, globalization, and a business-class society, the other increasingly unproductive, dependent on subsistence farming and marked by impoverishment.[5]

Instead, Orozco's film portrays the competition and clash of two cultures on Mexican soil and in the digital public sphere, whereby members of drug cartels "take advantage of the immediacy and vast dissemination of the Internet" to upload propagandistic films or raw-footage videos of torturous interrogations and assassinations on YouTube and other, less regulated, websites, such as the infamous *Blog del narco* (Narco's Blog),[6] the main source for trafficking-related news in Mexico and the primary forum for what Robert Gomez calls the "competition of video violence between cartels," not to mention a springboard to other sites that "are just one click away."[7] And while Orozco's film takes a sharp turn, the essayistic form persists. *Reality 2.0* remains an essay film, with "the look of a documentary filtered through a more or less personal perspective."[8] More precisely, with its digital form, *Reality 2.0* signals what Timothy Corrigan refers to as an "intriguing contemporary transformation" of the decades-long tradition of the cinematic essay film.[9]

Reality 2.0 visualizes in a spectacular way the common sentiment that Mexico – in its geographical and digital public spheres – is home to co-existing value systems: on the one hand, a "more restrained" culture based on traditional values, and, on the other, a fast-growing "deviant" form known as *narco cultura* (narcoculture).[10] As Bunker and John P. Sullivan write, this means that traditional values and ways of living are being replaced by the ideologies and value systems held by the most powerful narco groups.[11] What Orozco paints are nostalgia-tinged snapshots of traditional Mexican culture – from bullfighting and celebrations surrounding the national holiday *Día de los muertos* (Day of the Dead) to small/local business culture, using them as a visual starting point to communicate how spectatorship and entertainment, business, and even death has transformed under the influence of narcoculture; a new reality that for the director is foreign yet fascinating. But it is not unrecognizable. Orozco is not talking about a complete transformation of one set of ideologies and value systems to another altogether, but rather connections and continuities that are, to recall Bunker's term, "deviant."

Orozco is not alone in speaking of this transformation of Mexican culture through poetic language. For Robert J. Bunker, who has published widely on the topic, the cartels and gangs are akin to "cancerous organizational tumors" in the host "body" of Mexico.[12] These "cancerous" cartels, Bunker writes, are transforming the institutions and structures of Mexican government and society into their "own version of what the human condition and relationships should be."[13] In the opinion of this counterterrorism and international security professional, neither state nor society is immune to these tumours, and, what is more, they do not necessarily resist them. In short, for Bunker, no part of the Mexican body is beyond the reach, grasp and corrupting effect of Mexico's narcoculture, in which we see "the glorification of narco-violence, narco-corruption, narco-songs, narco-mansions, and narco-saints."[14] To Bunker's list we can add other objects and acts, such as those signalled by Gomez: *narco mantas* (narco-blankets), onto which messages are inscribed and which are left in the proximity of dead bodies, "function[ing] as a type of Narco public service announcement"; *narco tortura* (narco-torture); and *narco bloqueos* (narco-roadblocks).[15]

Like Bunker, María L. Christiansen turns to biology in search of a metaphor for the co-existence of Mexico's il/legal cultures, though she favours one that is less disparaging and more in line with Orozco's talk of "rabbits" and "rats." For Christiansen, narcoculture and official culture are "dos nichos ecológicos [en] un mismo ecosistema" (two ecological niches in the same ecosystem),[16] although there is blurring of the boundaries, or a "con-*fusión*" ("con-fusion") of the borders of the two cultural realms. As we shall soon see, Christiansen's description could is also apt for describing the use of rotoscoped animation in *Reality 2.0*. This technique becomes for Orozco a way of making visible the lens through which he views "his" Mexico, where there occurs not only a transformation of traditional values, but also a fusion of new reality and old to the point where the lines demarcating the one from the other are blurred beyond distinction.

The "two Mexicos" that Orozco illustrates are generational. Not having been born into what Bunker and Sullivan call the "prevailing narco status quo," Orozco, like many from his generation and those earlier still, experiences a "re-socialization" into a new value system, seeking, as Sullivan elsewhere writes with Rosales, "a viable place in the social strata … [of] an alternate reality that challenges Western state sensibilities."[17] Conversely, those born into this status quo readily accept it.[18] To this later generation, reality "2.0" is actually just reality, and narcoculture has always been their status quo, or, to use the neologism employed by some, "la narcotidianeidad" (roughly, "the narco-everyday-reality") in which they grow up.[19]

Although this is but an implicit argument in Orozco's essayistic film, it is explicitly highlighted in another recent documentary on the topic. In a scene from Shaul Schwarz's nearly two-hour *Narco cultura / Narco Culture* (USA/Mexico, 2013),[20] a live-action documentary film that will be discussed more thoroughly in a moment, we witness the hyperbolic ramblings of a star-struck teenage school girl, who suggests that *narcocorridos*, folk songs in a genre that glorifies drug violence as well as the lives of the larger-than-life cartel kingpins, are listened to and liked by almost everyone. Schwarz interviews the girl while she is waiting with her peers outside the gates of a set for a narco action film featuring a well-known *corrido* singer. She confesses her dream of becoming a drug trafficker's girlfriend, rationalizing that this is just a way of life; "No es nada malo" (It's not anything bad). When challenged by a few of her peers, she immediately flips her statement to admit that "tal vez sí es algo malo, pero es una forma de vida" (perhaps it's something bad, but it's a way of life). The girl's possibly wiser friend steps in to help her out, though much of what she says is left on the cutting-room floor, and all we are left with is the explanation that, in their Mexico, "es algo que es una cultura para nosotras" (it's something that is a culture for us; 00:42:10–42).

Orozco, though near the beginning of his career at the time of *Reality 2.0*'s release, belongs to an earlier generation for whom narcoculture is not the status quo, but rather a *transformed* reality. As this book has aimed to show, animation is a useful tool in documenting past and present realities, through a variety of styles and techniques that can trace political issues, actions, myths, and points of view through the numerous national histories across the Spanish-speaking world. In the case of Orozco's *Reality 2.0*, animation is the ideal tool to illustrate this *transformation* of reality from traditional culture into narcoculture; in other words, for teasing out this cultural transition for the viewer, who may or may not know anything other than this narco daily reality.

To be more specific, it is the animation technique of rotoscope, which draws into the film the underlying live-action footage, that allows for the visual communication of a transformation. The technique inherently requires that the animator engage in a process of transforming reality so that its presence (or absence) remains and yet the ensuing product is something more (or less). From a formal standpoint, Orozco's use of rotoscope is a stylistic choice that allows the montage of user-generated, live-action content to appear as a cohesive whole curated by Orozco's directorial hand. However, when considering the characteristics of rotoscoped footage – live-action scenes that are traced over with ink, whose components can be either emphasized or effectively erased depending on the qualities of this line and of the treatment of the various background elements, and to which hand-drawn elements can be added – it is easy to imagine the essayistic potential that this long-standing animation technique allows.[21]

If, as mentioned in the previous chapter, animated journalism is a "cousin" of the animated documentary, a distinct yet related form of animated non-fiction, the same kinship can be attributed to the animated essay, which shares an even closer bond and should perhaps be considered a "step-sibling," given its documentary roots. Yet this undertheorized form of film-making also shares ties with the graphic essay, which, as Jesús García Cívico writes, hinges on the possibility of thinking in images. Accepting that this is also the cornerstone of animated essay, Orozco's *Reality 2.0* emerges as extraordinarily essayistic given his choice of rotoscope as a narrational tool. That is, the Mexican film-maker was forced to engage in this process of thinking essayistically with (moving) images twice over: first, by thinking critically about the organization of the live-action found or filmed footage; and, in turn, considering how its treatment through animation would result in its resignification. In other words, in composing *Reality 2.0*, Orozco held in mind a vision of both a starting image and a final image that, in one single shot or sequence, could show the similarities and differences between thing A (traditional culture) and thing B (narcoculture), and more importantly, certain continuities in ideology and values from of the one to the other.

We see this in the Hamburg scene, with the added action of the bus and plane crash (as well as the elements of fire and smoke and all), not to mention the detail of the tabloid paper drawn into the hands of the bus driver, who in the original footage is seen keeping a firm grip on the steering wheel and a steady gaze on the road ahead. With the addition of these hand-drawn elements, Orozco draws connections between participation in popular culture, voyeurism, and violence to, on the one hand, forecast his intent to comment on the relationship between these elements in Mexico's narcoculture and, on the other, to illustrate the universality of the underlying theme of his essayistic film. That the constructed violence in the Germany segment is accidental and mechanical can be read as an allusion to the fact that the nation's main exports continue to be vehicles, machinery, and chemical goods, and serves to contrast the fact that the drug-related violence within Mexico's borders is ideological and human.

These brief moments of fictional violence (or hallucinated violence, we may wonder as Victor rubs his eyes to clear his vision) illustrate the relationship between voyeurism and violence, as well as the reach of narcoculture across geographical borders. They also forewarn the viewer of a thematic shift towards voyeurism and violence in general, as well as a contrasting of Mexico's traditional and narcocultures in particular. First, there is the explosion of the airplane, and second, a multi-car pile-up involving the bus on which Victor was travelling moments before. By yet another miracle, however, he appears in the foreground of this scene, a little sooty but again smiling as his gaze is set on the Hamburg cityscape before him (see figure 5.1).

Victor's close proximity to a third event of fictionalized/hallucinated traffic violence is presaged by the frantic ringing of a bicycle bell that reverberates off screen before we hear the thud of a body struck down and the dull clatter of a capsized bicycle. The off-camera action suggests that Victor has not escaped this third accident unscathed. But the next shot does not show Victor sprawled in the streets of Hamburg's Ulenhorst quarter, as anticipated by the viewer, but rather an unnamed cadaver in the blood-stained streets of Mexico. Immediately following these three violent events that forecast the sharp turn in the director's gaze, *Reality 2.0*'s thematic shift towards Mexico's drug-related violence is signalled by a thirty-second segment that shows the interrogation of four alleged Gulf cartel members, one of whom is executed at point-blank range on screen. The recycled footage, clipped and heavily altered through rotoscope, is a bridge from the short-lived Germany-Mexico comparison to that of Orozco's two Mexicos.[22] That this connection is made through a third site – the Internet – is fitting, as it is the Internet that became for Orozco the vehicle on which he was *transported* to this evolving Mexican culture, and the window through which he would once more "immerse" himself, as he says, in Mexican culture (00:02:20).

Shortly following this jarring transition, we become privy to Orozco's confession that "me transformé, sin dar me cuenta, en un obseso voyeurista" (I became, without realizing it, a voyeuristic freak; 00:02:18). However, it is not just the web, but specifically Web 2.0 that becomes a portal through which Orozco can enter what he calls "reality 2.0." What the Mexican film-maker comes to notice in poring over narco-related forums and blogs, YouTube videos, and daily news on national and international sites, is that the coming into existence of this new reality has not been a spontaneous occurrence, as were the traffic accidents in

Figure 5.1. Fictional or hallucinated violence punctuating Victor's arrival in Germany (00:01:22)

the German streets. What we read in the increasingly fast-paced video is that Mexico's "reality 2.0" has come into existence, in part, through the *evolution* of traditional values. Here again we can recall Orozco's – and Christiansen's – fitting use of biological metaphors to refer to this cultural transformation.

It should not come as a surprise that Orozco witnesses this fundamental shift in Mexican culture through Web 2.0, as user-generated videos in particular have become the latest vehicle to celebrate and document the deeds of Mexico's drug traffickers. These are "a new venue for spreading the mythology, allowing people who identify with one of the cartels to delight in humiliating their rivals,"[23] and a development from the *narcocorrido* that has long held popularity among Mexico's people. Echoing this from off screen, in an ever controlled and at times rhythmic voice Orozco admits that he grew sick of listening to these songs. On screen, a close-up shot captures the screen of Victor's computer, on which we see a video loading symbol and the frenetic waving of the cursor, accompanied by the sound of the impatient clicking of the mouse buttons (00:02:04–30; see figure 5.2). The implication is that it is not a question of growing sick of one genre of narcocultural production, but of finding another more readily satisfying, more conducive to connecting from afar and overall more participatory in regards to this new reality.

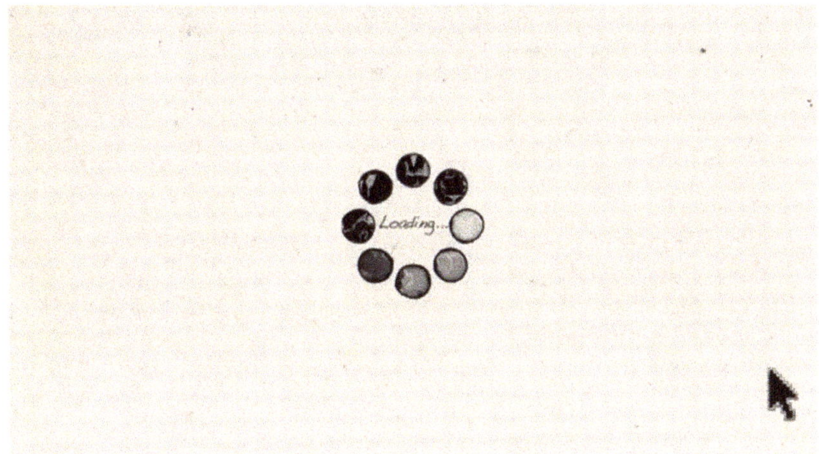

Figure 5.2. The spectator of narco-violence as a "cog" in the narco-machine (00:02:26)

Orozco's incorporation of this particular narco video at this transitional moment of the film does more than merely demonstrate this new obsession. Orozco narrates his obsession with viewing the acts of Mexico's drug war, and, by extension, his immersion into and even *participation* in narcoculture as one of many, to borrow the words of Christiansen, "engranajes que mueven día con día la 'narcomaquina'" (cogs that day by day move the "narco machine").[24] Nothing demonstrates this more clearly than the cog-like loading symbol, which plays a scene of violence in each "notch" like a queue of associated videos, whose circularity reiterates the notion of a continuous stream.

For Gomez, who interrogates the ways in which audience is "implicated" in the cartels' social-media-based system of violence, the participation of the viewer, whether they be a general audience, viewers with cartel allegiances, or participants in the cartel conflict, involves "consuming, demanding, and disseminating the cartels' performed acts of violence."[25]

Around the time that the execution video was uploaded by Dallas news, there occurred a steep rise in use among cartel members of social network sites from a smattering in 2005 to a full-fledged "heyday" by 2008 that includes the use of Twitter, Facebook, and YouTube accounts.[26] This uptick in narco-warfare through social media, what Gomez in the title of his essay calls "a new visual regime,"[27] coincided with an escalation of drug-related violence on Mexico's streets, as well as an increased use of websites for reporting on the Mexican drug war.[28] The players in this ongoing conflict include rival drug cartels, vying for regional control, as well as Mexican government forces and civilian vigilante groups.[29] Moreover, in 2006, the Mexican drug war could be seen as part of a two-sided coin, the other of which is the war on drugs waged by the Felipe Calderón presidency (2006–12).

Beyond these contextual cues, the Zetas' hitman execution clip signals a shift in the type of documentary materials featured in the remainder of his film. From this point onwards we get glimpses of more social media videos as Orozco explains the ways in which traditional Mexican culture has transformed into narcoculture, and his perception of its reach and effects. Yet these are but glimpses, as the view of Mexico's drug-related violence in *Reality 2.0* is both momentary (emerging through fragments of longer clips) and partial ("shielded" by a thick layer of animation).

The minimalist hand-drawn rotoscoping features a thin line tracing the basic outlines of the human figures, which are set against heavily blurred backgrounds. The resulting effect is that the animation acts as a protective veil, or "mecanismo de distanciamiento" (distancing mechanism), following Bruno Hachero Hernández, who writes on Folman's *Waltz with Bashir*, that allows the spectator of *Reality 2.0* to "soportar el horror" (bear the horror) of the violence in the clipped live-action footage.[30] But what Hachero Hernández does not consider is that the layer of rotoscoped animation on top of the live-action footage in films such as *Waltz with Bashir* and *Reality 2.0* might not only cover up the action to spare the viewer the explicitness of the violence, but also to protect them from their own instinctual attraction towards it. This is the dominant way in which *Reality 2.0* has been read: for Luc-Carolin Ziemann, for instance, the film places a "veil" over the various video snippets, many of which are "oozing with savagery" so that the content would no longer appeal "to the lowest instincts of the viewers" and as a result permit "a critical reflection of what had happened."[31]

There is then a dual purpose to the rotoscoped footage in the execution scene. No doubt, for the general viewer of *Reality 2.0*, the execution clip, like the brief murder scene that precedes it, would be encountered with shock, despite the forewarnings. The smooth layer of animation softens the viewer's landing, so to speak, into this new reality and the scenes of violence that fuel it. Meanwhile, the hazy aesthetic may confuse or even frustrate another set of viewers accustomed to streaming such videos, though as will be argued further on, obscuring the action causes such viewers (or voyeurs) to pause and reflect on the act of viewing such content.

While in the previous chapter's exploration of Aleix Saló's journalistic short *Spainistan* we saw how the digital public sphere has become a new realm for disseminating as well as archiving works of animated non-fiction, with Orozco's *Reality 2.0* we see the inverse. Here, content from social media sites is employed *as* archive. In other words, metaphorically, but also very literally with his animated treatment of the live-action footage, Orozco draws on what is now commonly referred to as archive 2.0: "The implementation of Web 2.0 tools in archives, such as launching wikis and blogs, contributing digitized content to social media sites such as Flickr and YouTube, and communicating with users through Facebook, Twitter, and other social networks."[32] This aesthetic decision in Orozco's *Reality 2.0* has important implications.

To start with, granting what Gomez says about the "new digital media regime [that] is emerging in Mexico," in which "cartels create their own power structures through the reality framing device of the digital video camera," it must be asked what *Reality 2.0* says about the power relationships between violence, culture, and digital space, which are, as Gomez concludes, being "redefined."[33] There is also the fact that, as this author further writes, "narco power effectively challenges both existing state power and cultural norms."[34] What Gomez makes clear in his article, and what Orozco similarly illustrates within his animated documentary film, is that the digital public sphere has become a central arena for the wielding of this power, and not just the challenging but the *changing* of cultural norms.

One consequence of narco-violence in the digital realm, as Gomez states, is that the videos are "infinitely reproducible and accessible."[35] But these digitally recorded, posted, viewed, and circulated acts of Mexico's drug-related violence not only contribute to a proliferation of narcoculture at present, but also influence its "imagined future." This is the term used by David Beer, following Jacques Derrida in "Archive Fever Revisited," who states that the archive "becomes a producer of our attempts to capture the present or the past for the purposes of an *imagined future*."[36] For Beer, this is especially the case for social media, which, despite appearing "instant … are often concerned with an imagined future use of the content in mind."[37]

An example given by Beer is the hashtag, which is "likely to be created or reused with a sense of an imagined future in which others use or through which the associated content is discovered."[38] In the case of Mexico's narcoculture, popular hashtags on social media sites such as Instagram, Facebook, and Twitter include #narcocultura, #narcostyle, and #narcomexico, as well as specific ones like #narcosinaloa, to denote Mexico's most dominant drug cartel. Beer and Gomez converge in their recognition that there are dynamics of power inherent to the recording (for Gomez) and archiving (for Beer) of lives on social media. For Gomez, this power is related to a new dimension of warfare, whereas Beer, still following Derrida, is concerned with the political power that ordinary people gain in the creation of "meaning, memory and knowledge ... within and through the social media archives."[39] By creating social media profiles, "ordinary" people assume the power-laden role of the archon, although this has been mutated in social media from the archon of centralized official archival spaces of the past. The power they wield is in deciding how content is "organized and rendered retrievable."[40]

The notion of the social media archon introduced by Beer is useful – essential even – for understanding the role of the cartels in Mexico's reality 2.0, which, according to Orozco, is heavily shaped by narcoculture's new visual regime. When Gomez speaks of Mexican drug cartels "wield[ing] digital cameras as instruments of power,"[41] disseminating their videos on social media with one eye towards rival cartels and the other towards general audiences,[42] we can see how they function as the "archons" of this "reality 2.0." Not to mention that a consideration of narcoculture in the digital realm shows how content is created and disseminated with the imagined future of associated content in mind when we read Gomez's assertion that the cartels "produc[e] increasingly gory and cinematic visualizations in their attempts to best each other in the raw power of their images."[43] In this sense, we can affirm Beer's assertion that social media archives "alter the way that [lives] are lived,"[44] while adding that, in the context of narco-violence as an alarming – and accelerating – process, which involves the dehumanization of its victims and a desensitization of its viewer to ever-increasing violence, they also alter the ways in which lives are ended.[45]

Central to Orozco's personal documentary narrative is an argument that, as participants in narcoculture through spectatorship in the digital realm, we play into this dehumanizing display of power. The word *play* is purposeful as there is also a direct correlation between spectatorship of narco-violence and seeking entertainment. This argument is made by Orozco in the arcade scene that unfolds throughout the second half of the documentary short. In a cleverly constructed series of shots that are woven together, we at first watch through rotoscoped shaky-cam footage as a pair of young boys engages in play with various arcade games. The camera captures the boys at a close distance, in either medium or close-up shots that show their interaction with the gaming machines, pushing the buttons as they battle space aliens and monsters, as we see through intermittent, subjective shots of these games that fill the frame (00:06:45–00:07:22). All the while, Orozco tells from off camera how Mexico's drug traffickers have developed their own "estética de horror" (aesthetics of horror; 00:07:38), one that echoes tactics used by Al-Qaeda, as they turn to YouTube to interrogate, torture, and execute hostages, portraying their "realidad inobjetable" (indisputable reality; 00:07:44). The cartels argue for this reality – reality 2.0, we hear Orozco state – from the comfort of Internet cafes, from where they deliver their "chingadazos" (hits; 00:07:52).

As this is told to us from off screen, the camera seamlessly leaves the arcade, and we now are presented with recorded footage from a first-person shooter game (again, rotoscoped but with softer lines and a heavier blur than the shots of the arcade games) that is tacked on to the scene. All the while, the camera maintains the subjective player shot so that what fills the frame is the action of each new game. From the slaying of unearthly creatures, we witness a player on a killing spree across several levels of an urban setting, then a transition to increasingly blurred footage of drug-related killings on Mexico's streets from footage featured on *Blog del narco*. While the scope of violence progresses from action against the non-human (space aliens and monsters) to the semi-human (realistic video game characters) to fully human (victims of narco-violence), the progressive dulling of the drawn line with each cut of the camera communicates the dynamics of desensitization/dehumanization noted by Gomez, as well as the blurring of ethical lines between finding entertainment in gaming violence, where the victims are *very clearly not human*, to online spectatorship of real-life narco-violence, where the victims are *not very clearly human* (see figure 5.3).

We can see why Paul Ward has suggested that animated documentary works performatively, causing audiences to "*think* and *feel* about that something and the way in which it has been communicated to us."[46] In short, the rotoscope *performs* a desensitization for its viewer. Ultimately, the conclusion that Orozco draws for his viewer within this scene – and what he challenges them to consider through the sensation that he transmits – calls to mind what Sullivan and Adam Elkus call the "increasing tempo of atrocity" in Mexico's narco-violence, as well as its "banalization" in mainstream culture.[47] Meanwhile, *Reality 2.0*'s arcade scene brings us to consider an important transformation in the places and spaces in which violence-as-entertainment is contained (or not). Starting from the enclosed space of the locally run arcade (and furthermore, within the individual arcade machines within this space), violent play gets literally closer to home as public arcade machine is substituted for private video game console, and ultimately the limitless container of the Internet. For Mexican culture, we are to read, the parallel

Figure 5.3. Desensitization and dehumanization in the arcade scene from *Reality 2.0* (00:06:45–00:08:45)

development of new technologies alongside the rise of narcoculture has paved a path for the transformation of violence-as-entertainment from quasi-innocent public pastime to spectacle in a new social reality, as well as its exploitation on social media by the cartels, who pump out streams of propagandistic videos that are, to recall Gomez's words, "infinitely reproducible and accessible."[48]

A common criticism of video games (from the arcade and beyond) is that they foster violence and aggression in their players,[49] but Orozco leads us to recognize that the seemingly passive role of social media spectator also involves a certain level of violent inter/action, such as giving a video a "hit" with the click of a button. Here, we can recall Victor's aggressive and impatient clicking of the mouse as he waits for a stream of narco-videos to load on YouTube, seen in figure 5.2 (00:02:06–30). With this moment still fresh in our mind's eye, we are further led to this consideration a few minutes later as midway through the arcade scene the camera jumps outwards from the gaming machines to capture first from a distance and then in extreme close-up the strategic pressing of the round red buttons that control the arcade games (00:06:45 and 00:07:00).

What Orozco presents is a shift in entertainment values for the general public, using as one example traditional gaming culture to show a *playing into* narcoculture, where what is at play is not fictional violence but rather real-world violence (or, to be more specific, the hyper-violent reality 2.0). The blurred animation that characterizes this scene also narrates the increasingly blurred lines between fictional and real violence for the spectator, as it moves from the controlled environment of the arcade to the control of the cartel archon in the digital realm. Orozco's documentary short is proof, however, that when it comes to narcoculture and the archive 2.0, the power-laden role of social media archon is not limited to the cartels that create the content. "Wielding" his camera, not to mention his equipment for hand-drawn animation as "instruments of power," to recall Gomez's words,[50] Orozco shows that the animated essayist – and animated documentarian by extension – is also a powerful archon of Mexican culture, or perhaps a counter-archon, as he *re*organizes, *re*signifies, and *re*distributes content on social media for a different ideological purpose.

Only recently has the notion of documentarians as "archons of the audiovisual" been introduced, by Duke scholar Gustavo Procopio Furtado, who writes in the context of documentary and film-making in contemporary Brazil that these directors "determine what will be remembered and what will not, opening up a passageway from the visible phenomenal world, always subject to change and inhering in the temporality of duration in the present, to the durable and fixed record of film."[51] What Furtado does not take into account, however, is that when the "fixed record" of live-action film footage falls into the hands of animators well-versed in the technique of rotoscoping, its record becomes once again fluid and malleable. In short, it seems, Orozco (re) captures the present with the purpose of, to recall Beer, an imagined future in mind.

This is precisely the case of *Reality 2.0*, as it redirects the source content back towards a faction of the original intended audience to make them see (by letting them not see clearly) how they have become inured to the violence and how they play into the dehumanization of its victims. That is, how they become cogs that grinds against the narco-machine. With this in mind, it should be noted that the release of *Reality 2.0* in Mexico's cultural sphere coincided with a pivotal moment in the sociopolitical sphere; a moment of hope for transformation regarding government strategies against Mexico's war on drugs and for diminishing of violence as the six-year Calderón presidential term was coming to an end. That is, the year 2012 saw the election of Enrique Peña Nieto (2012–18) as president, bringing with his rise to power an increase in hope for many citizens that, as Jonathan Rosen and Roberta Zepeda explain, there would be a change in strategy against the war against the cartels from the government realm and that, ultimately, there would be a reduction in violence.[52]

As it is comprehensible that Orozco's commentary on the transformation of Mexican culture into a hyper-violent narcoculture appeared right around this time of optimism, it should also come as no surprise that Orozco was not alone in commenting on Mexico's next-level but hopefully not enduring reality from this historical moment. Accordingly, *Reality 2.0* should be read in the context of other documentary films from national and international film-makers, who likewise broached the topic of narco-violence around this moment of anticipated transition on all levels of Mexican society, politics, and culture.

In Schwarz's aforementioned *Narco Culture*, for example, violence permeates nearly every scene. The documentary's dual-narrative thread follows in the footsteps of crime scene investigator Richi Soto as he responds to call after call of narco-related homicides, as well as the footsteps of lead singer of the *corridos* group BunKas de Culiacán, American-born Edgar Quintero, who writes ballads that glorify the violence as well as the cartel members by whose hand it is enacted. Conversely, Natalia Almada's *El Velador / The Night Watchman* (Mexico, 2011) does not feature any on-screen violence, at least not directly. The entire film is shot within Culiacán's Jardines del Humaya (Humaya Gardens) cemetery. Almada addresses the extreme violence without visually portraying any violence at all. Rather, it is only suggested through the radio broadcasts listened to by the cemetery's night watch man, Martín. For Martín, each sunrise in the *Jardín* brings a new wave of corpses to fill the newly constructed graves, contractors to build the increasingly opulent mausoleums, new waves of funeral processions, and the growing and transforming of the cemetery into a vast and continually expanding city of the dead; a narco-necropolis, to use another necessary neologism.

Orozco's, Schwarz's, and Almeda's documentaries display different approaches to the violence of Mexico's narcoculture. On the spectrum of filmic violence where, on the one end, Schwarz offers an overt, borderline pornography of violence, and, on the other end, Almeda's film presents an artistic visual/verbal allusion to violence, Orozco's *Reality 2.0* lies in the middle. Yet all three directors converge in the picture that they create that, as Sullivan and Rosales write, "every day is a virtual *Día de los Muertos*."[53] Schwarz's film, meanwhile, merits further mention for the fact that it also takes a comparative approach to depicting narcoculture in Mexico. For the Israeli American film-maker this means contrasting through alternating segments what have come to be called "Narcolandia" (roughly, "Narcoland") and "narcoinfierno" (narco-hell). For Christiansen, these terms refer to the pleasures and pains (and above all death) brought on by narcoculture; two sides of the cultural coin that are simultaneously admired and condemned by society at large.[54] In *Narco Culture* this means an on-screen juxtaposition of the lush life led by *corridos* singer Quintero and the sobering crime scenes investigated by Soto, by cutting back and forth between footage that captures these two "realms" of narcoculture.

Like Schwarz, Orozco employs a contrastive approach, yet unlike the USA-based director, he narrates cultural contrast by *animating* rather than alternating scenes, and he zeroes in on Mexico's "narcoinfierno." For Orozco, the so-called "narco hell" is synonymous with "reality 2.0." This becomes clear from the final seconds of the Plaza de Toros scene, which carries us to the halfway point of the film. A shot-reverse-shot technique, beginning and ending with an extreme close-up of Victor's face, captures his upward gaze while a subjective shot in between reveals that what has caught Victor's attention is the sight of a large, black bull with demon-like wings as it soars across the skies above (00:04:46–00:05:01). Here, Orozco's animation works evocatively, to recall Annabelle Honess Roe's term,[55] as the image of the flying bull drawn onto rotoscoped footage of a partially cloudy sky becomes symbolic of the sudden and sharp escalation of narco-violence on Mexican soil in 2006, and along with it, spectatorship in the digital public sphere as one facet of narcoculture.

This metaphorical moment is the culminating point in Orozco's treatment through rotoscope and the animation of additional elements, of footage of the infamous Mexican bull aptly named Pajarito (Birdie). As historical records (and the digital footage from many a camera) show, the enraged bull entered the ring of Mexico City's monumental Plaza de Toros on 29 January 2006, only to make a quick and memorable exit by charging towards the crowd of spectators. Pajarito flew two metres into the air, propelling his 1,100-pound body with his hind legs from one set of guard rails clear over the next, landing in the crowd as chaos ensued.

At the same time that Orozco traces for his viewer (literally and figuratively) the events surrounding Pajarito's historic "flight," he adds another, symbolic layer of narration through the incorporation of hand-drawn elements such as the bull's wings (00:04:34). The visual transformation of Pajarito into the demon-like bull serves as one of the first indicators in the film that its director is of the opinion that there has been a transformation of entertainment values in his home nation from traditional culture to that of this "narcoinfierno," where the spectacle of violence reaches new heights. In the build up to this moment, we are already introduced to the conceptual link between narco-violence, entertainment, and a "hellish" reality. On screen, in one of the film's most poetic moments, rotoscoped footage of a different event from the same iconic red ring shows a bullfighter performing acrobatics over a charging bull, while off screen Orozco rhythmically recounts that "cabezas, piernas, penes, manos, lenguas, y dedos empezaron a aparecer en las calles … y así se escaparon los demonios" (heads, legs, penises, hands, tongues, and fingers began to appear in the streets … and this is how the demons escaped; 00:03:51). The Plaza de Toros scene itself serves as a harbinger to traditional Mexican culture, in which the controversial sport has been a traditional form of entertainment for more than five centuries. Nevertheless, for some members of the Mexican public this and other cultural forms of entertainment, we are to understand, has been eclipsed by expressions of narco-violence, facing which they find themselves either turning away in horror, or "titillated by its lurid rebelliousness."[56]

It is through this symbolic lens, whose focus is sharpened by the animator's hand, that we can read the manipulated footage of Pajarito's 2006 escape from the ring as Orozco's indication that narco power was escaping the bounds of Mexican state authority, not to mention that violence-as-entertainment was soaring to new heights. Through rotoscope, Orozco transforms the bullfighting ring into a microcosm of Mexico, opening the scene with a prolonged shot of the Plaza de Toros, the largest bullfighting ring in the world, in which the empty stands are recoloured in the red, white, and green of the nation's flag. These are captured by a panning camera, which eventually comes to rest in front of the reserved seats marked *Autoridades* (Authorities). Although a mimetic rendering of the Plaza de Toros, the footage functions evocatively, where the empty box ascribed to authority alludes to the lack of definitive government following the controversial 2006 general election, in which Andrés Manuel López Obrador claimed to be the legitimate president, challenging Calderón's authority from the start of his official appointment. It is within this context of political upheaval and the declaration of war against the drug traffickers by a president who was, we hear, motivated but lacking in strategy (00:03:24) that the narco daily reality gained its wings.

The following scene reinforces Orozco's central argument that a transformation has taken place from one reality – albeit a nostalgic and idyllic one – to one that he views as a "narcoinfierno." The transition between scenes occurs with a quick jump from a close-up of Victor, clearing his vision with the palm of his hand as he stares after the airborne bull, to a wide-angle shot featuring head-on the entrance to a local *peluquería* (barbershop; 00:04:58–00:05:03). From our vantage point on the street, where the camera is placed, the first detail that calls our attention is the florescent blue sign that reads "El paraíso" (Paradise), the words seemingly inscribed by Orozco in cursive font across the building's façade. This detail, together with the soundtrack of singing birds and distant upbeat music, and the bright colour palette, asks the viewer to recall that, for the young director, there is another side, or a "before," to what he calls "reality 2.0."

Sure enough, the viewer is transported to this other side of "paradise," carried across the threshold of the barbershop thanks to another quick camera jump. Here, a low-angled shot directs our gaze up towards the face of a barber, who contentedly stares downwards, not to meet the spectator's gaze, but rather to focus his attention on the young customer sitting in his chair, whose dark head of hair fills the bottom third of the frame. The setting of this new scene once again serves as an indicator to traditional culture: on the one hand, to a local and legal business culture, and, on the other, to traditional cultural values. A calendar on the wall sets the date as the second of November – the Day of the Dead – while to the right of the calendar hangs a colourful tapestry of Santa Muerte (a folk saint who personifies death). Together, these elements visually reiterate what Orozco describes as "una macabre fascinación de los mexicanos por la muerte y el horror" (Mexicans' macabre fascination with death and horror; 00:05:50).

As our gaze continues travelling to the left of the frame (and to the right of the calendar and the tapestry), we encounter a shirtless young man swaying back and forth, eyes dull and mouth agape, seemingly in a drug-induced trance (00:05:36; see figure 5.4). In this shot we can find a second allusion in the barbershop scene to a cultural threshold that has been traversed. When we notice the intoxicated man's symbolic placement in the threshold of the interior doorway, as well as the fact that the placement of the Santa Muerte tapestry produces the effect that the female deity is directly gazing down at him, we come to realize that the *mise en scène*, the characters, and even the setting itself have again become symbolic and essayistic tools in the hands of the Mexican animator. All the while, Orozco's steady and soft-spoken voice relays to the viewer that the Day of the Dead is the "máxima expresión" (epitome) of this macabre fascination with death and horror (00:05:48). It is here, in the barbershop scene, that we most clearly read Orozco's assertion, echoing that of other inter/national documentarians, that in this new reality of narcoculture, every day is a Day of the Dead.

In the same way that we read the image of the bullfighting ring as a visual synecdoche for Mexico's entertainment culture, we can also find symbolic meaning in the setting of the barbershop. In other words, the animation in this scene again breaks with its mimetic function, taking on an evocative one, and it is now the inner space of the barbershop that

Figure 5.4. Becoming the "voyeuristic freak" (00:05:36)

becomes a microcosm of Mexican culture, and a space onto which Orozco can write a transformation. By the time we arrive at the second half of this scene, it has become clear that the boy's haircut – his physical transformation – symbolizes a cultural transformation of a much larger kind. By animating this act, Orozco alludes to the transformation of Mexico's social and political landscape into what has been called a "narcoscape"; that is, the political and social landscape of the nation's "drug war zone."[57]

The barber is seemingly done his work, as is signalled to us by a mid shot of him shaking out his white cape as its fabric stretches across the frame (00:06:04). Locks of the young customer's black hair fly into the air and fall to the floor, their landing captured by the camera that is now also at floor level, where it will remain for the rest of the scene. All the while, a soundtrack continues to play the violent "snip, snip, snip" of scissor blades as they come together over and over again, insinuating the cutting short of countless lives in this new, bloody landscape. Orozco confirms this from off camera, his voice competing with the sounds of the scissor blades, as he divulges that in the context of cartel violence, crime scenes have become theatres in which there is a calculated staging of bodies, which "se transforman en piezas de utilería" (are transformed into props; 00:06:27). Not so subtly reiterating this, strands and tufts of black hair rain down from the top of the shot at an alarming rate, covering the red tile floor so that, in the scene's final seconds, we are facing a thick, black carpet of hair and the visual iteration of a changing landscape.

Keeping in mind that, as Sullivan reminds us, the cartels' instrumental and symbolic violence is a tactic for gaining support and legitimacy in the geographic areas the cartels control, which specifically means gaining autonomy as well as economic control,[58] an even more nuanced reading of the barbershop scene reveals a connection between the metaphorical theatre of violence of which Orozco speaks and changing notions of socially acceptable business enterprise. Specifically, we can read a subtle nod to changing notions of economic activity, in which drug trafficking is considered a socially acceptable money-making endeavour, as Sullivan notes, rather than the criminal enterprise that it legally is.[59]

Further and more apparent meaning linked to the space of the barbershop is the fact that this particular place has a deep resonance for the director's personal journey towards becoming, to recall his words, the "voyeuristic freak" that he saw himself as at the moment of the film's conception. Beyond a general commentary on the coming into existence of Mexico's narcoscape, as well as shifting notions of legitimate (but illegal) business, the barbershop scene offers an autobiographical portrait, where both the young boy and the entranced man represent the director at two extremes of his journey.

It is not coincidental that Orozco zooms in on the hands of the young boy, from where he sits in the barber's chair, as he tells of his first encounter with voyeurism as a young boy himself, leafing through the pages of so-called "Red Press" tabloids at the local *peluquería*. Neither is it unintentional that he cuts from a close-up of the boy's curious gaze to the young man's transfixed stare, as we are called to see the one in the other, who seemingly sees nothing at all. The fact that this same character appears in a shot in the arcade scene that directly follows emphasizes the fact that it is in this desensitized (and not inebriated, as we first assumed) man that the director sees himself. Through this lens we can read the (animated) effects produced by the hair cut – a shower of infinite trimmings – in an additional way, that is, in terms of Orozco's account of immersing himself in narcoculture as a spectator of social media. As Gomez reminds us, "Social media allows the singular performance in physical space to manifest itself millions of times in digital space."[60] And when viewing this scene, especially from the perspective of an English-speaking spectator, one can find a connection between this massive amount of hair in the barbershop scene and the image of the proliferating *hare* in the early Germany scene. While the latter signifies cultural rebirth and recuperation, the former denotes deterioration. It is, after all, a reflection on such transformations that guides *Reality 2.0* right up to its conclusion.

The final scene begins with the repeated shout "¡Viva México!" (Long live Mexico!), as a rallying cry from the members of the Gulf cartel, whose crystal-clear words contrast with their blurred images in the footage taken from *Blog del narco* and animated into the end of the arcade scene. That this cry is heard during an extended fade-to-white transition, which bridges the arcade scene to the final one, gives it a double signification: on the one hand, it remains the propagandistic shout captured in the violent footage and, on the other hand, these words become resignified as Orozco's own words to his concluding scene. It is the cry "¡Viva México!" that ushers the viewer in to the final scene, which features rotoscoped footage of a funeral procession on the streets of Culiacán, along with the loud tune played out by a brass marching band. Here the camera pans over and above a multitude of citizens, some bearing coffins, until the crowd nearly disappears out the bottom of the frame as the camera moves upwards and zooms in, past the buildings that line the city streets, and towards the outskirts, where the Jardin del Humaya cemetery can be seen.

It is not this narco-necropolis, however, that becomes the focus of the penultimate shot; nor is it the Mexican Flag that rises above it. Rather, it is the backdrop of a brilliant red, pink, purple, and orange sunset that spans the length of the shot. Here we hear Orozco's realization that in Germany, the rabbits never evolved into rats, but instead, "en México, este país surrealista, nosotros hicimos que los conejos se transformaron en ratas" (in Mexico, this surreal country, we managed to transform the rabbits into rats; 00:10:11). Thus begins the director's final reflections on the transformation of Mexico's traditional culture values to those of narcoculture. And yet, *Reality 2.0*'s conclusion is not so disparaging, thanks to an idiomatic phrase that brings about a poetic conclusion to Orozco's essayistic documentary film.

In a subjective shot where we assume Victor's gaze (and thus Orozco's by extension), an extreme close-up of a thumb trying in vain to eclipse the brilliant sun calls to mind the Spanish idiom *tapar el sol con el dedo* (to bury one's head in the sand). After carefully tracing for us (literally and figuratively speaking) continuities that can be found in Mexico's narcoculture, those stemming from traditional values and ideologies, the director admits that he will selectively choose what he wants to see or remember. This final image makes us reflect back on the use of the adjective "2.0" in the title of the film. To those born into the narco status quo, this might seem superfluous – or perhaps even confusing. But Orozco makes it clear from the start that his documentary short is written from a personal perspective, and one belonging to a previous generation. Rotoscope – a traditional animation tool – serves the director in his quest for tracing the transformation of traditional values and ideologies into those of narcoculture, while allow for the illustration that these are not completely transformed from one culture to the other, but rather it is a question of continuities that can be traced back to a common (back)ground.

Rotoscope's magnificent ability to trace otherwise intangible ideas and concepts for the viewer also features in the analysis found in the final chapter of this study. Here, however, we are not talking about tracing cultural transformations, but rather the textures of private memory. Chapter 6 sheds light on an innovative anomaly in the realm of animated documentary: the television documentary series *Cuentos de viejos / Old Folks' Tales* (Colombia/Spain, 2013–19). This collaborative, transmedial documentary project by creative directors Laura Piaggio and Marcelo Dematei has four seasons of 2D-animated television episodes, as well as hundreds of raw (live-action) videos uploaded to a user-generated online platform. An analysis of this overlooked project is timely, given the recent critical attention to the convergence between memory, documentary, and animation.

Zeroing in on the project's televised component, my sixth and final chapter will ask how *Old Folks' Tales* trans-stylistic approach illustrates the difference of individual lived experiences that form a transnational collective memory, one that challenges, broadens, and at times counters Spain and Latin America's official twentieth-century histories. My analysis of a handful of key episodes will argue for animation's ability to illustrate the textures of private memory, here largely childhood memories of war and conflict, and thus will bring this study full circle. It will further be highlighted how the mnemonic medium of animation can also draw lines – both literally and metaphorically speaking – from one memory to another, doing the work of what has recently been called "visual collective memory."

Ultimately, the final chapter of this book works against the common claim that animation is unmoored from history, to show that it is, in fact, firmly moored to not just one history, but to many histories across the Spanish-speaking world. Yet I aim to show that the transmedial documentary project as a whole is also characterized by multiple unmoorings: memorialization from the state, memory from the collective – especially when we consider, as has Andrew Hoskins, that the term "memory of the multitude" better suits the participation of masses in memory activity within the online realm[61] – archive from the institution, animation style from the hand of the animator or the brand of the studio, and, finally, animated documentary from the vessel of cinema.

6 In Uncharted Waters and Totally Unmoored: The Transmedial Documentary Project *Cuentos de viejos / Old Folks' Tales* (2013–2019)

In his final words written in homage of the life's work of Tokyo-based animator Hayao Miyazaki, considered by many to be the Japanese Walt Disney, Anthony Carew assertively states that "animation is a place unmoored from history, from the physical laws of life on earth."[1] Carew's estimation of animation's role in narration is a general statement on the artistic medium, although it is no doubt shaped by his professional proximity to the Japanese animation director's body of work, in which the creation of fantasy worlds has been a unifying thread from the late 1970s into the 2010s, a time when the septuagenarian stepped back from his career. A driving factor in Carew's conclusion that animation is far-off from the real is the fact that Miyazaki's fantasy-based films characteristically "take audiences to unimaginable worlds and mythical realms." However, Carew's is no doubt a common view, and we can in fact recall from chapter 1 Judith Kriger's assertion that animation is predominantly associated with entertainment and escape from events of the real world, especially those related to unpleasant realities.[2]

Meanwhile, one aim of this study has been, and continues to be, to expand understanding of the opposite: that animation is (also) anchored to the representation of times past and present. This is true throughout the history of Western cinema, and is especially apparent in the proliferation of animated documentaries specifically, and of animated non-fiction more broadly that we are experiencing as twenty-first century spectators. Up to this point, this study has provided an exploration on how animation, regardless of style or technique, is a place in which counter-narratives of history – whether marginalized, myth-building, silenced, satirical, or countercultural – allows for the illustration of politics relating to both the past and the present of nations and generations across the Spanish-speaking world.

This sixth and final chapter aims to round out this argument through one final case study: the transmedial documentary project *Cuentos de viejos / Old Folks' Tales* (Columbia/Spain, 2013–19).[3] Coproduced by the national television channel Señal Colombia, the Colombian production company HIERROanimación, and Spain's cross-media production and design company Piaggiodematei, a fourth season of the television documentary series was released in the spring of 2019. Beyond its airing on television and its streaming and sharing on an online platform that was available during the show's seven-year run on television, there is the project's strong educational aim, as participation through the *Old Folk's Tales* online platform is intended to inspire and facilitate similar projects that feature high-level content at home and in the classroom.[4]

There is perhaps no way more fitting to end this study, as an analysis of *Old Folks' Tales* brings us full circle, from and back to the study of how private childhood memories – of conflict as well as of the everyday – are rendered visual and audible for the viewer. There is, however, a key difference between the two Colombia-based documentary projects. *Little Voices*'s collective testimonies were combined into a single animated narrative and its subjects drawn into the same story world with the purpose and effect, as mentioned, of protagonizing childhood as a whole. Conversely, the episodes of *Old Folks' Tales*, which employs a protagonist-narrator,[5] or dozens of protagonist-narrators, rather, makes use of abundant animation techniques and styles to illustratively capture the way that our individual lives become coloured – or shaped – by our lived experiences of what are, in many cases, common geographical places or shared historical experiences. Testimonies of tumultuous twentieth-century events such as the Spanish Civil War, Colombia's bipartisan violence and armed conflict, and the Second World War are woven together into a extensive transgenerational, transatlantic, and transnational memory that stems largely from Spain and Latin America, but is also fed by storytellers that reside beyond the geographical borders of the Hispanic world.

Recipient of multiple awards in the realms of animation, television, and transmedia, *Old Folks' Tales* was conceived as a collaborative (i.e., official and user-generated) and transmedial documentary with official animated episodes released annually on television, as well as hundreds of indexical (live-action) videos uploaded to its online platform. There, myriad stories were collected, but also connected through keyword tags, the Stories on the Map feature,[6] and the splicing together of certain stories under thematic titles such as "La educación es un derecho" (Education is a Right), "La revolución cubana" (The Cuban Revolution), and "Jugar sin juguetes" (Playing without Toys). The coproduced documentary project's complex and collaborative structure is one reason that we can firmly say that *Old Folks' Tales* exemplifies how a new generation of animated documentarians are venturing into uncharted waters.

Another chief reason for this claim is the fact that its televised documentary series component relies on a completely different animation style and technique combo for each of its forty narrative episodes;[7] five-minute micro shorts in which rotoscoped medium shots characteristic of talking-head interviews alternate with scenes constructed from 2D digital animation. As creative directors Laura Piaggio and Marcelo Dematei explain, "La primera resultó idónea para retratar al entrevistado, permitiendo rescatar la gesticulación y el lenguaje no verbal. Con el 2D se dio vida a los eventos de la historia" (The first seemed ideal to portray the interviewee, allowing gesticulation and other non-verbal language to be salvaged. The 2D gave life to the events of the story).[8] Transcending any unitary or specific animation style, then, which is characteristic of the feature films and digital shorts studied in the previous chapters, *Old Folks' Tales* moves freely from one 2D style to another, notably at a time in which traditional, hand-drawn 2D animation is starting to make a comeback in both mainstream and independent productions alike, as one unique characteristic of what Nichola Dobson, following Mihaela Mihailova calls a "renaissance of animation."[9]

The co-creators themselves of the documentary series explain the myriad animation techniques and styles as dozens of "soluciones creativas completas" (complete creative solutions) that respond, on the one hand, to the narrative intentions of each episode and, on the other, to the production capabilities and resources available to the team of animators.[10] It is because of this ever-changing aesthetic that the minds behind *Old Folks' Tales* denominate their own project an "antiserie de animación" (animated anti-series); an aesthetic choice they view as an enormous risk, but one that also stands as one of the series's chief virtues and main identifying features.[11] But perhaps, rather than a negative comparison to what has long been the standard in animation, where individual studios develop and establish their stylistic traits, stories, and characters as corporate identities,[12] *Old Folks' Tales* should be understood as avant-garde in the creative context in which it has knowingly placed itself.

And while *Old Folks' Tales* stands as proof that animation is in fact firmly moored to history, to borrow and amend Carew's statement, the transmedial documentary project is characterized by multiple unmoorings: memorialization from the state, memory from the collective, archive from the institution, animation style from the hand of the animator or the brand of the studio, and animated documentary from the vessel of cinema. Thus, we can open this final chapter's case study with the claim that *Old Folks' Tales* sits not only in uncharted waters, but, to rely on another nautical term, is totally unmoored. To understand just how fitting this metaphorical evaluation of the television documentary series is – and especially of the documentary project in its entirety – one need only to look so far as the program's title sequence.

At once evoking and far surpassing the metaphoric notion of a pool or well of memories, the program's title sequence centres on the actions of a young boy and his elderly self (the conceptual link made easy by the similarity between their black-and-white rotoscoped figures), who has transcribed a memory or testimony on to a piece of paper. The paper, which has already been fashioned into a boat, is released by the boy in one frame (and seemingly one era) into a large body of water and then retrieved in a later frame (and seemingly a later era) by the old man, although as man and child feature together in this final shot of the title sequence, the one passing the vessel to the other, the boy, who bends down to engage with the memory-boat, at once also comes to more broadly symbolize a next generation who do not just spectate, but rather *participate* in what Andrew Hoskins calls the "memory of the multitude," as part of "a new mass [who] constantly snap, post, record, edit, like, link, forward and chat in a digital ecology of media."[13]

As this action unfolds onscreen, the thirty-second instrumental opening song plays from off camera, an oneiric and melancholic staccato blend of strings, bells, and chimes. To this tune, the memory-boat sets sail on a stream of 2D paper cut-out waves, which in the following shot transform into photorealistic waves and again seconds later into swells of handwritten testimonies penned on yellowed leaflets, just like that of which the featured vessel is comprised. On top of and within this sea of testimonies can be seen swarms of twentieth-century iconography: antique toys and sporting goods bobbing in the waves, old-fashioned stamps taking the formation of schools of fish, and an archival photograph of a passenger ship that is likewise tossed about by the waves.

The waves of testimonies, which do not move along with the ocean current but rather constitute it, represent a boundlessness or a limitlessness that Hoskins notes to be characteristic of the memory of the multitude.[14] Although it would be tempting to view *Old Folks' Tales* as a collective memory project, we must recognize, as Hoskins has, the extent to which digital technologies and media have transformed remembering and forgetting.[15] There is also the fact that the term *collective memory* seems suddenly inadequate when one considers, as Hoskins continues, "the digital's ushering in of much more complex dialogic modes of communication, undermining previous configurations of individual–group–societal relations, and the forging of new flexible community types with emergent and mutable temporal and spatial coordinates."[16] Accordingly, Hoskin's titular term "memory of the multitude" seems more appropriate when referring to the project *Old Folks' Tales* as a whole, especially in light of one final consideration: that collective memory implies an audience who "share the temporality of simultaneity,"[17] while the multitude "is made through hyperconnectivity, with each other, with the network, with the archive."[18]

However, given these considerations, and especially the final criterion of *spectatorial* audience versus *participatory* multitude (two terms used by Haskins as one differentiating factor between the two),[19] we can draw a distinction between the *Old Folks' Tales* television series component and the documentary project as a whole, and classify the *Señal Colombia* series as a collective memory project within a larger project that, in its entirety, should be read through the lens of the memory of the multitude. And yet, these distinctions are not always so clear cut in the televised series. The aforementioned title sequence, for example, seems to speak to the scope of the whole transmedial project, as the thirty-second segment strongly evokes the memory of the multitude, which is, in the words of Hoskins, "all over the place, scattered yet simultaneous and searchable: connected, networked, archived."

If the ocean in this segment visually represents the container in which these archives are connected and networked, one global commons that stands in as substitute for that of cyberspace, the tossing waves of seemingly endless testimonies can be read as a visual representation of key characteristics of the multitude such as "the sharing in the contagion of the propulsion of data"[20] and "an obsession over recording."[21] Yet the rotoscoped figures of the young boy and his elderly self become the archetypal "old folk," and can be read as affirmation that "memory of the multitude is bound to the singularity of the individual as fundamentally the new centre of media and tied to the rapid proliferating media of the self, yet inextricable from the complex hyperconnectivity of digital networks and traces (that make us findable and memorable)."[22]

Having made these distinctions, it should be easily comprehended why I choose to read the animation-based televised component of the *Old Folks' Tales* documentary project, which is the focus of this chapter, through the lens of collective memory. Accordingly, critical attention to this almost entirely underappreciated series need take into account the recent critical attention to the interrelation of animation and memory, which has its roots in a handful of publications.[23] Namely, we can look to Victoria Grace Walden's study of the ways in which the medium of animation emphasizes the fragile materiality of Holocaust memory while also engages spectators with the materiality of memory.[24] In the Spanish-speaking context, there is Vicente Fenoll's exploration of the theme of memory within an array of animated representations of the Chilean dictatorship.[25] We are also seeing this conceptual pairing in book chapters such as Walden's more recent "Animation and Memory" in *The Animation Studies Reader*.[26] Most notable, however, is Maarten van Gageldonk, László Munteán, and Ali Shobeiri's seminal book *Animation and Memory*,[27] a follow-up to and expansion upon Walden's earlier article of the same title.

It is beyond question that from this edited volume, a wealth of additional studies will spring up, which continue the work of drawing on the dual fields of animation and memory studies to interpret animated audiovisual projects that address various forms, methods, and contexts of remembering and forgetting. As these authors write in the introduction to the volume,

> Memory studies, especially recent work on the transnational, multidirectional, affective, and material dimensions of memory, provides novel theoretical and methodological frameworks to study animation as a mnemonic medium. In its potential to preserve, transmit, and mediate memories, animation constitutes a mediating technology that, often sharing intermedial relationships with photography, literature, and live action film, plays an integral role in the performance of personal and collective memories.[28]

One branch of exploration in *Animation and Memory* has been precisely the convergence between memory, documentary, and animation, which "explores how animation can comment on the collective memories of the past through exploring the documentational capacities of the medium."[29] The sixth and final chapter of this book draws on these interlaced theoretical frameworks, fitting squarely into the area of animated documentary and memory research, while also expanding this strand of research to include Hoskins's notion of the "memory of the multitude," which remedies this from what Hoskins calls the "hangover of the collective in memory studies."[30] The main purpose here is to explore how the televised series *Old Folks' Tales* engages in a "performance of personal and collective memories," to recall the words of van Gageldonk, Maarten, and Shobeiri,[31] within and across the Hispanic world. My analysis of the *Old Folks' Tales* program centres on a handful of episodes that, like the series as a whole, largely feature elderly subjects from Spain and Latin America. I ask how *Old Folks' Tales* trans-stylistic approach, together with what Paul Wells in

Understanding Animation calls the "dynamics of musicality,"[32] work in tandem to illustrate the difference of individual lived experiences that form this collective memory.

Broadly speaking, I argue for animation's unparalleled ability to perform private memory. For, while memories are often shared in an oral capacity, in life as in the arts, they are a highly visual phenomenon; a reality that gets lost in their oral transmission, save for live-action re-enactments that fail to illustrate the textures of memory in the same powerful way that animation has proven effectively capable of doing. Turning to a number of concrete examples, I illustrate how the animated "antiaesthetic" that characterizes *Old Folks' Tales* makes the textures of the protagonist-narrators' memories visible for the spectator, thereby rendering *invisible* the performance of the animator's hand. Finally, I highlight how *Old Folks' Tales* series demonstrates that the mnemonic medium of animation also has the ability to draw traceable lines – both literally and metaphorically speaking – from one memory to another, doing the work of what has recently been called "visual collective memory"[33] within the largely accessible, collaborative, and traceable realm of a so-called (but not unproblematically so) "online collective memory."[34]

Elderly Subjects, Young Animators: "So Whose Memory Is It?"

That *Old Folks' Tales* animates the memories of its elderly subjects, placing old age centre stage while drawing (on) current topics such as memory in general and historical memory in particular, is significant but not surprising. The televised docuseries joins a growing list of notable titles of animated films from the Hispanic world and beyond that focus on the relationship between memory and later life.[35] What is more, *Old Folks' Tales* participates in a larger cinematic, televised, and digital media movement that uses animation to challenge the societal (in)visibility of the aging body as well as the stigmatization of elderly citizens.[36]

Yet encountering elderly persons as key subjects in animated documentary is a relatively new phenomenon, especially in the Hispanic world.[37] When it comes to *Old Folks' Tales,* however, the made-for-television animated documentary exists in a league of its own, for the aforementioned reason that it signals an unmooring of the animated documentary genre from the vessel of cinema. In this same vein, *Old Folks' Tales* broadens the horizons of television animation, given its creative conception at a moment in which, as Dobson points out, "the cartoon continues to dominate the Western TV landscape" despite the fact that there now exist a wide variety of animated television genres.[38] The

Old Folks' Tales televised program is evidence of what Dobson calls "a rise in innovative TV animation, for both children and adults" due to the growth in animated television generally, and the increase in platforms for viewing on cable and streaming television as well as Internet channels.[39] And while Dobson notes that at this twenty-first-century moment there exists a diversity in genres of television animation, and that new transnational, increasingly experimental television animation is emerging, the existence of animated television documentaries appears to be overlooked or unperceived. Perhaps this is because, until now, in the realm of television documentary, animation has primarily been integrated into otherwise live-action productions and, in turn, has been solely studied for this particular use.[40]

As for where in particular this expansion of the animated horizon is unfolding, it should not come as a surprise that the territory of transnational television animated documentary featuring elderly subjects is now being traversed by Colombia and Spain together. These two nations are linked by their status as currently having the top-billing animation sectors in the Spanish-speaking world and having already produced award-winning animated documentaries, as well as by being two territories that face the same demographic crisis: a rapidly aging population.[41] There is also the important fact that the current elderly populations of both Spain and Colombia have respectively lived through the Spanish Civil War and a decades-long Franco dictatorship that ensued (1936–75), and a ten-year period of political unrest in Colombia commonly referred to as *La Violencia* (The Violence, 1948–58), which was closely followed by the decades-long armed conflict that broke out in the mid-1960s.

These respective periods of civil unrest shaped much of their twentieth-century histories, and, in the case of Colombia, the first two decades of the present century. And, senior subjects residing on Spanish and Latin American soil, whose lives have been duly shaped by war and conflict, have similarly experienced a politics of silence and impunity that, for many years, rendered their stories untold, often to their own families, and especially through channels such as cultural products like the animated documentary that challenge official narratives. What is more, the importance of capturing these testimonies increases along with the age of the subjects who lived them so that private memory would not only persist – here, in easily accessible, consumable, and sharable channels of the digital public sphere – but also compete against the official narratives of Spain and Colombia's twentieth-century histories as new forms of archive, or memorialization, unattached from the state.

This urgency can be read in the title and content of a special episode from the first season, "Capítulo 14: Las historias no contadas" (Chapter 14: Stories Untold), a ten-minute special that weaves together raw footage from the live interviews and animated segments from the opening season's twelve narrative episodes that specifically recall affected childhoods within the contexts of the Spanish Civil War, Colombia's bipartisan violence and armed conflict, and the Second World War. While the episode's title no doubt signals the inclusion of eleven additional testimonies that did not make the final cut, or rather, that did not make it to the literal drawing board for the first season's twelve micro-filmic narratives, it also holds a double – and ironic – meaning as a great number of the testimonies featured within this special episode are not in fact *untold* as they belong to roughly half of the six-minute testimonial narratives animated throughout the season. Rather, the episode's title nuances the larger aim that the transnational and transmedial project *Old Folks' Tales* holds, that is, compiling and articulating stories of Spain's civil war, the Second World War, and Colombia's bipartisan violence and subsequent prolonged armed conflict that are untold in the sense that official histories do not reflect these private memories, of which there are too many to be counted or measured.

This is evidenced by the hundreds of testimonial clips on the *Old Folks' Tales* online platform – largely user-generated content from Spanish-speaking countries such as Colombia, Spain, Argentina, Chile, and Mexico, and also places as seemingly disparate to the Hispanic world as Russia, Uzbekistan, and Nepal. The diverse geographical origins of subjects within the proliferating testimonial clips point to migrations to, from, and within the Spanish-speaking world for reasons like the turbulent sociopolitical events listed above, among others.

The first season, for example, offers a childhood memory belonging to Nety, a native of Colombia's Valle de Tenza (Tenza Valley), who at a young age moved to Garagoa in the department of Boyacá, only to see violence unfold there soon after due to the town's strong conservative ties and the attacks on liberalism.[42] The threat of persecution ultimately led to Nety's decision to flee and undertake a precarious journey across a river and through the mountains, where she would live in hiding for years. Select scenes in Nety's story are portrayed in black and white, representing the seemingly black-and-white nature of the bipartisan violence, while other scenes, or select elements in otherwise colourless scenes, are rendered in an array of solid and bright colours. These are reserved largely for the simplistic, cartoon-like protagonist, animals, trees, flowers, and sunshine that reflect Nety's Garden of Eden–esque idealization of her home, in a similar fashion to the child narrators' depiction of their homelands, as described in chapter 1's analysis of *Little Voices*. Yet in this episode of *Old Folks' Tales*, the juxtaposition of colour and a lack thereof ultimately reflects how Nety remembers a vibrant childhood interrupted – or tainted, we are to understand – by a life altering suffering caused by *La Violencia*.

The same season also offers the story of Roser, specifically, her remembered experience of being sent thousands of kilometres from her family as a young girl when the Spanish Civil War reached her city of Barcelona, as she recalls how, for years, she was unable to return home.[43] The storybook aesthetic features realistic, if not picturesque characters within a hand-drawn, but highly detailed landscape. This is captured by a travelling camera that creates the majority of the movement in each scene as it soars over 2D cut-outs of ocean waves and 2D bridges, and through the archways of 2D buildings. The travelling camera creates the feeling of a 3D story world much like that of a pop-up fairy tale book, while the dark skies of the night-time setting, a maudlin soundtrack, and the testimony recounted by the voice-off reiterate that, for Roser, this recollection very much resembles an "unfairy tale," to borrow the term from the discussion of *Little Voices*.

Conversely, in a narrative of emigration to the Hispanic world, season 2 features an episode based on a series of three-minute interview clips uploaded by the Barcelona-based Buddhist monk Thubten Wangchen.[44] Wangchen's episode tells of his birth in Tibet in the 1950s, only four short years before he would flee the country with his father following unrest and oppression from the Chinese occupation. Wangchen also recounts his upbringing in India, where he formed close ties to the Dalai Lama. Following this, we hear, the monk would leave India for Spain, where he founded the Tibetan House in Barcelona that serves as the setting of his live-action interviews. The handful of three-minute live-action interviews with Wangchen, housed on the digital platform, are characterized by an unmoving camera and a medium shot that captures the traditionally clad and bald-headed monk from where he sits in a plush armchair in front of a brightly painted wall. Partially visible on screen is the bottom half of a mural featuring a mountain scene, which sits behind the interviewee's head in the top third of the shot (see figure 6.1). Meanwhile, the interview segments in Wangchen's animated episode place the mural centre stage, or rather, draw Wangchen into the ornate background, doing away with the subject's chair and transposing his rotoscoped figure directly onto the mural, which is highly stylized to nostalgically reflect Buddhist thangka art (see figure 6.2).

Figure 6.1. Thubten Wangchen's interview, titled "La escuela de la India, años 50."

Figure 6.2. "Thubten: ¡Adiós Tíbet!" / "Thubten: Goodbye, Tibet!"

The "risky" use of trans-stylistic animation briefly described in these few examples is precisely what makes *Old Folks' Tales* successful in the performing of many individual and subjective memories. It also works against a recent criticism of animation and memory: Walden notes the increasing number of animated documentaries, and the fact that animation helps draw attention to an individual's subjective response to events, yet this author problematizes the idea of these films "simply as an exchange between the testifier and the viewer," as one cannot ignore the animator or the animation that lies in between. As Walden aptly writes, "What we see on screen is not simply the testimony – unless the animation is also created by the person telling their story – so whose memory is it?"[45]

Thus far, we have implicitly addressed this question in chapter 1's study of *Little Voices* and chapter 3's analysis of the graphic novel documentary *30 Years of Darkness*. It was argued, for example, that the animated aesthetic in *Little Voices*, which both integrates and imitates the testimonial drawings made by the displaced children, functions in tandem with their recorded testimonies as children's political articulations. That is, as their own visualizations and verbalizations of their memories of the violent conflict that displaced them from their homes to the city of Bogotá. In this child-centred narrative, the animation is necessarily manipulated by the adult production team, in what should be understood as an adult's engagement with the child's world, and the offering of an image of children's politics. The adverse, and more common tendency in Latin American film and beyond, is that adult film-makers impose their world upon children and use the image of children as politics.

Accordingly, *Little Voices* is exactly the case that Walden theorizes about: as long as animation is also created by the person telling their story, what we see on screen *is* the testimony. It was also argued in chapter 3 that the use of a contemporary aesthetic and the voice and face of contemporary popular actor Juan Diego to relate Manuel Cortés's testimony of decades spent in hiding as a political *topo* (mole) in the landscape of post-war Spain communicates a ghostly imbrication of Spain's past and present; what has been called the "spectral nature" of Spain's twentieth-century past surfacing in the twenty-first century as private testimonies at long last proliferate in the wake of the (historical) memory boom.

Yet in the case of *Old Folks' Tales*, the question "Whose memory is it?" is an especially apt one, as the role of the animator and animation is unmistakable in the forty self-contained micro shorts. And yet, the trans-stylistic animation points away from the hand of the animator and towards, rather, the personal memory belonging to each individual interviewee. This strategy goes well against the grain noted by German screenwriter, director, and animator Felix Gönnert during an interview with Meike Uhrig, where studios seemingly "pick a style and then create a story for it," and, in the process, style is ultimately subordinated to story despite the fact that "the story should determine everything in a production of an animation project: character design, colors, character animation, production design, voices, music, sound design, and so forth."[46] It is for these reasons and others that Wells, in his recent "Animation Manifesto," calls animation "the inclusive art," which is "to be used as a radical tool in the reinvention, re-engagement or reinterpretation of social, cultural and historical materials," particularly in the production of animated documentaries.[47]

It is precisely for the fact that *Old Folks' Tales* follows this ideal outlined by Gönnert that it also merits the status as totally unmoored and in uncharted waters. The process of going back to the drawing board for each new episode, despite, in the words of Gönnert, "the immense effort" that animated productions require in the creation of whole worlds,[48] reflects this innovation and quality. In short, Piaggio and Dematei's television documentary series reveals in the maximum way possible that style need not be subordinated to story, but rather that in animated cinematic and televised productions, they can exist in a mutual and parallel relationship. It also evidences that animation, being "el medio ideal para representar la memoria: polimorfa, difusa, proclive a distorsiones y mezclas inesperadas" (the ideal medium to represent memory: polymorphous, diffuse, prone to unexpected distortions and mixtures),[49] need not interfere between testifier and the viewer, but rather facilitates the understanding of exactly *whose memory it is* that is being illustrated.

The fact that the vast majority of episodes throughout the four seasons of *Old Folks' Tales* display a childlike, often simplistic and cartoonish style of animation on the 2D, historical level of the narratives, despite their otherwise individualized characteristics, colour palettes, and soundscapes, can be seen as a reflection of the assertion made within a special episode in season 1 that "los viejos cuando cuentan sus historias, vuelven a ser niños; niños traviesos, curiosos o asustados, y muy sabios" (the elderly, when they tell their stories, become children once again; mischievous, curious or frightened children, and very wise).[50] As Piaggio and Dematei further reveal in their article on the series, the animated testimonies featured within the televised episodes are chosen from the hundreds of user-generated web content for their relevance and originality, the narrative richness brought by the protagonist, the presence of an appropriate dramatic arc, and their aesthetic and plastic potential.[51]

As I have already began to argue, and will further elaborate on here, the aesthetic and plastic potential is not realized, however, to reflect the artist (or number of artists) behind the episode, as is often the case with experimental animated filmic and television productions. Wells, in his notes towards a theory of animation, differentiates between traditional, or orthodox, animation and experimental animation. Whereas one is narrative, the other is interpretive. While the former features a unity of style, the latter plays with multiple styles. While the one features dynamics of dialogue, the other features dynamics of musicality. While the idiosyncratic "graphic trace" of the individual artist – to borrow a term often employed in comics studies to denote the cartoonist's individual style, which highlights the constructedness of a comic by pointing to the hand of the author-artist (a strong expectation in the medium, as Kai Mikkonen observes in *The Narratology of Comic Art*[52]) – is absent or obscured in orthodox animation,[53] it is present and highly evident in experimental animation. As Wells further notes on this last difference, more recent cartoon animation, and especially more personal "auteurist" animation, reveals the presence of an individual artist in creating the work.[54]

By this measure, it can be said that *Old Folks' Tales* defies and even transcends categorization as, while it is not non-narrative and does not resist telling stories, the animation still requires audience interpretation – or what Ward calls "emotional engagement," as will soon be discussed.[55] Further, while the project rejects a unity of style, it does not simply feature multiple styles, but rather myriad and ever-changing styles. What is more, the "graphic trace" of the artist(s) get(s) obscured in this constant exchange of style, ultimately diverting attention to the episode's constructedness away from the artist and towards each individual protagonist and the traces of their private memories.

It is animation's ability to make visible the intangible phenomenon of the traces of memory, or the "texture of a memory," to use Ward's term,[56] that becomes exceedingly evident within the very first episode of season 1 of *Old Folks' Tales*. "Ysabel: El miedo baja del cielo" (Ysabel: Fear Comes Down from the Sky) narrates the memory that Ysabel Santamaría Erdaide holds of living in Bilbao, Spain, as a seven-year-old child in the early years of the Spanish Civil War, during which time she experienced systematic bombings of her city, one of the first ordered by General Francisco Franco and carried out with the help of German and Italian air forces.[57] Ysabel and her family are drawn as overly simplistic, black-and-white figures shaped largely through geometrical forms, while the details of her memory are textured by excessive cross-hatching (see figure 6.3). These fast and loose scribbles in thin-lined black ink quiver constantly, at times constituting the main or even the only action within the shot. The aesthetic at once conveys the young girl's innocence as well as both the physical tremors from the bombings and the trembling of the frightened young girl as an emotional response to the event.

Figure 6.3. Simplistic figures and excessive cross-hatching in "Ysabel: El miedo baja del cielo" / "Ysabel: Fear Comes Down from the Sky" (00:01:20)

The soundscape of Ysabel's episode equally communicates this fear, as her oral testimony is largely accentuated by sound effects: the low roar of plane engines; the distant sound of bombs exploding; a muffled roar of a crowd; and, the muted but sharp sound of civil defence alarms and civilian screams. Just past the one-minute mark the narrative also incorporates melodramatic piano music, playing softly and slowly as Ysabel begins to tell of how, at the sound of the warning alarms, she and her family would descend the stairs of their apartment building to take cover at street level. In a re-enactment scene, the music not only compliments or competes with the testimony, but is also at times challenged by the even louder and more urgent sound of Ysabel's heaving breath as she descends the stairs in fear. Here, the momentarily subjective camera shows the dizzying and frantic descent to find refuge before switching to an objective shot that zeroes in on the girls face and wide eyes, as seen in figure 6.3. This moment in Ysabel's episode, along with many moments throughout the four seasons demonstrate the fact that, as Wells first theorized, "experimental animation has a strong relationship to music."[58] And, it should be added, to other elements of the soundscape in general. Ysabel's episode is a particularly good example of the fact that, as Wells continues, "there is a psychological and emotional relationship with sound and colour which may be expressed through the free form which characterises animation."[59]

The constant quiver of the thin black lines on screen paired with the predominantly black-and-white palette and a low-level rumbling noise evokes the phenomenon of television static and white noise resulting from signal interference. This purposeful aesthetic reflects the way that Ysabel's childhood memory still interferes in her mind, many decades later. In fact, around the one-minute mark a convergence occurs between the visual aesthetics of the 2D animated memory and the rotoscoped interview, as Ysabel tells of the daily fly-bys of what are visually depicted as Heinkel He 111 bomber planes. The elderly Ysabel vocally imitates the drone of their engines by emitting a prolonged "rrrrr," and simultaneously signals their flight with a rapid sweep of her left arm across her body. Concurrent to this gesture, a drawing of one such plane appears, following the trajectory of her hand until it flies over the elderly woman's right shoulder, dropping a bomb before continuing on its course exiting the shot to the left side of the screen. The bomb bursts into a small swirl of black scribbles near the bottom of this same side of the screen, quickly unfurling and spreading across the shot, at first behind the protagonist but moments later rising up in front of Ysabel's torso, bubbling up like a sea of black ink, and growing more active and threatening as the woman, struggling for the right words, narrates that the city used a system of sirens "como avisándote que venían y que te preparara" (as though warning you that they were coming and that you should prepare yourself). It is at this moment that the sea of scribbles nearly fills the screen, ready to engulf the figure of the elderly woman before they are swept away and out of the shot with another wave of her left hand (see figure 6.4).

On the one hand, the sloshing, wave-like motion of these thick memory lines poignantly illustrates that memory "is not fixed, but rather it is fluid," not to mention "messy."[60] Meanwhile, Ysabel's animated – in the other sense of the word – body language to which the animation is choreographed, highlights how memory "refers to our bodily and sensual relations to events that have previously happened."[61] Here, the black lines from the representational space of past experience in the foreground of the shot leap seamlessly on to the rotoscoped arm of the present-day subject, dripping off of Ysabel's raised elbow as a visual communication that "memory is something felt."[62]

Above all, this scene, like many others in the series, makes clear that memory is best understood as "our experience of the past in the present."[63] Figure 6.4 unmistakably shows how animation allows for the literal drawing of the past into the present to symbolically illustrate the ephemeral overlap of past experiences in present moments that occur during the phenomenon of remembering. The particularly

Figure 6.4. Sweeping away memories in "Ysabel: El miedo baja del cielo" / "Ysabel: Fear Comes Down from the Sky" (00:01:03)

solid, expressive black lines in this scene visually communicate that the memory is clearly etched into the protagonist's mind, while the shaky, two-tone black-and-white aesthetic of the 2D animation, which takes on an early twentieth-century archival quality, signals the distance of the event and its ability to be pushed aside despite the fear and vulnerability that the subject once felt. In this way, the animation can be said to work evocatively, in Annabelle Honess Roe's terms,[64] illustrating through its expressive tone and style the textures of Ysabel's fear-filled memory, evoking this unfilmable – but not *unanimatable* – subjective experience of a fear-filled past experience.

Yet the animation also works mimetically in the sense that it visually recreates the action for which no archival footage exists. Piaggio and Dematei themselves state animation's twofold function by noting of the series in general that animation is "una herramienta que permite reconstruir los relatos recordados no solo en su dimensión histórica, sino más especialmente, *en su dimensión emotiva*, poniendo a la vez de relieve los mecanismos de la memoria" (a tool that allows for the reconstruction of remembered stories not only in their historical dimension, but especially *in their emotional dimension* while highlighting the mechanisms of memory).[65]

These animated memories, especially those with an emotional dimension relating to war and trauma, are recent evidence of, as Hillary Chute says of comics in *Disaster Drawn*, "how war generates new forms of visual-verbal witness."[66] The *verbal* in the case of comics is what is written, inscribed on the page, with size, colour, tone, and line of font contributing to the communication of verbal testimony. In the case of animated documentary, however, the verbal becomes even more complex: there is tone and volume of voice, the pace at which one recounts an experience, and the dynamics of musicality and sound effects added by the production team to heighten the verbal – all of which play out in Ysabel's narrative. If drawing takes the lead in a comics narrative, as it is widely argued to do, it can be said that in animated documentary, the visual and verbal work in tandem, just as has already been argued of the story and style.

A viewing of the following episode in season 1 immediately makes clear the extent of animation's versatility and suitability to performing of the textures of a memory. While Ysabel's chiefly black-and-white frenetic drawing style communicates the nightmarish fear she faced as a young girl living in Bilbao during the systematic bombing raids, in the bright, multicoloured episode that directly follows, war and death are more abstract for the young protagonist from Mompox, Colombia; a source of vivid curiosity rather than terror. "Hernán: El niño y los muertos" (Hernán: The Boy and the Dead) animates the memories of a man who spent his childhood during the 1940s and 1950s in the colonial town nestled near the nation's northern Caribbean coast.[67] As we hear, Hernán's childhood was relatively unaffected by *La Violencia* until it arrived in Mompox in the form of "los chulavitas"; an irregular armed faction of the Colombian government that functioned like a police force, searching out supporters of the former Liberal presidential candidate Jorge Eliecer Gaitán, whose assassination in 1948 spurred the ten-year period of political unrest.

Hernán's testimony is centred on his curiosity over the funeral proceedings for two citizens from his town that were systematically assassinated by the chulavitas, yet addresses his larger fascination with death, despite, as he says, the constant reminders from home that he should not go out into the streets "porque había que tener miedo de la muerte ... porque había la violencia" (because one had to fear death ... because of the violence that was there). The latter part of Hernán's testimony consists of an anecdote about a clandestine night-time excursion into the Mompox cemetery, where, as he narrates, he rested on a tomb waiting to see if he would become frightened. In the end, however, upon leaving the cemetery at dawn, it is an encounter with a large dog that finally frightens Hernán, who immediately believes it to be "el diablo que me estaba persiguiendo" (the devil that was pursuing me). This anecdote that closes Hernán's testimony, together with the

Figure 6.5. "Hernán: El niño y los muertos" / "Hernán: The Boy and the Dead" (00:00:40)

opening scene, in which an extreme long shot shows the young boy running playfully in the streets of Mompox, oblivious to the mournful mood of all others around him, frames his childlike curiosity of but also aloofness to the reality of death.

This is nuanced by the fact that Hernán holds high a toy-sized Heinkel He 111 plane as he runs on the sidewalk in front of a row of colourful colonial-style buildings, before a jump to an extreme close-up zeroes in on the toy bomber in the left hand of the boy as he enters a wake and, approaching the open casket, begins to describe how "parece que me perseguía … la imagen de la muerte" (it seemed as though … the image of death was haunting me; see figure 6.5). Although, as the elderly narrator continues to share from later in life, as a young boy he did not yet understand mourning or the meaning of death. The detail of the bomber plane establishes an immediate link with Ysabel's episode, juxtaposing the machine as an instrument of certain fear and threat of death for the young girl living in the heart of the civil war in Spain while the same plane imagined as a toy for Hernán, symbolizes the young boy's fascination but not fear of death, as well as his more distant relationship to a national conflict and a lesser affected childhood.

In this sense, the juxtaposition of Hernán's brightly coloured narrative against Ysabel's largely black-and-white animated memory also communicates these two children's disparate understandings of death and of their respective national conflicts. In other words, the colour(lessness) communicates how their respective worldviews have either been shaped or not by the sociopolitical context in which their childhood played out. While the vivid colours of the costumbrista animation no doubt mimetically reconstruct Mompox's Sevillian colonial architecture, they also become evocative of childhood where life is thought to be colourful, metaphorically speaking, as a child's worldview is not so black and white, given that young children have not yet necessarily distinguished between good and bad.

Hernán and his surroundings within the colourful memory scenes exist in opposition to the adult figures that are collectively portrayed in an array of solid, cool hues of blue, purple, and green, as seen in figure 6.5. The representation of the grown-ups in this manner should be read as a communication of "el tono luctuoso del contexto político" (the sorrowful tone of the political context), of which they are fully aware and which affects them.[68] The use of cool colours specifically reiterates the mind/body effect that psychologists ascribe to this portion of the colour wheel, thought to have a subduing effect on the body and believed to suppress emotions, ultimately contrasting and underscoring the boy's zest for life, his appetite for adventure, and his childlike curiosity surrounding death.

The marginality of *La Violencia* to Hernán's childhood is highlighted by the narration of a joyful memory as the now-old man tells how within this same era, he began to know "el valor de la música" (the value of music), having lived with his aunts, who practised piano, violin, and guitar. What fascinated Hernán the most, we learn, was listening to his relatives interpret the symphonies of Beethoven and Mozart, among other classical musicians, in the *tertulias* (get-togethers) his family would host. In the scene recreating one of these gatherings, the grown-ups that play and listen to the music are conversely portrayed in warm hues of orange, yellow, and red; the emotion that the musical gatherings provided, we are to understand, was felt by all. Beyond the use of colour in the visual language, this sentiment is communicated through the dynamics of musicality as a harmonious rendition of Beethoven's ode to joy plays while Hernán nostalgically recalls the memory of these parties at an unhurried pace.

The pairing of colourful animation along with the dynamics of musicality to portray the texture of a melancholic or nostalgic memory plays out to an even greater extent in a notable episode from the second season, crafted from one of the most popular and commented on interviews from the formerly active *Cuentos de viejos* online platform: "José María: Historia con acordeón" (José María: Story with an Accordion).[69] This popular episode paints – literally, with its watercolour aesthetic – a

Figure 6.6. "José María: Historia con acordeón" / "José María: Story with an Accordion" (00:01:55)

picture of José María Díaz Oñate's childhood in San Juan del Cesar, a municipality in the south of Colombia's La Guajira department. What is portrayed is a very local story, achieved by the watercolour scenery that recreates San Juan del Cesar's lush agricultural landscape, and didactic elements in black ink that outline the cultivation of tobacco, in which José María worked with his mother from the young age of eight as "jefe de la familia" (head of the family) following his father's untimely death. When we view the young José María reach for his deceased father's hat, which sits atop a wooden stool, while his mother and two younger siblings huddle in the background crying together (see figure 6.6), we cannot help but recall the similar moment of symbolism in *Little Voices*, depicted in figure 1.4 from chapter 1.

It is, however, the fluid integration of *Vallenato*, Colombia's popular folk music autochthonous to the Caribbean region, where José María grew up, that completes the local flavour of the memory as the protagonist shares portions of his story through song, self-accompanied by his accordion. José María's child-self, along with the figures representing his siblings and mother, are composed of charcoal-lined brown paper cut-outs, which then move across the landscape, seemingly a rapidly composed afterthought in the visual narration and thus arguably setting up rural life – full of textures and colour and local sounds – as the true protagonist of José María's memory.

At the same time, the simplistic, rudimentary black-ink character drawings on unbleached paper represent the nostalgic tone of the memory for the subject, as the pre-digital drawing form communicates a longing for simpler times housed in the past. As Walden notes on animation's paradoxical capacity to represent nostalgia, "It is often digital media, such as Pixar animations, that offer nostalgic value … However, they are also products of modern advancement … and their means of production (computer-generated animation) technologically threaten the existence of the old media forms that characterized the eras to which we often longingly look back."[70] José María's episode is evidence that *Old Folks' Tales* intentionally works against this paradox in nostalgia-tinged memories, once again allowing style and story to play equal roles in the creative production of the episode.

A final notable example of animation's ability in *Old Folks' Tales* to evoke the subjective texture of a memory can be seen in an episode from the third season, "Alejandro: Por los aires" (Alexander: In the Air).[71] The episode is narrated by Alejandro Valsuani (1934–2016), an Argentine from Buenos Aires equally passionate about his career as a historian as he was about his hobby as a parachutist, earning fame for a jump in 1960 from over 26,500 feet, with which he broke South America's standing record for the highest jump. On the one hand, Alejandro's episode communicates this sense of adventure through an aesthetic that is highly evocative of *The Adventures of Tintin*, the internationally popular comic book series created by Belgian cartoonist known as Hergé (born Georges Prosper Remi) around the same time that the protagonist was a child. Alejandro's memory is drawn in the same clean line and realistic style, and he features a similar round face, black-dot eyes, and single tuft of hair atop his forehead to the title character. Most notable, however, are his rust-colour plus fours and brown loafers and spirit of adventure.

On the other hand, the episode captures Alejandro's enthusiasm for the archival, by superimposing real images of the boy's childhood hero and inspiration, the late Argentine parachutist Tomás Picasso, into the colourful world of his memory. As depicted in figure 6.7, at certain moments the animated and the archival become inextricably intertwined, as both aesthetics prove integral to the communication of the young boy's twin passions.

Alejandro's episode is also worth mentioning for the fact that it highlights that not all testimonies animated in the episodes throughout the four seasons of *Old Folks' Tales* are textured by war and conflict. Some, like Hernán and Alejandro's narratives, also – or even exclusively – reveal childhood adventure or curiosity as another important theme.

Figure 6.7. "Alejandro: Por los aires" / "Alexander: In the Air" (00:01:20)

In the final episode of the first season, likewise Argentine-born Susana remembers her upbringing in her grandfather's travelling circus and her close relationship with one of the performing elephants.[72] In season 2's opening episode, Inés, who grew up in Colombia's capital, Bogotá, reveals how her curiosity about her city led her to frequently sneak out of her home, anecdotally highlighting the time that she encountered Margarita "la Loca" Villaquirá (1860–1942), one of the city's infamous Liberal fanatics from within the two decades leading up to *La Violencia*.[73] In the fourth episode from the most recent season, Carlos, a Cuban-born man hailing from the port town of Nuevitas, recalls one of his habitual fishing excursions with his father in which they were caught in a storm that left them stranded for some time from his mother and siblings.[74]

Beyond animation's capacity to evoke emotions tied to individual memory, however, the trans-stylistic quality of *Old Folks' Tales* makes evident the recently noted fact that animation can also evoke an emotional response from viewers. This potentiality has, on the one hand, been attributed to animated fiction. As Dobson writes, "Beyond the style and technique used in animation, there can be a combination of factors – sound, voice, performance, and color that can influence the level of emotional response,"[75] despite audience awareness of the fictional nature of the characters whose emotional journey they are accompanying. On the other hand, and more pertinent to the case study here, scholars of animated documentary have recently been theorizing how the animated aesthetic of a filmic narrative can elicit a different type of emotional response from the viewer. Ward, for example, highlights "the extent to which animated documentaries foreground their constructedness and the emotional effect this has on the viewers."[76] For Ward, who proposes that we think about animated documentary *performatively*, animation does not aim to merely make visible for the viewer straightforward facts, but rather intends to, "through a highly self-conscious foregrounding of the interplay between animator and animated, with the status of the animated being further complicated by its reenacted relationship vis-à-vis the real world," make the audience "*think* and *feel* about that something and the way in which it has been communicated to us."[77] This becomes evident through the analysis of the four principal examples above. While we may or may not feel Ysabel's fear, Hernán's vivid curiosity, José María's nostalgia for his homeland, or Alejandro's sense of adventure, we can undoubtedly understand that, through the highly intentional construction of each short episode, the series aims to portray the subjective and individual emotions that these memories hold for different protagonists.

Having thoroughly discussed the private memory-performing capacity of the 2D animation in the television documentary series *Old Folks' Tales*, it remains to be said how the rotoscoped interviews – a unifying factor that visually links the forty episodes – contributes to the series's overarching project of collective memory. This term, popularized by sociologist Maurice Halbwachs, is meant to suggest that our personal remembrance of the past is affected and informed by memories that we have collected and recollected as part of a society.[78] More recently, the discourse surrounding collective memory has theorized that this phenomenon is central to identity formation, in the sense that it is "less fixed to a specific notion of identity and more fluid, melding together the recollections and experiences of different individuals and things."[79]

No doubt, as Ward also notes, rotoscoped animation has a "vexed reputation," often considered "cheating" or "not proper animation" or thought to inhibit performance and action.[80] Rotoscoped animation's reputation becomes even thornier in the particular case of the animated documentary, in which live-action bodies "clash" with animated ontologies, and it is in these cases, Ward suggests, that rotoscoping either succeeds or fails to work. In the case of *Old Folks' Tales*, the rotoscoped aesthetic very much works, and, what is more, it works with a very particular purpose: towards communicating the construction of collective memory, again, a "melding together [of] the recollections and experiences of different individuals and things."[81]

The thick, black lines that trace the bodies of the elderly protagonists in the rotoscoped talking-head shots repeatedly link one episode to the next, becoming like rhizomatic memory lines that constitute the base – or borders – of the collective memory being mapped out through the televised documentary project. While these proliferating dark lines can be said to trace the outline of this figurative map, each episodic site of memory ("les lieux de mémoire"), to borrow French historian Pierre Nora's term,[82] are uniquely textured by emotions tied to the interviewees' individual experiences of places or events related to the Hispanic world's twentieth-century history. The rotoscoped live-action footage also contributes to the representation of the oneiric quality inherent to the act of remembering, thus highlighting another common characteristic ascribed to rotoscoped animation: the dream-like effect that this technique can have for the viewer as it simultaneously blurs some features while bringing others to the fore. In the case of *Old Folks' Tales*, the dream-like quality can be read as a visual iteration that the elderly protagonists participate in the act of remembering, as it is their past experiences – their recollections of childhood, specifically – that are portrayed as more vivid and more concrete, highlighting the fact that the action of these micro-filmic documentary episodes is anchored in the past.

These communicated memories of the past, however, are subject to one's predisposition to both blur and highlight, or mistake and overemphasize, specific details from one's own memory. As Piaggio and Dematei note, "La memoria de los ancianos puede ser frágil, o confusa, pero eso es justamente lo interesante. [Cada historia es] un retrato, uno entre miles, todos son individuales y entre todos construyen una historia colectiva" (The memory of the elderly can be fragile, or confused, but this is exactly what is most interesting. [Each story is] a snapshot, one among thousands, they are all individual and between them all they construct a collective story).[83]

And yet, one of the three aims of the project, as outlined in the beginning of this chapter, was not only to collect stories, but to have users connect and share these, as well as inspire the creation of further narratives that would add to a collective memory. With this aim, Piaggio and Dematei's project exists not only as transnational and transmedial, but also as transgenerational. While it is the older generation that tells their stories, it is the users of the interactive documentary project, young and old alike, which interact with the plethora of short videos and thus acquire the memories of their compatriots or ancestors.

While the series's titular sequence no doubt communicates the circularity of life and the passing on of memory into the hands of the next generation, a more nuanced reading reveals a metatextual commentary on the series's deconstruction of predominant correlations between age and animation, those that, as previously mentioned, remain predominant on the small screen. The introductory sequence alerts the viewer to an intermingling of the animated and the archival, in both verbal and visual terms, as well as the idea that animation in this series is not entertainment for children but rather a method of performing the personal memories of the Hispanic world's oldest generations. That the opening sequence itself is trans-stylistic, relying on rotoscoping, cut-out animation, montage, CG, and traditional hand-drawn animation, further suggests that animation is not only an apt aesthetic for the cultural representation of and reception by the aged (social) body, but one that allows us to draw (on) the textures of private memory and draw together a collective memory that is remarkably visual and acoustic.

That visual culture plays a key role in collective memory formation is not a novel notion. However, its theorization under the umbrella of the term *visual collective memory* is an emergent tendency. In particular, two recent dissertations explore the role of social representations that rely on visual images – namely, photographs – in communicating and creating conceptions of a common past and a group identity,[84] and even to create meaning of a geographical or architectural place.[85] *Old Folks' Tales* stands out as a case of exceptional visual collective memory for its non-indexical and highly varied aesthetic. It seems paradoxical to believe that a broad group of people can find common meaning in a media representation that relies on an exponentially diverse visual aesthetic. And yet, *Old Folks' Tales* is proof that the medium of animation, with its capacity to infinitely illustrate the textures of private memory, retains the essence of the individual as part of the broader collective within social representations that host and foster collective memory.

In other words, as a tool of visual collective memory, that *Old Folks' Tales* relies on animation to draw together – pun intended – common past experiences is novel. While current theorizations of visual collective memory place a single photographic image at its centre, an artefact upon which myriad unspecified spectators gaze in order to find group meaning, *Old Folks' Tales* illustrates how visual collective memory can work in the opposite direction. The series's animators highlight the role of the individual, and of private memory within the creation of a picture of a cohesive common past. In short, this tapestry effect retains the aesthetics of individual threads of private memory.

Add to this alternative understanding of visual collective memory the recent opening up of "online collective memory" as a topic of interest,[86] and a more nuanced understanding of *Old Folks' Tales* as a tool of collective memory shaped by media and new technologies can be had.

These authors show how, in sites of online collective memory such as Wikipedia, hyperlinks play a key role in the user's ability to comprehend a source article (generally a current or recent event) in the context of target articles (generally similar past events in terms of time, geography, and topic). In a similar way, the aforementioned "tags" used in *Old Folks' Tales*'s Stories on the Map online tool allowed for individual past experiences to be understood in the context of other testimonies that share a geography, time, and/or topic, though perhaps this is best understood under the framework of the memory of the multitude. These hundreds of tags played a key role in not only digitally connecting and collecting these stories, but also allowing them to be recollected in a meaningful way, which varied according to the pathway choices made by each individual user, who participated from their own unique spatial and temporal coordinates. And if animation, as Fenoll repeatedly states throughout his article, allows for new generations to connect with themes of memory,[87] something that rings true of *Old Folk's Tales*'s televised episodes, which attract viewers of all ages, so too does the *onlineization*, so to speak, of the hundreds of recorded testimonies in the interactive story map aspect of the documentary project.

No doubt this new strand of memory-related research opened up by García-Gavilanes et al. is proof that much remains to be said about the multifaceted and collaborative documentary project *Old Folks' Tales*. The aim here, however, has been to focus on one specific branch of this innovative project: the animated television documentary series. This chapter has joined in a recent effort to explore the convergences between animation, documentary, and memory. I have pointed out animation's ability to illustrate the textures of private memory; exponentially so when aided by dynamics of musicality and other aspects of soundscape. Further, I argued for the importance of this transgenerational project in both Spain and Colombia alike, given the ticking clock on recording these remembrances of past experiences of war and conflict, as well as of childhood in general and childhood adventure specifically, that challenge or expand official histories within the Spanish-speaking world and beyond, given the threat of losing these memories along with the aging minds and bodies of those who carry them. I have also aimed to show how part of a political project that undoubtedly underlies the *Old Folks' Tales* collaborative documentary project is its transgenerationality; bringing these "untold stories" into the reach of audiences from new generations through an animated aesthetic on television, as well as by the onlineization of its untouched, recorded testimonies.

I have further said that if the ever-changing aesthetics make *Old Folks' Tales* an animated anti-series, as the creators themselves suggest of their risky aesthetic choice, perhaps this is not a negative thing as the term suggests, but rather an example for future animated series, whether they be documentary or fictional in nature. The trans-stylistic television series ultimately transcends what has been called one of "the most widespread and compelling forms of animated documentary," being productions that use an animated aesthetic to interpret the testimony or reminiscence of a real person.[88] *Old Folks' Tales* does this forty times over and in forty unique ways. What is more, amid the proliferation of the animated documentary genre, especially in the post-truth era, as Nea Ehrlich notes, *Old Folks' Tales* stands as proof that the transgressive potential of animated documentary remains by allowing "viewers [to] see realities anew through innovative representation that breaks with conventions."[89] The Colombian-Spanish transnational, trans-stylistic, and transgenerational animated television documentary series evidences the fact that the future of *politically animated* depictions of actuality is vibrant in the Hispanic world, whether or not these be multicoloured or black and white (or both), hand-drawn or CG (or both), media-specific, intermedial, or even transmedial (or a blend of these), and whether or not they reach us through the big, small, or digital screen.

Notes

Introduction: Towards Expansion and Liberation in the Field of Animated Documentary

1 Amago and Marr, *Consequential Art*.
2 A single surviving tape is a copy of the short film *El mono relojero / The Monkey Watchmaker* (Argentina, 1938), a cinematic adaptation of Constancio C. Vigil's children's story of the same title. At the time of the fire, the Uruguyan-Argentine writer had a personal copy in his possession. Regrettably, although the surviving film is tangible proof of Cristiani's work as an animator, it is not representative of his style, being thematically different and lacking the element of political satire characteristic of his other films. Nevertheless, a great effort to document Cristiani's creative legacy was recently made by Italian film-maker Gabriele Zucchelli, who directed *Quirino Cristiani: The Mystery of the First Animated Movies* (UK, 2007).
3 In this film Cristiani once again draws on the subject of the presidency of Irigoyen, who at the time was fulfilling a second term. Increasingly ambitious, the eighty-minute *Peludo City* centres on governmental corruption and popular rights accompanied by synchronized sound and music on disc.
4 Three years after becoming personally acquainted with the then octogenarian Cristiani in 1980, Bendazzi would publish a biography in his native Italian, under the title *Quirino Cristiani, Due voite l'oceana* (Quirino Cristiani, Twice the First). For an English edition, see Bendazzi, *Twice the First*, and for a Spanish-language version, see Bendazzi, *Quirino Cristiani*. And, although Cristiani's films were lost, his creative legacy was recently documented by Italian film maker Gabriele Zucchelli in *Quirino Cristiani: The Mystery of the First Animated Movies* (see n. 2 above).
5 Bendazzi, *Foundations*, 86.
6 Bendazzi, 86.

7 Bendazzi notes a number of animated shorts made by Cristiani that seem to verge on the genre of animated documentary. These include films about current events, including sports, notably the fights of boxer Luis Ángel Firpo (*Firpo-Brennan* and *Firpo-Dempsey*, both Argentina, 1923) and a portrayal of the victory of the Uruguay soccer team (*Uruguayos Forever*, Argentina, 1924). The same year, Cristiani would produce *Humberto de garufa / Little Umberto's Frolic* (Argentina, 1924), a short film inspired by the visit of Umberto of Savoy, the young and carefree crown prince of Italy; see Bendazzi, *Foundations*, 87.

8 Marr, "Building a Home," 144. Marr refers specifically to the work of well-known American documentarian Michael Moore, drawing comparisons to the "activist spirit of satire" in the work of Spanish cartoonist and film-maker Aleix Saló, whose viral short film *Españistan: De la burbuja inmobilaria a la Crisis / Spainistan: From the Real-Estate Bubble to the Crisis* (Spain, 2011) will be the subject of exploration in chapter 4 of this study.

9 A three-pronged definition was originally put forth by leading animated documentary scholar Annabelle Honess Roe in 2011. Honess Roe includes as the final criterion that the audiovisual work ought to have "been presented as a documentary by its producers and/or received as a documentary by audiences, festivals, or critics." The intention of this third criterion for classification, as Honess Roe continues, "helps to narrow the field; advertising, scientific, educational and public service films, arenas in which animation is frequently utilized, fall beyond what I would consider an animated documentary because they are neither intended, nor received as documentaries." See Honess Roe, "Absence, Excess and Epistemological Expansion," *Animation* 6, no. 3 (2011): 217. Paul Ward has most recently summarized this now common understanding of animated documentary and the role of the animator, but has likewise taken into consideration the oft-overlooked role of the viewer in the meaning-making process: "Viewers 'take up' and understand the animation in relation to the real world events and people"; animated documentary "mak[es] us think and feel about that something and the way in which it has been communicated to us." See Ward, "Animated Documentary: Viewer Engagement," 96, 99.

10 McKinney and Richter, *Spanish Graphic Narratives*; Magnussen, *Spanish Comics* (the contents of this edited collection were published a handful of years prior as two special issues of *European Comics Art*; see Magnussen, "Spanish Comics, Part I" and "Spanish Comics, Part II"); and Fraser, *Art of Pere Joan*. These four books published within the same number of years – *Consequential Art* included – demonstrate that the study of Spanish comics has recently experienced a definitive shift from historical and narratological approaches to schematic and thematic analyses of contemporary comics. Notable examples of earlier historical approaches include Pérez-del-Solar, *Imágenes del desencanto*; and Merino, *El cómic hispano*.

11 L'Hoeste and Poblete, *Redrawing the Nation*; Catalá-Carrasco, Drinot, and Scorer, *Comics and Memory*; King and Page, *Posthumanism and the Graphic Novel*; and Scorer, *Comics beyond the Page*.
12 On the themes of animation, documentary, and journalism, see González Monaj and Lorenzo Hernández, "Animación y periodismo"; and González Monaj "Animando realidades."
13 See García López, "El documental de animación."
14 See Pinotti, "La animación no ficcional"; and Pinotti, "Los documentales animados."
15 See Fenoll, "Animación, documental y memoria"; and Fenoll, "La representación de la dictadura."
16 See Trombetta, "Lenguaje de animación"; and Trombetta, "La ficción y su función de memoria."
17 Honess Roe, *Animated Documentary*.
18 Murray and Ehrlich, *Drawn from Life*.
19 Ehrlich, *Animating Truth*.
20 Formenti, *Classical Animated Documentary*.
21 Wells, "Animation Manifesto."
22 Ward, *Documentary*, 85.
23 Honess Roe, *Animated Documentary*, 22.
24 Nash, Hight, and Summerhayes, *New Documentary Ecologies*.
25 See Ward, "Animating with Facts"; and Ward, "Animated Documentary: Viewer Engagement."
26 Ward, "Recollection, 'Re-enactment' and Temporality."
27 See, e.g., Buchan, "Animated Spectator"; Davis and Vladica, "Consumer Value"; and Landesman and Bendor, "Animated Recollection."
28 Honess Roe, "Against Animated Documentary?"
29 Ehrlich, "Conflicting Realisms," 27.
30 Ehrlich, "Animated Documentaries," 266–7.
31 Honess Roe, "Interjections and Connections," 284.
32 Ehrlich, "Conflicting Realisms," 36.
33 Chute, *Disaster Drawn*, 5.
34 Mickwitz, *Documentary Comics*.
35 Gauthier, "On 'Institutionalization,'" 367.
36 Gauthier, 374.
37 Chute, "Comics as Archives."
38 Wells, "Never Mind the Bollackers."
39 To view the videocomic in its entirety, see Sastre and Sedano, "Videocómic: La batalla de Mosul."
40 Wells, "Animation Manifesto," 99.
41 Chute, *Disaster Drawn*, 5, 7.
42 Buchan, "Animation, in Theory," 119.
43 As quoted in Buchan, 121.

44 Bendazzi, *Foundations*, 86.
45 Bendazzi, 190.
46 Bendazzi, 95.
47 As quoted in Bendazzi, *Birth of a Style*, 410.
48 Bendazzi, 422.
49 Bendazzi, 417.
50 To view the documentary in its entirety, see IDM, *LAS TABAS*.
51 Bendazzi, *Contemporary Times*, 318. To view the animated documentary in its entirety, see L'Ami, *Mi historia es tu historia*.
52 Locuviche, "Latin American Animation Leaders."
53 To access the animated documentary in its entirety, see Orozco, *Reality 2.0*.
54 See Fenoll, "Animación, documental y memoria."
55 Wells, "Animation Manifesto," 96.
56 See Honess Roe, "Interjections and Connections."
57 See Sebreli, *Deseos imaginarios*.
58 Martí López, "MAKUN (No llores)," 20.
59 Honess Roe, "Interjections and Connections," 284.
60 Caron, *Satire*, 2.
61 Caron, 33.
62 See Hoskins, "Memory of the Multitude."

1. Animating Agency: Children's Articulated and Embodied Politics in Jairo Carrillo and Oscar Andrade's *Pequeñas voces / Little Voices* (2010)

1 Carrillo and Andrade, *Pequeñas voces*. Note that the animated documentary in its entirety can also be seen on Vimeo at https://vimeo.com/207047394.
2 The 2003 short film of the same title premiered at the Venice Festival and was the winner of eight international awards.
3 Consultoría para los Derechos Humanos y el Desplazamiento, "De la seguridad a la prosperidad democrática."
4 See UNHCR, *Forced Displacement in 2015*.
5 See UNHCR, *Forced Displacement in 2019*.
6 See Durán, "Las potencias," 44.
7 According to the final box-office and ticket sales published in editions 536 and 518 of the online newspaper *Pantalla Colombia*, respectively. See "Estadísticas del cine colombiano: Taquilla y box office finales de la película colombiana *Pequeñas voces 3D*" and "Estadísticas del cine colombiano: Taquilla y box office finales de la película colombiana *Los colores de la montaña*."
8 Kriger, *Animated Realism*, 61.

9 Ospina, "Natural Plots," 253.
10 Randall, *Children on the Threshold*, 76–9.
11 See Elwood and Mitchell, "Mapping Children's Politics."
12 See, e.g., Kallio, "Body as a Battlefield"; Kallio and Häkli, "Political Geography in Childhood"; Kallio and Häkli, "Are There Politics in Childhood?"; Kallio and Häkli, "Tracing Children's Politics"; and Lind, "Duality."
13 Skelton, "Young People, Children, Politics and Space."
14 Kallio and Häkli, "Tracing Children's Politics," 104–5.
15 Elwood and Mitchell, "Mapping Children's Politics," 5.
16 Kallio, "Body as a Battlefield," 294.
17 Kallio and Häkli, "Political Geography in Childhood."
18 See Lind, "Duality."
19 Kallio and Häkli, "Are There Politics in Childhood?," 26 (emphasis in original).
20 Bosco, "Play, Work or Activism?," 385.
21 Kallio and Häkli, "Tracing Children's Politics," 100.
22 See Karlsson, "'Do You Know What We Do?'"
23 Sköld and Söderlind, "Agentic Subjects."
24 See Lind, "Duality."
25 See Elwood and Mitchell, "Mapping Children's Politics."
26 See Kallio, "Body as a Battlefield."
27 Honess Roe, "Interjections and Connections," 284.
28 See Kallio and Bartos, "Children's Caring Agencies."
29 Brocklehurst, *Who's Afraid of Children?*, 33.
30 Denov, *Child Soldiers*, 16 17.
31 Paz-Mackay and Rodríguez, *Politics of Children*.
32 Paz-Mackay and Rodríguez, ix.
33 Paz-Mackay and Rodríguez, xv.
34 Paz-Mackay and Rodríguez, xv.
35 Paz-Mackay and Rodríguez, xv.
36 Paz-Mackay and Rodríguez, xviii.
37 López Zúñiga, "Oscar Andrade."
38 Although the names of these four characters are never mentioned within the film or listed in the closing credits, these are the names employed by the film's synopsis and promotional materials and are employed here for clarification purposes.
39 See, e.g., UNICEF's *Unfairy Tales*, which spotlight the youngest victims of the ongoing Syrian refugee crisis.
40 Honess Roe, "Absence, Excess and Epistemological Expansion," *Animation* 6, no. 3 (2011): 229.
41 Andrade Salazar, "Manifestaciones proyectivas," 6.

42 As reported by Andrade in López Zúñiga, "Oscar Andrade."
43 See, e.g., Andrade Salazar, "Manifestaciones proyectivas"; and Andrade Salazar, Bustos Rojas, and Del Guzmán Jiménez, "Análisis de la figura humana."
44 Schöb, "Memory Building," 30.
45 López Zúñiga, "Oscar Andrade."
46 Honess Roe, "Against Animated Documentary?," 23.
47 Geist and Carroll, *They Still Draw Pictures*.
48 Geist and Carroll, book jacket.
49 Kallio and Häkli, "Tracing Children's Politics," 100.
50 Sköld and Söderlind, "Agentic Subjects," 41.
51 Sköld and Söderlind, 41. See Ferrière, "Voice of the Innocent."
52 As quoted in Sköld and Söderlind, "Agentic Subjects," 41.
53 Hast, "Children Witnessing War," 215.
54 Hast, 215.
55 Hast, 206.
56 Hast, 212.
57 Elwood and Mitchell, "Mapping Children's Politics," 9 (emphasis in original).
58 Elwood and Mitchell, 1.
59 Elwood and Mitchell, 11.
60 Elwood and Mitchell, 8.
61 Geist and Carroll, *They Still Draw Pictures*, 34.
62 Elwood and Mitchell, "Mapping Children's Politics," 11.
63 Elwood and Mitchell, 4.
64 Kallio, "Body as a Battlefield," 285.
65 Sköld and Söderlind, "Agentic Subjects," 29.
66 See Kallio, "Performative Bodies."
67 Lind, "Duality," 288.
68 Lind, 299.
69 Forceville, "Metaphor and Symbol," 254.
70 Wells, *Understanding Animation*, 6.
71 Lind, "Duality," 293.
72 Lind, 289.
73 Lind, 299.
74 Karlsson, "'Do You Know What We Do?,'" 322.
75 Schöb, "Memory Building," 40.
76 Ibáñez and Vélez, "Civil Conflict and Forced Migration," 661.
77 Kallio and Häkli, "Tracing Children's Politics," 102.
78 Kallio and Häkli, 104 (emphasis in original).
79 Kallio and Bartos, "Children's Caring Agencies," 148.
80 See Kallio, "Between Social and Political."

81 Sköld and Söderlind, "Agentic Subjects," 29.
82 Kallio and Bartos, "Children's Caring Agencies," 148.
83 Kallio and Bartos, 149.
84 Kallio and Bartos, 148–9.
85 Bosco, "Play, Work or Activism?," 385.
86 Forceville, "Metaphor and Symbol," 254.
87 Brocklehurst, *Who's Afraid of Children?*, 16.
88 Gómez, "*Pequeñas Voces.*"
89 Other Colombian directors, in turn, have provided their takes on forced displacement in Colombia from the adult perspective, including Luis Alberto Restrepo (*La primera noche / The First Night*, 2003; and *La pasión de Gabriel / The Passion of Gabriel*, 2008) and Carlos Gaviria (*Retratos en un mar de mentiras / Portraits in a Sea of Lies*, 2009).
90 As quoted in Gómez, "*Pequeñas voces.*"
91 Ortiz de Urbina, *Diccionario Akal*, 235.
92 Brocklehurst, *Who's Afraid of Children?*, 35.
93 Brocklehurst, 35.
94 Brocklehurst, 36. See Bellamy, *State of the World's Children 1996*.
95 Brocklehurst, *Who's Afraid of Children?*, 36.
96 Wyness, "Childhood, Human Rights and Adversity," 350. See Utas, "Victimcy, Girlfriending, Soldiering."
97 Wyness, "Childhood, Human Rights and Adversity," 353.
98 Wyness, 350.
99 Wyness, 348.
100 According to the US Committee for Refugees's World Refugee Survey 2001, cited in Ibáñez and Vélez, "Civil Conflict and Forced Migration," 662.
101 Denov, *Child Soldiers*, 280.
102 Denov, 282.
103 Denov, 286.
104 See, e.g., Kaduson and Schaefer, *Play Therapy Techniques*, 159–62.
105 Andrade Salazar, "Manifestaciones proyectivas"; and Andrade Salazar, Bustos Rojas, and Del Guzmán Jiménez, "Análisis de la figura humana."
106 Elwood and Mitchell, "Mapping Children's Politics," 12.
107 Elwood and Mitchell, 12.

2. What's in a "cómic animado" (Animated Comic)? Poetics, Politics, and Personal Myths of Peronism in María Seoane's *Eva de la Argentina / Eva from Argentina* (2011)

1 Seoane, *Eva de la Argentina*. Note that the film in its entirety can also be seen on Vimeo at https://vimeo.com/238121820.

2 Clément and Kristeva, *The Feminine and the Sacred*, 126.
3 Eva, the only one to ever hold this honorary position, was granted this title by her husband on 7 May 1952, her thirty-third (and final) birthday.
4 Ranzani, "Toda la vida de Evita es cinematográfica."
5 Scolari, "*El Eternauta*," 56. Scripted by Héctor Germán Oesterheld, *The Eternaut* was serialized between 1957 and 1959 with a sequel released in 1976. Meanwhile, a remake of the original also appeared in 1969, this time featuring illustrations by Alberto Breccia. This new version, which was published in the magazine *Gente*, is widely considered to feature a stronger political tone, although this notion is recently being challenged; see, e.g., Scolari, 60–1, as well as Palacios, "'The Nestornaut.'" Since then, the story that follows the adventures of protagonist Juan Salvo fighting for survival in the midst of an extraterrestrial invasion in the streets of Buenos Aires has been subjected to numerous extensions, notably under the series *Universo Eternauta* (Eternaut Universe), which ran from 1997 to 2010 (see Scolari, "*El Eternauta*," 62, for a table chronologically outlining the entire comic narrative universe of El Eternauta across seven decades). Solano López again played a key role in illustrating these stories; however, they did not feature the name of *The Eternaut*'s original author, who was disappeared in 1977 along with his four daughters and two sons-in-law. Rather, the new series is written by varying national authors including Pablo "Pol" Maiztegui and Juan Sasturain. Meanwhile, in 2020, another adaptation was devised when the streaming platform Netflix bought the rights to adapt *The Eternaut* as a small-screen series, which as of 2023 is still in production.
6 Page, "Intellectuals, Revolution and Popular Culture," 45.
7 Foster, El Eternauta, Daytripper, *and Beyond*, x.
8 Misemer, *Secular Saints*, 98.
9 Ranzani, "Toda la vida de Evita es cinematográfica."
10 Pérez, *La taquilla de cine*.
11 Noriega, "Eva de la Argentina."
12 Seoane, *La noche de los lápices*.
13 On 22 March 2021 Seoane was given the title "Ciudadana Ilustre" (Illustrious Citizen) by Buenos Aires's legislature for her distinguished and still ongoing career as author, journalist, economist, and film-maker, among other roles, as well as her commitment to the fight for human rights.
14 Trombetta, "Lenguaje de animación."
15 Trombetta, "La ficción y su función de memoria."
16 Sebreli, *Deseos imaginarios*.
17 Ortiz, *Eva Perón*, 46.
18 Tekiner, "Back-to-Roots Again?," 275.

19 Beasley-Murray, *Posthegemony*, 35.
20 Sebreli, *Deseos imaginarios*, 19–20.
21 Scorer, "Latin American Comics," 2.
22 Scolari, "*El Eternauta*," 62.
23 As quoted in Kidd, "Eva Perón se transforma."
24 Honess Roe, *Animated Documentary*, 72.
25 Honess Roe, 26.
26 Honess Roe, "Interjections and Connections," 283–4.
27 It would be a number of years before an uptick in the appearance of animated biographical films would occur. We can recall, for example, Dorota Kobiela's *Loving Vincent* (Poland/UK/USA, 2017), which portrays the life and mysterious death of Vincent van Gogh in the world's first fully painted feature film. In a similar vein, French directors Eric Warin and Tahir Rana's *Charlotte* (Canada/France/Belgium, 2021) is a Second World War–themed animated feature portraying the life of German Jewish artist Charlotte Salomo. The film tells Salamo's story by animating and interpreting the artist's own paintings. Around 2016, development began for *Bubbles*, a stop-motion film about the life of Michael Jackson as told from his pet chimp's perspective, though production of the project came to a halt in 2019. On Spanish soil, we can mention Salvador Simó's *Buñuel en el laberinto de las tortugas / Buñuel in the Labyrinth of the Turtles* (Spain, 2018), a cinematic adaptation of the 2008 comic of the same title by Fermín Solís.
28 Formenti, "Sincerest Form of Docudrama," 105–8.
29 Serrano Abarca, "Retórica de la facticidad," 20.
30 See, e.g., Honess Roe, *Animated Documentary*, 4. *Eva from Argentina* is the most recent Argentine film to follow the hybridization trend to tell the former first lady's story, yet displays qualities that link it to notable predecessors in the documentary genre. The use of drawings to give further meaning to the archival images on screen is a shared characteristic with Leonardo Favio's nearly six-hour documentary that covers six decades of Argentine history, *Perón, sinfonía del sentimiento / Perón, Symphony of Feeling* (Argentina, 1999). To make up for a lack of newsreel clips with which to build the plot, Seoane's film features a prevalence of photographs as an alternative resource, which is also a technique employed in Mazzorotol's *Evita, Another Look*. Likewise, *Eva from Argentina* turns to (animated) re-enactment to fill in the gaps, much like Bauer's *Evita, the Tomb without Peace*, which recreates a *mise en scène* reminiscent of the mid-1950s using live actors and period-appropriate scenery. Although animation is an altogether different form of re-enactment from live action, the animation style inspired by the drawings of Solano López is equally reminiscent of this mid-century era.

31 Misemer, *Secular Saints*, 99–100.
32 Wright, "Hand of God," 22.
33 Honess Roe, "Interjections and Connections," 273.
34 See Seoane and Santa María, *Eva Perón. Esa mujer*.
35 As quoted in Marziotta, "María Seoane."
36 Barthes, *Camera Lucida*, 77 (emphasis in original).
37 Bazin and Gray, "Ontology of the Photographic Image," 8.
38 See Martínez, *Santa Evita*.
39 Trombetta, "Lenguaje de animación," 372.
40 Ortiz, *Eva Perón*, 207–8.
41 Trombetta, "Lenguaje de animación," 372.
42 Paz-Mackay and Rodríguez, *Politics of Children*.
43 Rey, "Argentina's Evita Remembered."
44 See Pelegrinelli, "República de los Niños."
45 Pelegrinelli, 40.
46 Gambini, *Historia del Peronismo*, 198.
47 Beasley-Murray, *Posthegemony*, 243.
48 Journalist Héctor Daniel Vargas places Eva in Junín, likely in her mother's house, by proof of her signature on an official document, though the document was never published. See Vargas, "Qué hizo Evita el 17 de octubre." Vargas hypothesizes a return from Junín to Buenos Aires by midday, but affirms that she never went out into the streets or entered the plaza; her interaction with Perón that day, if any, was limited to a telephone call from the house of her actress friend Pierina Dealessi, and hearing his infamous speech on the radio en la Casa de Gobierno.
49 Rosa, "Popularidad de Perón" (emphasis in original).
50 Literally translated as "passionflower," the term references the nickname bestowed upon Dolores Ibárruri Gómez to immortalize the Basque communist politician and Republican fighter from the Spanish Civil War of 1936–9. Ortiz affirms that it was actually Isabel Ernst, who would later become an assistant to Eva Perón, who was the "Pasionaria of the revolution of October 17"; Ortiz, *Eva Perón*, 121. Ortiz further points out a jealousy on Evita's part of the natural blonde, and that it was Ernst's style of "gray suits, linen-colored hair, and discreet makeup" that would inspire the image of Evita. Evita would then in a sense become an uncanny double to the natural blonde, who as her assistant and advisor often stood "one behind the other, identical in everything: same suit and sometimes same hat (the only difference was that the German woman was four inches taller than Eva)"; Ortiz, 151.
51 Ortiz, 297–8.
52 In her biography of Eva Perón, Ortiz also signifies a third myth, the black myth, which rendered the former first lady a "prostitute, a social climber thirsting for power"; Ortiz, 296.

53 Beasley-Murray, *Posthegemony*, 66.
54 Trombetta, "Lenguaje de animación," 376.
55 See, e.g., Scalabrini Ortiz, *El hombre que está solo y espera*, 245.
56 Other intertextual references that substantiate this claim likewise emerge primarily through Rodolfo's narrations, as he cites, for example, Walsh's *Esa Mujer / That Woman* (1965) and *Operación massacre / Operation Massacre* (1957), as should be expected, as well as Eva Perón's *La razón de mi vida / The Reason for my Life* (1951) and José Pablo Feinmann's essay *La sangre derramada / For the Blood Shed* (1998). Not to mention the frequent use of reconstructed newspapers, such as the one that opens this scene, by the director, who remains a prominent figure in Argentine journalism today.
57 Vázquez, *Intervenciones intelectuales*.
58 Trombetta, "Lenguaje de animación," 374.
59 Trombetta, 374.
60 Seoane, "Ni a Palos."
61 Oloixarac, "A New Evita Rises."
62 Wells, "Animation Manifesto," 99.
63 Wells, 99.
64 Palacios, "'The Nestornaut,'" 179.
65 To view the image, see Nestornaut Advertising Campaign.
66 See, e.g., Fernández and Gago, "Historieta y mitos políticos"; Palacios, "'The Nestornaut'"; and Francescutti, "Del Eternauta al 'Nestornauta.'"
67 Palacios, "'The Nestornaut,'" 179–80.
68 Palacios, 180.
69 Wells, "Animation Manifesto," 99.
70 Foster, "Masculinity," 97.
71 Beasley-Murray, *Posthegemony*, 243–4.
72 Beasley-Murray, 243 (emphasis in original).
73 See Tekiner, "Back-to-Roots Again?"
74 Tekiner, 257.
75 Seoane, "Ni a Palos."
76 Historians agree that the pair were married five days following the strike, on 22 October 1945, though details surrounding the exact location remain foggy. However, as Ortiz notes, the official version of story places the civil marriage ceremony in Junín; Ortiz, *Eva Perón*, 133.
77 Oesterheld and Solano López, *El Eternauta: 1957–2007*, 2.
78 Page, "Intellectuals, Revolution and Popular Culture," 57.
79 Page, 47.
80 Trombetta, "Lenguaje de animación," 373.
81 Ranzani, "Toda la vida de Evita es cinematográfica."
82 Trombetta, "Lenguaje de animación," 374.

3. Animating Autobiography: Historical Memory and Catharsis in Manuel H. Martín's Graphic Novel Documentary *30 años de oscuridad / 30 Years of Darkness* (2012)

1 Martín, *30 años de oscuridad.*
2 The use of the term "mole" is attributed to the novel *Los topos / The Moles* (1977) by journalists Manuel Leguineche and Jesús Torbado, the latter a central narrator within the film through live interview segments. See Torbado and Leguineche, *The Moles.*
3 Resina, *Ghost in the Constitution*, 2.
4 Labanyi, "Engaging with Ghosts," 7.
5 As stated in the DVD booklet; see "Notas sobre la película," 6.
6 Chute, *Disaster Drawn*, 16.
7 "Notas sobre la película," 8.
8 Schlichting and Schmid, "Graphic Realities."
9 See 30deoscuridad, *Trailer 30 años de Oscuridad.*
10 See, e.g., Labanyi, "Memory and Modernity," 103; and Colmeiro, "Nation of Ghosts?," 28.
11 de la Fuente Soler, "La memoria en viñetas," 260.
12 Amago, "Drawing (on) Spanish History," 56.
13 Wells, "Animation Manifesto," 99.
14 Aldama, "Comics Studies Here and Now," 3.
15 Carrera Garrido, "El dolor del pasado," 38.
16 Labanyi, "Memory and Modernity," 95; and Labanyi, "Languages of Silence," 26.
17 Labanyi, "Politics of Memory," 119.
18 Tahmassian, "*Espacios en blanco*," 29. It should be noted from the outset that the widely used but not unproblematic or uncontroversial term *historical memory* refers exclusively to the determined period of twentieth-century Spanish history of the Spanish Civil War and immediate post-war period, becoming, as Labanyi notes, synonymous with the civic duty of recalling the repression carried out during these four decades, largely, although not exclusively, by addressing the repression of *Republican memory*, and ultimately with the goal of *national* reconciliation. See Labanyi, "Historias de víctimas," 87–90 (emphasis in original).
19 Tahmassian, "*Espacios en blanco*," 29.
20 Tahmassian, 29.
21 Tahmassian, 45.
22 Chute, *Disaster Drawn*, 4.
23 Ausente, "La memoria gráfica," 126.
24 Martín, "Para iniciar el despegue."
25 See, e.g., Kearney, "Narrating Pain"; and Kearney "Writing Trauma."

26 Kearney, "Narrating Pain," 61 (emphasis mine).
27 Bernecker, "La memoria histórica en España," 134.
28 Bernecker, 120.
29 See, e.g., Hirsch, "Family Pictures."
30 Hirsch, *Generation of Postmemory*, 9.
31 Tahmassian, "*Espacios en blanco*," 34.
32 See, e.g., Tronsgard, "Drawing the Past."
33 Martín, "Para iniciar el despegue," 6.
34 Suárez Vega, "Memoria histórica en viñetas," 286–7.
35 Aldama, "Comics Studies Here and Now," 1.
36 Wells, "Animation Manifesto," 95.
37 Honess Roe, *Animated Documentary*.
38 Chute, *Disaster Drawn*, 2.
39 Groensteen, *System of Comics*, 11.
40 Altarriba, "Los años que vivimos en viñetas," 161.
41 Gowdy, "Meaning from Movement," 180.
42 Gowdy, 179–80.
43 Gowdy, 183.
44 Gowdy, 184.
45 Gowdy, 178.
46 Gowdy, 186.
47 Gowdy, 184.
48 Keller, *Ghostly Landscapes*, 8.
49 Keller, 15. While Keller's 2016 seminal study evidences the perpetuation of the hauntological perspective introduced by Labanyi in the early 2000s, I would be remiss not to note that this debate has been met with some criticism. Notably, Ángel G. Loureiro labels figures of speech such as the *return of the repressed* "poor metaphors for extremely complex, multilayered and contentious historical or cultural processes," for, as he argues, "physical and psychical pathologies that pertain to individuals … cannot be easily translated to social bodies or processes"; see Loureiro, "Pathetic Arguments," 225. Meanwhile, others have attempted to dialogue with the hauntological perspective in order to broaden its application: echoing Loueiro, Juan F. Egea, in his reading of Ricardo Franco's documentary *Después de tantos años / After So Many Years* (Spain, 1994) calls such metaphors "ruinous" for that fact that they are, in his esteem, more aptly symbolic of "futuros perdidos" (lost futures) rather than of repressed pasts (see Egea, "Después de tantos años," 170), and, while Santiago Morales Rivera does not object to psychoanalytic readings of traumatic symptoms in Spain's cultural products from the final two decades of the twentieth century, he aims for a rereading that rather approaches melancholy through lenses such as that of ironic humour;

see Morales Rivera, *Anatomía del desencanto*. Nevertheless, the release of *30 Years of Darkness* in 2012, just following the apex of the swing towards spectrality in the realms of Spanish media and scholarship alike, no doubt reveals it as a cultural product that reflects and signifies a major ideology in contemporary Spanish society, and accordingly warrants reading in this light.

50 Labanyi, "Memory and Modernity," 109.
51 Amago, "Drawing (on) Spanish History," 32.
52 See Winter, "'Localizar a los muertos' y 'reconocer al otro,'" 19.
53 Resina, *Ghost in the Constitution*, 4.
54 Keller, review of *Ghost in the Constitution*, 805.
55 Colmeiro, "Nation of Ghosts?," 31.
56 Ferrándiz, "Return of Civil War Ghosts," 10.
57 Gordon, *Ghostly Matters*, 24. It is this "special instance" that for Gordon defines the ghost.
58 Colmeiro, "Nation of Ghosts?," 28.
59 Chute, *Disaster Drawn*, 142.
60 Derrida, *Specters of Marx*, 11 (emphasis in original).
61 Torbado and Leguineche, *The Moles*.
62 As the text on the book jacket of Torbado and Leguineche's *The Moles* describes, while many of these "forgotten men" were Republican soldiers who fought against Franco's Nationalist forces, others were prominent Socialist leaders and activists, whose pre-war authority was seen as a threat to the new regime, while others were peasants and artisans who were recruited against their will to what would end up being the losing side.
63 Although the Law's full title is "Ley por la que se reconocen y amplían derechos y se establecen medidas en favor de quienes padecieron persecución o violencia durante la guerra civil y la dictadura" (Law for Recognizing and Broadening Rights and Establishing Measures in Favour of Those Who Suffered Persecution or Violence during the Civil War), it quickly became known as the "Ley de memoria histórica" (Historical Memory Law) by the Spanish communications media. As Labanyi succinctly outlines in the opening paragraph of her article "The Politics of Memory in Contemporary Spain," the Historical Memory Law was "proposed by the PSOE government initially in 2004; first published in July 2006 to outcries from the Partido Popular and the right-wing media; finally approved by Congress on 31 October 2007 after last-minute revisions to secure the support of Izquierda Unida; and implemented on 26 December 2007"; see Labanyi, "Politics of Memory," 109.
64 The effort, led by journalist Emilio Silva, founder of the Association for the Recovery of Historical Memory, started as an attempt to identify the

remains of his grandfather, who was executed during the war. Guided by historical records, a team of biologists, anthropologists, and researchers located and excavated a mass grave, ultimately unearthing thirteen skeletons. The following year, a DNA match was established between Silva and some of the remains; the first DNA-aided identification of Spanish Civil War remains.

65 Chute, *Disaster Drawn*, 252 (emphasis in original).
66 Honess Roe, *Animated Documentary*, 22.
67 Honess Roe, "Uncanny Indexes," 31.
68 Chute, *Disaster Drawn*, 142.
69 Amago, "Drawing (on) Spanish History," 33.
70 Freud, "The Uncanny (1919)," 241.
71 Freud, 234.
72 Honess Roe, *Animated Documentary*, 24.
73 Honess Roe, 25.
74 Honess Roe, 25.
75 Chute, *Disaster Drawn*, 27.
76 Colmeiro, "Nation of Ghosts?," 25.
77 Keller, *Ghostly Landscapes*, 5.
78 See "Contra la impunidad" to view Rodríguez's film. The short documentary features personalities such as Pedro Almodóvar, Maribel Verdú, Javier Bardem, Almudena Grandes, Juan Diego Botto, María Galiana, Carmen Machi, Juan José Millás, Aitana Sánchez-Gijón, Paco León, Pilar Bardem, José Manuel Seda, Hugo Silva, and Miguel Ríos.
79 Derrida, *Specters of Marx*, 10 (emphasis in original).
80 Ribas-Casasayas and Petersen, "Theories of the Ghost," 2.
81 In fact, the 2010 version of Torbado and Leguineche's *The Moles*, published by Capitán Swing, adopts a similar image on their cover: an eye, peering out from its hiding place, is painted over in the colours of the flag of the Second Spanish Republic.
82 Freud, "The Uncanny (1919)," 219.
83 Labanyi, "History and Hauntology," 69.
84 Chute, *Disaster Drawn*, 17.
85 Keller, *Ghostly Landscapes*, 4 (emphasis in original).
86 Colmeiro, "Nation of Ghosts?," 29.
87 Derrida, *Spectres of Marx*, 11.
88 Derrida, 175.
89 Ferrándiz, "Return of Civil War Ghosts," 10.
90 Resina, *Ghost in the Constitution*, 2.
91 Keller, review of *Ghost in the Constitution*, 805.
92 Honess Roe, *Animated Documentary*, 167.
93 Gordon, *Ghostly Matters*, xix.

94 Gordon, xix.
95 Gordon, 102–3.
96 Derrida, *Spectres of Marx*, 175.
97 Chute, *Disaster Drawn*, 18–19.
98 Respectively, Sommerland and Wallin Wictorin, "Writing Comics," 1; and Rippl and Etter, "Intermediality, Transmediality, and Graphic Narrative," 197.

4. Simply A-musing: Aleix Saló's *Españistan / Spainistan* (2011) as Animated Journalism in Spain's Comic Public Sphere

1 Saló, *Españistán, de la Burbuja Inmobiliaria a la Crisis.*
2 Amago and Marr, "Comics in Contemporary Spain," 18.
3 Alba MA, comment on Saló, *Españistán, de la Burbuja Inmobiliaria a la Crisis.* To date, the film has reached nearly six and a half million hits on YouTube.
4 de la Coba, "Españistán."
5 Respectively see, e.g., "'Españistán. Este país se va a la mierda'"; "'Españistán,' un divertido vídeo"; and Aranda, "Dibujos para entender la crisis."
6 Marr, "Building a Home," 144. While some scholars and critics have tended not to translate the title *Españistán* into English, others have translated this neologism as "Spainistan," as I have done here. In its original form, Javier Muñoz-Basols and Marina Massaguer Comes skillfully deconstruct the term pointing out that "the morphological crossing between the noun 'España' [Spain] and the suffix '-stán' is easily identifiable with former Soviet republics in Central Asia (Kazakhstan, Kyrgyzstan, Tajikistan, Turkmenistan, Uzbekistan) or with countries like Pakistan or Afghanistan, which frequently appear in the media as political conflict areas. Indeed, the humorous new word *Españistán* in the title might make audiences curious about what this 'new country' would be like." On the other hand, these authors also conjecture that an inspiration "may have been the 10 December 2001 cover of the *New Yorker* with the comical name 'New Yorkistan,'" although they also acknowledge that in the introduction to *Simiocracia*, Saló himself "explains that this title is an adaptation of the word Hispanistán, which appeared on Burbuja.info, an Internet forum that started to warn people about the effects of the property bubble well before the mass media began to speak about it openly." See Muñoz-Basols and Massaguer Comes, "Social Criticism through Humour," 119.
7 Marr, "Building a Home," 155.
8 See, e.g., the playlist category titles on the main page of Saló's YouTube channel: "Aleix Saló."

9 Ehrlich, "Indeterminate and Intermediate," 49.
10 Porter, "Animation."
11 "Introducing TomoNews."
12 "Un vídeo cómico de animación." The video is featured at the beginning of this news article.
13 Ehrlich, "Indeterminate and Intermediate," 54.
14 Weber and Rall, "Comics Journalism and Animated Documentary."
15 Weber and Rall.
16 Martí López, "MAKUN (No llores)," 20.
17 Martí López, 39.
18 See Honess Roe, "Interjections and Connections."
19 Víctor Sampedro and Mayra Martínez Avidad, for example, argue for the emergence of an alternative digital public sphere in Spain as a key resource for subaltern publics, pinpointing the emergence of such to the 2004 terrorist attacks in Madrid and a gain in influence in the context of the 15-M in 2011 to the point where these alternative discourses were proven to not only express an unofficial public opinion consensus, but also reframe public debate and change the electoral map. See Sampedro and Martínez Avidad, "Digital Public Sphere."
20 Caron, *Satire*, 2.
21 Honess Roe, "Interjections and Connections," 284.
22 Arrese, "Spanish Press," 94.
23 Arrese also signals a sixth debate, which arose one year after the appearance of *Spainistan*, "Waiting for a Bailout" (2012), in which national and international media discussed the possible bailout of the Spanish economy of up to €100 billion by the European Union, although this course of action would ultimately not be requested; Arrese, "Spanish Press," 97–8. In a more recent article he adds two more recent debates to this list: "Austericidio y corrupción" (Austericide and Corruption, 2013–14) and "Recuperación y fin de la crisis, o no" (Recuperation and End, or Not, of the Crisis, 2015–17). See Arrese, "La crisis económica española."
24 Arrese, "Spanish Press," 98.
25 See, e.g., "Españistán: ¿Un vídeo parcial?"; and Ruiz Bartolomé, "Desmontando Españistán (1)."
26 Marr, "Building a Home," 137.
27 Marr, 139.
28 Marr, 144. Marr further highlights how "the viability of the comparison also rests on both figures' adept construction of an intermedial platform for their respective projects of satirical pedagogy."
29 Weber and Rall, "Comics Journalism and Animated Documentary."
30 Saló, *Españistán: Este país se va a la mierda*.

31 As the closing soundtrack plays, a written message appears, stating that "la historia continúa en *Españistán: Este país se va a la mierda* … y en … burbujainmobilaria.com" (the story continues in *Spainistan: This Country Is Going to Hell* … and at … burbujainmobilaria.com; 00:06:31–45).
32 As quoted in Jiménez, "'Españistán. Este país se va a la mierda.'"
33 Arrese, "La crisis económica española," 9.
34 See Méndez, "Cannibal Wave."
35 Matthew J. Marr, for example, adeptly highlights how Saló's satirical text "unfolds as a mock-epic quest narrative with ironic nods to a variety of literary, cinematic, and televisual intertexts including *Don Quijote*, *The Lord of the Rings*, *The Wizard of Oz*, *Harry Potter*, and even the *Odyssey*"; "Building a Home," 146.
36 Saló, "*Españistán* simplifica por su formato."
37 Muñoz-Basols and Massaguer Comes, "Social Criticism through Humour," 109.
38 The promotional videos are titled after the comics, respectively *Simiocracia* and *Europesadilla*, and are available for viewing on Saló, "Brooktrailers de mis libros."
39 Javier A, comment on *Cambios de Humor Colectivos*.
40 Sainz Borgo, "Aleix Saló."
41 See, e.g., Soto, "Retrato de la generación de 'Guatepeor.'"
42 Sainz Borgo, "Aleix Saló."
43 Marr, "Building a Home," 152–3.
44 Sainz Borgo, "Aleix Saló."
45 Marr, "Building a Home," 145.
46 Domènech, "Esta crisis."
47 Respectively, see "'Españistán,' un divertido vídeo"; and Aranda, "Dibujos para entender la crisis."
48 Saló, "Important Problems Explained."
49 Domènech, "Esta crisis."
50 Caron, *Satire*, 33.
51 Caron, 5.
52 de Chávez, "De la Transición a Twitter," 67.
53 de Chávez, 81; and Caron, *Satire*, 5.
54 See Arrese, "Spanish Press."
55 See Arrese, 94.
56 See Arrese, 99.
57 Arrese and Vara-Miguel, "Comparative Study of Metaphors," 149.
58 Arrese and Vara-Miguel, 150.
59 Arrese and Vara-Miguel, 151.
60 Arrese and Vara-Miguel, 150.
61 Chute, *Disaster Drawn*, 252 (emphasis in original).

62 Chute, 162.
63 As Arrese notes, Zapatero "portrayed the image of a robust economy during the general election in 2008, when he argued that there was no risk of an economic crisis. In June that year, as news organizations and public opinion explicitly talked about the crisis, Zapatero said that 'it was arguable that there was actually a crisis' (*El País*, 28 June 2008), and pleaded for the avoidance of doom-laden and unpatriotic statements. In July, as reporters persisted in using the term, 'crisis,' Zapatero, in a televised interview, finally acknowledged that there was an economic crisis, 'as they called it' (El Mundo, 9 July 2008). Of course, the Lehman Brothers collapse came soon afterwards." See Arrese, "Spanish Press," 95.
64 See Pano Alamán, "La negación."
65 Arrese, "La crisis económica española," 11.
66 As quoted in Arrese, 11.
67 Arrese, 14–15.
68 As quoted in Arrese, "Spanish Press," 96.
69 See, e.g., Méndez, "Cannibal Wave."
70 As quoted in "*Españistán*: ¿Un vídeo parcial?"
71 Muñoz-Basols and Massaguer Comes, "Social Criticism through Humour," 119.
72 Arrese, "Spanish Press," 96.
73 See, e.g., Seoane Pérez, "'Spain Is Not Greece.'"
74 Arrese and Vara-Miguel, "Comparative Study of Metaphors," 149.
75 *Greek Crisis Explained.*
76 Arrese, "Spanish Press," 96.
77 Arrese, "La crisis económica española," 12.
78 Sánchez, "Editorial."
79 Arrese, "La crisis económica española," 12.
80 Arrese, "Spanish Press," 98.
81 "Santiago Niño-Becerra."
82 As quoted in "Niño Becerra: '¿Engañados?'"
83 Arrese, "Spanish Press," 98.
84 Arrese, 92.
85 Catalá-Carrasco, "Neoliberal Expulsions," 174.
86 Marr, "Building a Home," 137.

5. Tracing Cultural Continuities: Rotoscope, Archons, and Archive 2.0 in Victor Orozco's Essayistic *Reality 2.0* (2012)

1 To access the animated documentary in its entirety, see Orozco, *Reality 2.0.*
2 These can be seen on the page dedicated to *Reality 2.0* on the film director's personal website; see "Short Film Reality 2.0."

3 See "Victor Orozco."
4 Tolliday, "Enterprise and State," 273.
5 See, e.g., Imison, "How NAFTA Explains the Two Mexicos,"; Bolio et al., "Tale of Two Mexicos"; and Correa-Cabrera, *Democracy in "Two Mexicos."*
6 Howard Campbell and Tobin Hansen, who denote these two basic genres of online narco videos, also name an emerging third genre in which the lines between user-created content and the official media become blurred as members of drug cartels create and disseminate their own pseudo-press conferences, complete with microphones and bottled water. See Campbell and Hansen, "Is Narco-violence in Mexico Terrorism?," 166.
7 Gomez, "New Visual Regime," 195.
8 Corrigan, *Essay Film*, 4.
9 Corrigan, 7. As Corrigan notes, precursors can be found in early documentary and avant-garde traditions, though we can pinpoint its "full visibility" in Western cinema to the 1940s and 1950s.
10 Bunker, "Criminal (Cartel & Gang) Insurgencies," 11.
11 Bunker and Sullivan, "Cartel Evolution Revisited," 44.
12 Bunker, "Criminal (Cartel & Gang) Insurgencies," 7. See also Bunker and Sullivan, "Cartel Evolution Revisited," 48.
13 Bunker, "Criminal (Cartel & Gang) Insurgencies," 11.
14 Bunker, 11.
15 Gomez, "New Visual Regime," 209n3.
16 Christiansen, "¿Narcoinfierno o narcolandia?," 144.
17 Sullivan and Rosales, "Ciudad Juárez."
18 Bunker and Sullivan, "Cartel Evolution Revisited," 44.
19 See, e.g., Christiansen, "¿Narcoinfierno o narcolandia?"
20 Schwarz, *Narco Cultura*. The version cited here can be found on YouTube at https://www.youtube.com/watch?v=7l8pfRZgwVE&.
21 Patented in 1917 by American film-maker Max Fleischer, who worked closely with his brother Dave, the hand-drawn animation technique used as a starting point frames of live-action footage to create more lifelike movements for characters in animated films.
22 As Orozco narrates in this segment, over the muffled sounds of the video, "In June 2005, the newspaper *The Dallas Morning News* uploaded to their website [this] video where a hitman of the Zetas gang is executed" (00:01:40).
23 Tobar, "Mexico's Brutality."
24 Christiansen, "¿Narcoinfierno o narcolandia?," 132.
25 Gomez, "New Visual Regime," 198–200.
26 Monroy-Hernández and Daniel Palacios, "Blog del Narco," 83.
27 See Gomez, "New Visual Regime."
28 Monroy-Hernández and Daniel Palacios, "Blog del Narco," 83.
29 De Choudhury, Monroy-Hernández, and Mark, "'Narco' Emotions," 3564.

30 Hachero Hernández, "Deformar a la Gorgona," 118.
31 Ziemann, "Victor Orozco Ramírez."
32 Theimer, "What Is the Meaning of Archives 2.0?," 59.
33 Gomez, "New Visual Regime," 192.
34 Gomez, 193.
35 Gomez, 192.
36 Beer, "Archive Fever Revisited," 104 (emphasis mine).
37 Beer, 105.
38 Beer, 105.
39 Beer, 109.
40 Beer, 109.
41 Gomez, "New Visual Regime," 190.
42 Gomez, 192.
43 Gomez, 202.
44 Beer, "Archive Fever Revisited," 109.
45 Gomez, "New Visual Regime," 192, 202.
46 Ward, "Animated Documentary: Viewer Engagement," 99 (emphasis in original).
47 Sullivan and Elkus, "Barbarization and *Narcocultura*."
48 Gomez, "New Visual Regime," 192.
49 See, e.g., Cuenca Orozco, "Usos y gratificaciones," 7.
50 Gomez, "New Visual Regime," 190.
51 Furtado, *Documentary Filmmaking in Contemporary Brazil*, 5–6.
52 Rosen and Zepeda. "Una década de narcoviolencia."
53 Sullivan and Rosales, "Ciudad Juárez."
54 Christiansen, "¿Narcoinfierno o narcolandia?," 130.
55 Honess Roe, *Animated Documentary*, 26.
56 Campbell, "Narco-propaganda," 64.
57 Sullivan, "Criminal Insurgency."
58 Sullivan.
59 Sullivan.
60 Gomez, "New Visual Regime," 195.
61 See Hoskins, "Memory of the Multitude."

6. In Uncharted Waters and Totally Unmoored: The Transmedial Documentary Project *Cuentos de viejos / Old Folks' Tales* (2013–2019)

1 Carew, "Wind Rises," 15.
2 Kriger, *Animated Realism*, 61.
3 *Cuentos de viejos.*
4 In their expository article, Marcelo Dematei and María Laura Piaggio visually communicate this tripartite aim through the infographic "Transmedia Approach": Dematei and Piaggio, "Cuentos de viejos," 92.

5 Castellanos, Montoya, and Páez, "Discurso narrativo audiovisual," 29–30.
6 The Stories on the Map tool was one of many interactive features once available to users of the online platform. Users could manipulate the map to view stories that are connected in various ways. As of the end of the year 2019, for example, there were 240 stories tagged "Colombia" and 22 tagged "España" (Spain), while other locations were featured, such as France and Mexico (10 tags each), Equatorial Guinea (4 tags), Chile (2 tags), and Uzbekistan and China (1 tag each). Users could also explore the story map by topic, choosing to view all the stories centred on the Spanish Civil War (17 tags), the Second World War (20 tags), or *La Violencia* in Colombia (47 tags), or even themes such as *amistad* (friendship; 61 tags), *enfermedades* (illnesses; 17 tags), *plantas medicinales* (medicinal plants; 8 tags), or *música* (music; 33 tags). One could also simply choose the "Todas" (All) icon to simultaneously view the hundreds of stories on the world map.
7 The first season features twelve individual episodes, each one less than six minutes long, as are the episodes in the following seasons (fourteen in season 2, fourteen in season 3, and ten in season 4). However, season 1 features three promotional and behind-the-scenes episodes: "Capítulo 13: Una historia demasiado grande" (Chapter 13: A Story That Is Too Big; ten minutes), "Capítulo 14: Las historias no contadas" (Chapter 14: Stories Untold; ten minutes), and "Capítulo 15: Así hicimos *Cuentos de viejos*" (Chapter 15: How We Made *Cuentos de viejos*; twenty-five minutes).
8 Dematei and Piaggio, "Cuentos de viejos," 92.
9 Dobson, "Creating (Artificial) Emotion," 125. See Mihailova, "Mastery Machine."
10 Dematei and Piaggio, "Cuentos de viejos," 98.
11 Dematei and Piaggio, 98–9.
12 Uhrig, "'Portraying Emotions,'" 221.
13 See Hoskins, "Memory of the Multitude."
14 Hoskins, 106.
15 Hoskins, 85.
16 Hoskins, 85–6.
17 Hoskins, 100.
18 Hoskins, 92.
19 Hoskins, 100.
20 Hoskins, 100.
21 Hoskins, 101.
22 Hoskins, 92.
23 To date, a single exception (to the best of my knowledge) can be found in Castellanos, Montoya, and Páez, "Discurso narrativo audiovisual." This trio of authors uses digital documentary technology to analyse the

second season of the series and formulate two main conclusions: one, the series employs a protagonist-narrator; and, two, the primary theme is political conflicts, while a secondary theme is religious conflicts. While theirs is a thorough and interesting study of the series's narrative structure, content, and theme, these authors demonstrate a perpetuation of the tendency lamented by Wells in his animation manifesto, as we have already discussed, that "when an animated film of any sort [or series, we might add], and about any subject, is finally celebrated, it is usually recognised for its narrative or content, and rarely for its status as 'animation'" (Wells, "Animation Manifesto," 95).

24 Walden, "Animation: Textural Difference."

25 Fenoll, "Animación, documental y memoria."

26 Walden, "Animation and Memory."

27 van Gageldonk, Munteán, and Shobeiri, *Animation and Memory*.

28 van Gageldonk, Munteán, and Shobeiri, 2.

29 van Gageldonk, Munteán, and Shobeiri, 14.

30 Hoskins, "Memory of the Multitude," 85.

31 van Gageldonk, Munteán, and Shobeiri, *Animation and Memory*, 2.

32 Wells, *Understanding Animation*, 45–6.

33 Hakokõngäs, "Visual Collective Memory"; and van den Heuvel, "Picturing Landscape."

34 See, e.g., García-Gavilanes et al., "Memory Remains."

35 Chief among these is Spanish director Ignacio Ferreras's double Goya Award–winning feature film *Arrugas / Wrinkles*, a cinematic adaptation of Paco Roca's homonymous comic about Alzheimer's and aging (Spain, 2011 and 2007, respectively), winner of Spain's 2008 National Comics Prize. On a global scale, *Old Folks' Tales* joins a corpus of animated shorts such as Taiwanese animator Po Chou-Chi's nearly seven-minute 3D computer-animated *The Drawer of Memory* (Taiwan, 2006), an independent, internationally award-winning Dalinian take on an elderly woman's efforts to remember her deceased husband, which has seen hundreds of thousands of hits on YouTube since its publication there in 2007. More recently, we have seen Franck Dion's ten-minute short *The Head Vanishes / Une tête disparaît* (Canada/France, 2016), a poetic short that invites us to share the journey of Jacqueline, an elderly woman living with degenerative dementia yet determined to go on vacation alone, and who thus sets off by train.

36 From the Hispanic world is worth mentioning a short film produced by Spanish director Ignacio Ferreras, nearly a decade before his Oscar-contending *Wrinkles*, "How to Cope with Death" (2002), protagonized by a feisty elderly female in her (literal) fight against the film's only other character, death, who is personified as a skeletal angel. Likewise there

is the Mexican transmedial project *La vejez cuenta*, which can fittingly be translated either as "Old Age Counts" or "Old Age Tells," and which is probably, although fiction, closest in nature to *Old Folks' Tales*. *La vejez cuenta*, launched by Mexico's Canal Once Instituto Politécnico Nacional, where it has been transmitted between programming since February of 2018, consists of dozens of self-contained animated micro shorts that are meant to – as the production blurb informs – promote understanding, respect, patience, care and inclusion of the elderly while also making visible and dignifying the image of this demographic on a societal level. The project, with titled episodes such as "Alimentación adecuada" (Appropriate Diet), "Seguir trabajando" (Continuing to Work), and "Visitar a los familiares" (Visiting Family Members) also features on social media platforms such as Facebook, Twitter, and Instagram, marked by the hashtag #LaVejezCuenta. And, looking just north on the same continent, one of course cannot conclude this list without mentioning Disney/Pixar's *Up* (USA, 2009), recipient of the Academy Award for best animated feature film.

37 Two exceptions, to the best of my knowledge, are Liz Blazer's acclaimed six-minute *Backseat Bingo* (USA, 2004) and Iranian-born UK director Afarin Eghbal's *Abuelas / Grandparents* (UK, 2011). The former is a computer-animated project that interviews a handful of retirees on their personal attitudes and values about sex, romance, and aging; these interviewees are, in turn, kept anonymous through highly stylized and even "cutesy" animated avatars, although still portrayed in the traditional talking-head interview style. Meanwhile, the twelve-minute *Grandparents* relies on pixilation and stop-frame animation along with mixed media to address themes of memory, repression, and loss in the context of the thousands of Argentine civilian "disappearances" under General Videla's military dictatorship from 1976 to 1983.

38 Dobson, "TV Animation and Genre," 181–2.

39 Dobson, 186–7.

40 See, e.g., Hight, "Primetime Digital Documentary Animation"; Campbell, "Analysing Impossible Pictures"; Honess Roe, "Absence, Excess and Epistemological Expansion," *Animation* 6, no. 3 (2011); Honess Roe, *Animated Documentary*; and Honess Roe, "Absence, Excess and Epistemological Expansion," in Dobson, *Animation Studies Reader*.

41 Since the late twentieth century, Spain, for example, has experienced a marked growth in population of its senior citizens. Matthew J. Marr refers to this as "the rise of senescence in contemporary Spain"; Marr, *Politics of Age and Disability*, 68. Relying on statistical reports, Marr outlines this context by highlighting unprecedented shifts in national age demographics that can be traced back to the early 1990s, a time when Spain's

senior population doubled in size from what it had been at the mid-century mark. This phenomenon, coupled with a historically low fertility rate in younger generations resulted in demographic projections that by the year 2020 nearly one-third of all Spaniards would be senior citizens; a marked jump from the one-in-five ratio of the 1990s. Elsewhere, and more recently, it has been stated that Spain's population is continuing to age, and long-term projections have reported that by the year 2066, this statistic will surpass the one-third mark, with a projected 34.6 per cent of the population expected to be over the age of sixty-five; see Abellán García et al., *Perfil de las personas mayores*. In the case of Colombia, Pablo Rodríguez Jiménez and Fernán Vejarano Alvarado point out that the Latin American nation has always been considered a young country – childish, even – perhaps due to a proliferation of street children; see Rodríguez Jiménez and Vejarano Alvarado, "Presentación," 19. And, as these authors continue, although Colombia is not facing the same demographic crisis as Japan or European countries (like Spain), by 2015 citizens over the age of sixty comprised over 15 per cent of the population, and this number is expected to grow to encapsulate one-third of the population within half a century. Meanwhile, a report from the same year by Flórez et al. places the number of Colombia's citizens above and beyond the age of sixty at only 10 per cent of the population, yet converges in the assertion that the country is considered to be in an advanced stage of demographic transition due in part to decreasing fertility rates like Spain; see Flórez et al., *El proceso de envejecimiento*, 8–9, coupled with a greater life expectancy that has seen men and women living seven years longer than they did in 1990, now on average reaching the age of seventy-two and seventy-eight and a half, respectively, and projects that the life expectancy for both groups will increase another five years by 2050; see Flórez et al., 58.

42 *Cuentos de viejos*, season 1, episode 4, "Nety: Nueva York en los llanos."
43 *Cuentos de viejos*, season 1, episode 9, "Roser: Las trenzas."
44 *Cuentos de viejos*, season 2, episode 11, "Thubten: ¡Adiós Tíbet!"
45 Walden, "Animation and Memory," 85.
46 As quoted in Uhrig, "'Portraying Emotions,'" 221.
47 Wells, "Animation Manifesto," 99.
48 As quoted in Uhrig, "'Portraying Emotions,'" 221.
49 Dematei and Piaggio, "Cuentos de viejos," 92.
50 *Cuentos de viejos*, season 1, episode 13, "Una historia demasiado grande."
51 Dematei and Piaggio, "Cuentos de viejos," 91.
52 Mikkonen, *Narratology of Comic Art*, 196.
53 Wells, *Understanding Animation*, 36.
54 Wells, 38.

55 See Ward, "Animated Documentary: Viewer Engagement."
56 Ward, "Animated Documentary: Viewer Engagement," 87.
57 *Cuentos de viejos*, season 1, episode 1, "Ysabel: El miedo baja del cielo."
58 Wells, *Understanding Animation*, 46.
59 Wells, 46.
60 Walden, "Animation and Memory," 82.
61 Walden, 81.
62 Walden, 82.
63 Walden, 81.
64 Honess Roe, *Animated Documentary*, 26.
65 Dematei and Piaggio, "Cuentos de viejos," 92 (emphasis mine).
66 Chute, *Disaster Drawn*, 5.
67 *Cuentos de viejos*, season 1, episode 2, "Hernán: El niño y los muertos."
68 Dematei and Piaggio, "Cuentos de viejos," 97.
69 *Cuentos de viejos*, season 2, episode 9, "José María: Historia con acordeón."
70 Walden, "Animation and Memory," 88.
71 *Cuentos de viejos*, season 3, episode 4, "Alejandro: Por los aires."
72 *Cuentos de viejos*, season 1, episode 12, "Susana: Mi mejor amiga."
73 *Cuentos de viejos*, season 2, episode 1, "Inés: La niña de Bogotá."
74 *Cuentos de viejos*, season 4, episode 4, "Carlos: Mi capitán."
75 Dobson, "Creating (Artificial) Emotion," 124.
76 Ward, "Animated Documentary: Viewer Engagement," 84.
77 Ward, 85, 99 (emphasis in original).
78 Halbwachs, *On Collective Memory*, 38.
79 Walden, "Animation and Memory," 86.
80 Ward, "Animated Documentary: Viewer Engagement," 87.
81 Walden, "Animation and Memory," 86.
82 See, e.g., Nora, "Between Memory and History."
83 Dematei and Piaggio, "Cuentos de viejos," 91.
84 Hakokõngäs, "Visual Collective Memory."
85 van den Heuvel, "Picturing Landscape."
86 See, e.g., García-Gavilanes et al., "Memory Remains."
87 Fenoll, "Animación, documental y memoria."
88 Ward, *Documentary*, 87.
89 Ehrlich, "Conflicting Realisms," 27.

Bibliography

Abellán García, Antoni, Alba Ayala García, Julio Pérez Díaz, and Rogelio Pujol Rodríguez. *Un perfil de las personas mayores en España, 2018. Indicadores estadísticos básicos*. Informes Envejecimiento en red, no. 17. Madrid: Envejecimiento en red, 2018. https://envejecimientoenred.es/un-perfil-de-las-personas-mayores-en-espana-2018-indicadores-estadisticos-basicos/.

Aldama, Frederick Luis. "Comics Studies Here and Now: An Introduction." In *Comics Studies Here and Now*, edited by Frederick Luis Aldama, 1–6. New York: Routledge, 2018.

"Aleix Saló." YouTube, accessed 6 March 2023. https://www.youtube.com/user/aleixsalo.

Altarriba, Antonio. "Los años que vivimos en viñetas. Breve sociología sentimental del tebeo en tiempos de Franco." *CuCo, Cuadernos de cómic*, no. 2 (2014): 160–3. https://doi.org/10.37536/cuco.2014.2.1318.

Amago, Samuel. "Drawing (on) Spanish History." In Amago and Marr, *Consequential Art*, 31–64. https://doi.org/10.3138/9781487531386-004.

Amago, Samuel, and Matthew J. Marr. "Comics in Contemporary Spain." In Amago and Marr, *Consequential Art*, 3–28. https://doi.org/10.3138/9781487531386-003.

–, eds. *Consequential Art: Comics Culture in Contemporary Spain*. Toronto: University of Toronto Press, 2019. https://doi.org/10.3138/9781487531386.

Andrade Salazar, José Alonso. "Manifestaciones proyectivas de conflicto psicológico en el dibujo de la figura humana de niños y niñas desplazados en Colombia." *Psicología, conocimiento y sociedad* 3, no. 1 (2013): 5–40. https://www.redalyc.org/pdf/4758/475847409002.pdf.

Andrade Salazar, José Alonso, Juan Sebastián Bustos Rojas, and Pamela Del Guzmán Jiménez. "Análisis de la figura humana en niños y niñas desplazados en Colombia." *El Agora USB* 15, no. 1 (2015): 255–68. https://doi.org/10.21500/16578031.13.

Aranda, José Luis. "Dibujos para entender la crisis." *El País*, 21 June 2011. https://elpais.com/politica/2011/06/21/actualidad/1308688459_242294.html.

Arrese, Ángel. "La crisis económica española: De la burbuja a la recuperación." *Nuevas tendencias*, no. 99 (2017): 9–14. https://doi.org/10.15581/022.34292.

– "Spanish Press. No Illusions." In *The Media and Financial Crisis*, edited by Steven Schifferes and Richard Roberts, 87–102. London: Routledge, 2015.

Arrese, Ángel, and Alfonso Vara-Miguel. "A Comparative Study of Metaphors in Press Reporting of the Euro Crisis." *Discourse & Society* 27, no. 2 (2015): 133–55. https://doi.org/10.1177/0957926515611552.

Ausente, Daniel. "La memoria gráfica y las sombras del pasado." In *Supercómic. Mutaciones de la novela gráfica contemporánea*, coord. Santiago García, 107–35. Madrid: Errata Naturae, 2013.

Barthes, Roland. *Camera Lucida: Reflections on Photography*. Translated by Richard Howard. New York: Hill and Wang, 1981.

Bazin, André, and Hugh Gray. "The Ontology of the Photographic Image." *Film Quarterly* 13, no. 4 (1960): 4–9. https://doi.org/10.2307/1210183.

Beasley-Murray, Jon. *Posthegemony: Political Theory and Latin America*. Minneapolis: University of Minnesota Press, 2011.

Beer, David. "*Archive Fever* Revisited: Algorithmic Archons and the Ordering of Social Media." In *Routledge Handbook of Digital Media and Communication*, edited by Leah A. Lievrouw and Brian D. Loader, 99–111. London: Routledge, 2020.

Bellamy, Carol. *The State of the World's Children 1996*. New York: Oxford University Press, 1996.

Bendazzi, Giannalberto. *Animation: A World History*. Vol. 1, *Foundations – The Golden Age*. Boca Raton: CRC Press, 2015.

– *Animation: A World History*. Vol. 2, *The Birth of a Style – The Three Markets*. Boca Raton: CRC Press, 2016.

– *Animation: A World History*. Vol. 3, *Contemporary Times*. Boca Raton: CRC Press, 2016.

– *Quirino Cristiani, pionero del cine de animación (Dos veces el océano)*. Buenos Aires: Ediciones de la Flor, 2008.

– *Twice the First: Quirino Cristiani and the Animated Feature Film*. Boca Raton: CRC Press, 2018.

Bernecker, Walthier L. "La memoria histórica en España: Un pasado más actual que nunca."*Versants* 3, no. 67 (2020): 119–41. https://doi.org/10.22015/V.RSLR/67.3.10.

Bolio, Eduardo, Jaana Remes, Tomás Lajous, James Manyika, Eugenia Ramirez, and Morten Rossé. "A Tale of Two Mexicos: Growth and Prosperity in a Two-Speed Economy." *McKinsey Global Institute*, 1 March 2014. https://www.mckinsey.com/featured-insights/americas/a-tale-of-two-mexicos.

Bosco, Fernando J. "Play, Work or Activism? Broadening the Connections between Political and Children's Geographies." *Children's Geographies* 8, no. 4 (2010): 381–90. https://doi.org/10.1080/14733285.2010.511003.

Brocklehurst, Helen. *Who's Afraid of Children? Children, Conflict and International Relations*. New York: Routledge, 2017.

Buchan, Suzanne. "The Animated Spectator: The Quay Brothers' 'Worlds.'" In *Animated "Worlds,"* edited by Suzanne Buchan, 15–38. Eastleigh: John Libbey, 2006.

– "Animation, in Theory." In *Animating Film Theory*, edited by Karen Beckman, 111–27. Durham, NC: Duke University Press, 2014.

Bunker, Robert J. "Criminal (Cartel & Gang) Insurgencies in Mexico and the Americas: What You Need to Know, Not What You Want to Hear." *Has Merida Evolved? Part One: The Evolution of Drug Cartels and the Threat to Mexico's Governance*, Congressional testimony before the House Foreign Affairs Subcommittee on the Western Hemisphere, Washington, DC, 13 September 2011. https://scholarship.claremont.edu/cgu_fac_pub/155/.

Bunker, Robert J., and John P. Sullivan. "Cartel Evolution Revisited: Third Phase Cartel Potentials and Alternative Futures in Mexico." *Small Wars & Insurgencies* 21, no. 1 (2010): 30–54. https://doi.org/10.1080/09592310903561379.

Campbell, Howard. "Narco-propaganda in the Mexican 'Drug War': An Anthropological Perspective." *Latin American Perspectives* 41, no. 2 (2014): 60–77. https://doi.org/10.1177/0094582X12443519.

Campbell, Howard, and Tobin Hansen. "Is Narco-violence in Mexico Terrorism?" *Bulletin of Latin American Research* 33, no. 2 (2014): 158–73. https://doi.org/10.1111/blar.12145.

Campbell, Vincent. "Analysing Impossible Pictures: Computer Generated Imagery in Science Documentary and Factual Entertainment Television." In *Visual Communication*, edited by David Machin, 463–82. Berlin: de Gruyter, 2014.

Carew, Anthony. "The Wind Rises, a Genius Departs." *Screen Education*, no. 74 (2014): 8–15.

Caron, James E. *Satire as the Comic Public Sphere: Postmodern "Truthiness" and Civic Engagement*. University Park: Pennsylvania State University Press, 2021. https://doi.org/10.5325/j.ctv1k03g04.

Carrera Garrido, Miguel. "El dolor del pasado: *Insensibles* (2012) y los mecanismos de lo fantástico y el terror al servicio de la recuperación de la memoria histórica." *Sociocriticism* 32, no. 1 (2017): 11–44.

Carrillo, Jairo and Oscar Andrade, dirs. *Pequeñas voces*. Bogotá: Cinecolor Films, 2010. DVD.

Castellanos, Javier, Julieta Montoya, and Ángel Páez. "El discurso narrativo audiovisual en la serie de televisión 'Cuentos de viejos.'" *Temas de comunicación*, nos. 38–9 (2019): 22–48.

Catalá-Carrasco, Jorge L. "Neoliberal Expulsions, Crisis, and Graphic Reportage in Spanish Comics." *Romance Quarterly* 64, no. 4 (2017): 172–84. https://doi.org/10.1080/08831157.2017.1356139.

Català-Carrasco, Jorge, Paulo Drinot, and James Scorer, eds. *Comics and Memory in Latin America*. Pittsburgh: University of Pittsburgh Press, 2017.

Christiansen, María L. "¿Narcoinfierno o narcolandia? Una epistemología intempestiva sobre el relato oficial de la violencia en México." *European Scientific Journal* 12, no. 11 (2016): 129–55. https://doi.org/10.19044/esj.2016.v12n11p129.

Chute, Hillary. "Comics as Archives: Meta*MetaMaus*." *E-misférica* 9, nos. 1–2 (2012). https://hemi.nyu.edu/hemi/en/e-misferica-91/chute.

– *Disaster Drawn: Visual Witness, Comics and Documentary Form*. Cambridge, MA: Belknap Press of Harvard University Press, 2016.

Clément, Catherine, and Julia Kristeva. *The Feminine and the Sacred*. Translated by Jane Marie Todd. New York: Columbia University Press, 2001.

Colmeiro, José. "Nation of Ghosts?: Haunting, Historical Memory and Forgetting in Post-Franco Spain." *452°F*, no. 4 (2011): 17–34. https://452f.com/en/a-nation-of-ghosts/.

Consultoría para los Derechos Humanos y el Desplazamiento. *De la seguridad a la prosperidad democrática en medio del conflicto*. Documentos CODHES, no. 23. Bogotá: CODHES, 2011. https://www.acnur.org/fileadmin/Documentos/Publicaciones/2012/8445.pdf?view=1.

"Contra la impunidad: Personalidades de la cultura encarnan a quince personas que fueron ejecutados durante la Guerra Civil y la dictadura." *El País*, 14 June 2010. https://elpais.com/elpais/2010/06/14/videos/1276503418_870215.html.

Correa-Cabrera, Guadalupe. *Democracy in "Two Mexicos": Political Institutions in Oaxaca and Nuevo León*. New York: Springer, 2013.

Corrigan, Timothy. *The Essay Film: From Montaigne, after Marker*. New York: Oxford University Press, 2011.

Cuenca Orozco, David. "Usos y gratificaciones de los videojuegos en la Ciudad de México: El caso de las 'arcadias.'" PhD diss., Universidad Autónoma de la Ciudad de México, 2011.

Cuentos de viejos. Seasons 1–4, created by Laura Piaggio and Marcelo Dematei. RTVC Sistema de Medios Públicos, 2013. https://www.rtvcplay.co/series-de-ficcion/cuentos-de-viejos.

Davis, Charles H., and Florin Vladica. "Consumer Value and Modes of Media Reception: Audience Response to *Ryan*, a Computer-Animated Psycho-realist Documentary and Its Own Documentation in Alter Egos." *Palabra Clave* 13, no. 1 (2010): 13–30. https://doi.org/10.5294/pacla.2010.13.1.1.

de Chávez, Daniel Córdoba González. "De la Transición a Twitter: La sátira como vehículo de identidades políticas y culturales." *Caracteres* 7, no. 1 (2018): 67–99.

De Choudhury, Munmun, Andrés Monroy-Hernández, and Gloria Mark. "'Narco' Emotions: Affect and Desensitization in Social Media during the

Mexican Drug War." In *Proceedings of the SIGCHI Conference on Human Factors in Computing Systems*, 3563–72. New York: ACM, 2014.

de la Coba, Paco. "Españistán, la burbuja inmobilaria desde la sátira y la ironía."*El Ibérico*, 18 June 2011. https://www.eliberico.com/espanistan-la-burbuja-inmobiliaria-desde-la-satira-y-la-ironia/.

de La Ferrière, Alexis Artaud. "The Voice of the Innocent: Propaganda and Childhood Testimonies of War." *History of Education* 43, no. 1 (2014): 105–23. https://doi.org/10.1080/0046760x.2013.816879.

de la Fuente Soler, Manuel. "La memoria en viñetas: Historia y tendencias del cómic autobiográfico." *Signa*, no. 20 (2011): 259–76.

Dematei, Marcelo, and María Laura Piaggio. "Cuentos de viejos: Los relatos de la memoria." *Con A de Animación*, no. 5 (2015): 88–101. https://doi.org/10.4995/caa.2015.3541.

Denov, Myriam. *Child Soldiers: Sierra Leone's Revolutionary United Front*. Cambridge: Cambridge University Press, 2010.

Derrida, Jacques. *Specters of Marx: The State of the Debt, the Work of Mourning, and the New International*. Translated by Peggy Kamuf. New York: Routledge, 1994.

Dobson, Nichola. "Creating (Artificial) Emotion in Animation through Sound and Story." In *Emotion in Animation Studies*, edited by Meike Uhrig, 124–40. New York: Routledge, 2018.

– "TV Animation and Genre." In Dobson et al., *Animation Studies Reader*, 181–9.

Dobson, Nichola, Annabelle Honess Roe, Amy Ratelle and Caroline Ruddell, eds. *The Animation Studies Reader*. New York: Bloomsbury Academic, 2019.

Domènech, Albert. "Esta crisis no tiene grandes culpables, sino grandes aprovechados." *La Vanguardia*, 7 May 2012. https://www.lavanguardia.com/cultura/20120503/54288840141/entrevista-aleix-salo-simiocracia.html.

Durán, Mauricio. "Las potencias de la imagen animada." *Cuadernos de cine colombiano*, no. 20 (2014): 35–45.

Egea, Juan F. "*Después de tantos años*: Filme espectral y metaforicidad ruinosa en la España post-92." *Journal of Spanish Cultural Studies* 17, no. 2 (2016): 163–76. https://doi.org/10.1080/14636204.2016.1165853.

Ehrlich, Nea. "Animated Documentaries: Aesthetics, Politics and Viewer Engagement." In *Pervasive Animation*, edited by Suzanne Buchan, 248–71. New York: Routledge, 2013. https://doi.org/10.4324/9780203152577.

– *Animating Truth: Documentary and Visual Culture in the 21st Century*. Edinburgh: Edinburgh University Press, 2021.

– "Conflicting Realisms: Animated Documentaries in the Post-truth Era." *Studies in Documentary Film* 15, no. 1 (2019): 20–40. https://doi.org/10.1080/17503280.2019.1663718.

– "Indeterminate and Intermediate or Animated Non-fiction: Why Now?" In Murray and Ehrlich, *Drawn from Life*, 47–68.

Elwood, Sarah, and Katharyne Mitchell. "Mapping Children's Politics: Spatial Stories, Dialogic Relations and Political Formation." *Geografiska Annaler: Series B, Human Geography* 94, no. 1 (2012): 1–15. https://doi.org/10.1111/j.1468-0467.2012.00392.x.

"'Españistán. Este país se va a la mierda,' el retrato social de Aleix Saló." *RTVE.es*, 26 May 2011. https://www.rtve.es/noticias/20110526/espanistan-este-pais-se-va-mierda-retrato-social-aleix-salo/434796.shtml.

"'Españistán,' un divertido vídeo de YouTube explica la burbuja inmobiliaria." *La Verdad*, 27 May 2011. https://www.laverdad.es/murcia/20110527/gente/espanistan-youtube-burbuja-inmobiliaria-201105271230.html.

"Españistán: ¿Un vídeo parcial sobre la situación inmobiliaria?" *elEconomista.es*, 30 May 2011. https://www.eleconomista.es/espana/noticias/3113944/05/11/Espanistan-una-vision-parcial-de-la-situacion-Espanola.html.

"Estadísticas del cine colombiano: Taquilla y box office finales de la película colombiana *Los colores de la montaña*." *Pantalla Colombia*, no. 518, 1–8 July 2011. https://www.proimagenescolombia.com/secciones/pantalla_colombia/breves_plantilla.php?id_noticia=3425.

"Estadísticas del cine colombiano: Taquilla y box office finales de la película colombiana *Pequeñas voces 3D*." *Pantalla Colombia*, no. 536, 4–11 November 2011. https://www.proimagenescolombia.com/secciones/pantalla_colombia/breves_plantilla.php?id_noticia=3683.

Fenoll, Vicente. "Animación, documental y memoria. La representación animada de la dictadura chilena." *Cuadernos.info*, no. 43 (2018): 45–56. https://doi.org/10.7764/cdi.43.1381.

– "La representación de la dictadura en el cine de animación argentino." *Vivat Academia*, no. 149 (2019): 45–66. https://doi.org/10.15178/va.2019.149.45-66.

Fernández, Laura Cristina, and Sebastian Gago. "Historieta y mitos políticos: La relectura oficial de El eternauta en la argentina democrática." *Anagramas* 10, no. 20 (2012): 117–28. https://doi.org/10.22395/angr.v10n20a8.

Ferrándiz, Francisco. "The Return of Civil War Ghosts: The Ethnography of Exhumations in Contemporary Spain." *Anthropology Today* 22, no. 3 (2006): 7–12. https://doi.org/10.1111/j.1467-8322.2006.00437.x.

Flórez, Carmen Elisa, Leonardo Villar, Nadia Puerta, and Luisa Berrocal. *El proceso de envejecimiento de la población en Colombia: 1985–2050*. Bogotá: Editorial Fundación Saldarriaga Concha, 2015.

Forceville, Charles. "Metaphor and Symbol: SEACHING FOR ONE'S IDENTITY IS LOOKING FOR A HOME in Animation Film." *Review of Cognitive Linguistics* 11, no. 2 (2013): 250–68. https://doi.org/10.1075/rcl.11.2.03for.

Formenti, Cristina. *The Classical Animated Documentary and Its Contemporary Evolution*. London: Bloomsbury Academic, 2021.

Formenti, Cristina. "The Sincerest Form of Docudrama: Re-framing the Animated Documentary." *Studies in Documentary Film* 8, no. 2 (2014): 103–15. https://doi.org/10.1080/17503280.2014.908491.

Foster, David William. El Eternauta, Daytripper, *and Beyond: Graphic Narrative in Argentina and Brazil*. Austin: University of Texas Press, 2016.

– "Masculinity as Privileged Human Agency in H.G. Oesterheld's *El Eternauta*." *TRANSMODERNITY* 3, no. 1 (2013): 81–101. https://doi.org/10.5070/T431020837.

Francescutti, Pablo. "Del Eternauta al 'Nestornauta': La transformación de un icono cultural en un símbolo político." *CIC*, no. 20 (2015): 27–43. https://doi.org/10.5209/rev_ciyc.2015.v20.49477.

Fraser, Benjamin. *The Art of Pere Joan: Space, Landscape, and Comics Form*. Austin: University of Texas Press, 2019.

Freud, Sigmund. "The Uncanny (1919)." In *The Standard Edition of the Complete Psychological Works of Sigmund Freud*, vol. 17, *An Infantile Neurosis and Other Works*, edited and translated by James Strachey, 219–52. London: Hogarth Press, 1955.

Furtado, Gustavo Procopio. *Documentary Filmmaking in Contemporary Brazil: Cinematic Archives of the Present*. New York: Oxford University Press, 2019. https://doi.org/10.1093/oso/9780190867041.001.0001.

Gambini, Hugo. *Historia del Peronismo: El poder total (1943–1951)*. Buenos Aires: Vergara, 2017.

García, Santiago. *La novela gráfica*. Bilbao: Astiberri, 2010.

– *On the Graphic Novel*. Translated by Bruce Campbell. Jackson: University Press of Mississippi, 2015.

García-Gavilanes, Ruth, Anders Mollgaard, Milena Tsvetkova, and Taha Yasseri. "The Memory Remains: Understanding Collective Memory in the Digital Age." *Science Advances* 3, no. 4 (2017): e160236. https://doi.org/10.1126/sciadv.1602368.

García López, Sonia. "El documental de animación: Un género audiovisual digital." *ZER* 24, no. 46 (2019): 129–45. https://doi.org/10.1387/zer.20396.

Gauthier, Philippe. "On 'Institutionalization': From Cinema to Comics." *International Journal of Comic Art* 12, no. 2/3 (2010): 367–75.

Geist, Anthony L., and Peter N. Carroll. *They Still Draw Pictures: Children's Art in Wartime from the Spanish Civil War to Kosovo*. Urbana: University of Illinois Press, 2002.

Gomez, Robert. "A New Visual Regime: Narco Warfare through Social Media." In *Sightlines 2012: Visual and Critical Studies*, coordinated by Kate Moore, 186–209. San Francisco: California College of the Arts, 2012.

Gómez, Verónica. "Pequeñas voces, la primera película animada colombiana en 3D." *El País*, 1 September 2011. https://www.elpais.com.co/entretenimiento/pequenas-voces-la-primera-pelicula-animada-colombiana-en-3d.html.

González Monaj, Raúl, ed. "Animando realidades." Special issue, *Con A de Animación*, no. 12 (2021). http://polipapers.upv.es/index.php/CAA/issue/view/1032.

González Monaj, Raúl, and María Lorenzo Hernández, eds. "Animación y periodismo." Special issue, *Con A de Animación*, no. 11 (2020). http://polipapers.upv.es/index.php/CAA/issue/view/987.

Gordon, Avery. *Ghostly Matters: Haunting and the Sociological Imagination*. Minneapolis: University of Minnesota Press, 2011.

Gowdy, Joshua. "Meaning from Movement: Blurring the Temporal Border between Animation and Comics." *Studies in Comics* 9, no. 2 (2018): 177–92. https://doi.org/10.1386/stic.9.2.177_1.

Greek Crisis Explained: Trilogy, The. *NOMINT*. Accessed 24 April 2023. https://nomint.com/work/the-greek-crisis-explained-trilogy?play=the-greek-crisis-explained-trilogy.

Grierson, John. "The Documentary Producer." *Cinema Quarterly* 2, no. 1 (1933): 7–9.

Groensteen, Thierry. *The System of Comics*. Translated by Bart Beaty and Nick Nguyen. Jackson: University Press of Mississippi, 2007.

Hachero Hernández, Bruno. "Deformar a la Gorgona: La imagen animada como estrategia para documentar el horror." *Con A de Animación*, no. 5 (2015): 114–25. https://doi.org/10.4995/caa.2015.3542.

Hakoköngäs, Eemeli. "Visual Collective Memory: A Social Representations Approach." PhD diss., University of Helsinki, 2017.

Halbwachs, Maurice. *On Collective Memory*. Edited and translated by Lewis A. Coser. Chicago: University of Chicago Press, 1992.

Hast, Susanna. "Children Witnessing War: Emotions Embodied in the Theatre Play *Wij/Zij*." In *Art as a Political Witness*, edited by Kia Lindroos and Frank Möller, 199–217. Opladen: Barbara Budrich, 2017. https://doi.org/10.2307/j.ctvdf0047.17.

Hight, Craig. "Primetime Digital Documentary Animation: The Photographic and Graphic within Play." *Studies in Documentary Film* 2, no. 1 (2008): 9–31.

Hirsch, Marianne. "Family Pictures: *Maus*, Mourning, and Post-memory." *Discourse* 15, no. 2 (1992): 3–29.

– *The Generation of Postmemory: Writing and Visual Culture after the Holocaust*. New York: Columbia University Press, 2012.

Honess Roe, Annabelle. "Absence, Excess and Epistemological Expansion: Towards a Framework for the Study of Animated Documentary." *Animation* 6, no. 3 (2011): 215–30. https://doi.org/10.1177/1746847711417954.

– "Absence, Excess and Epistemological Expansion: Towards a Framework for the Study of Animated Documentary." In Dobson et al., *Animation Studies Reader*, 111–32.

– "Against Animated Documentary?" *International Journal of Film and Media Arts* 1, no. 1 (2016): 20–7.

– *Animated Documentary*. Basingstoke: Palgrave Macmillan, 2013. https://doi.org/10.1057/9781137017468.

– "Interjections and Connections: The Critical Potential of Animated Segments in Live Action Documentary." *Animation* 12, no. 3 (2017): 272–86. https://doi.org/10.1177/1746847717729552.

– "Uncanny Indexes: Rotoshopped Interviews as Documentary." *Animation* 7, no. 1 (2012): 25–37. https://doi.org/10.1177/1746847711428851.

Hoskins, Andrew. "Memory of the Multitude: The End of Collective Memory." In *Digital Memory Studies: Media Pasts in Transition*, edited by Andrew Hoskins, 85–109. New York: Routledge, 2017.

Ibáñez, Ana María, and Carlos Eduardo Vélez. "Civil Conflict and Forced Migration: The Micro Determinants and Welfare Losses of Displacement in Colombia." *World Development* 36, no. 4 (2008): 659–76. https://doi.org/10.1016/j.worlddev.2007.04.013.

IDM. *LAS TABAS (Documental completo)*. YouTube video, 53:35, 20 March 2016. https://www.youtube.com/watch?v=Vi03cXmEWkk.

Imison, Paul. "How NAFTA Explains the Two Mexicos." *The Atlantic*, 23 September 2017. https://www.theatlantic.com/international/archive/2017/09/nafta-mexico-trump-trade/540906/.

"Introducing TomoNews, the New Brainchild of the Taiwanese Animators." *PRNewswire*, 20 August 2013. https://www.prnewswire.com/news-releases/introducing-tomonews-the-new-brainchild-of-the-taiwanese-animators-220326381.html.

Javier A. (2020). Comment on *Cambios de Humor Colectivos*, YouTube video, https://www.youtube.com/watch?v=pe-97uKdaIw&t=45s.

Jiménez, Jesús. "'Españistán. Este país se va a la mierda,' la crisis según Aleix Saló." *Viñetas y bocadillos* (blog). *RTVE.es*, 26 May 2011. https://blog.rtve.es/comic/2011/05/mileurismo-telebasura-corrupci%C3%B3n-paro-espa%C3%B1a-tiene-problemas-y-el-dibujante-aleix-sal%C3%B3-se-ha-ocupado-de-plasmarlo.html.

Kaduson, Heidi Gerard, and Charles E. Schaefer. *101 More Favorite Play Therapy Techniques*. Lanham, MD: Jason Aronson, 2010.Kallio, Kirsi Pauliina. "Between Social and Political: Children as Political Selves." *Childhoods Today* 3, no. 2 (2009): 1–22. https://urn.fi/urn:nbn:uta-3-414.

Kallio, Kirsi Pauliina. "The Body as a Battlefield: Approaching Children's Politics." *Geografiska Annaler: Series B, Human Geography* 90, no. 3 (2008): 285–97. https://doi.org/10.1111/j.1468-0467.2008.293.x.

– "Performative Bodies, Tactical Agents and Political Selves: Rethinking the Political Geographies of Childhood." *Space and Polity* 11, no. 2 (2007): 121–36. https://doi.org/10.1080/13562570701721990.

Kallio, Kirsi Pauliina, and Ann E. Bartos. "Children's Caring Agencies." *Political Geography*, no. 58 (2017): 148–50. https://doi.org/10.1016/j.polgeo.2016.09.009.

Kallio, Kirsi Pauliina, and Jouni Häkli. "Are There Politics in Childhood?" *Space and Polity* 15, no. 1 (2011): 21–34. https://doi.org/10.1080/13562576.2011.567897.

– "Political Geography in Childhood." *Political Geography* 29, no. 7 (2010): 357–8. https://doi.org/10.1016/j.polgeo.2009.11.001.

– "Tracing Children's Politics." *Political Geography* 30, no. 2 (2011): 99–109. https://doi.org/10.1016/j.polgeo.2011.01.006.

Karlsson, Sandra. "'Do You Know What We Do When We Want to Play?' Children's Hidden Politics of Resistance and Struggle for Play in a Swedish Asylum Centre." *Childhood* 25, no. 3 (2018): 311–24. https://doi.org/10.1177/0907568218769353.

Kearney, Richard. "Narrating Pain: The Power of Catharsis." *Paragraph* 30, no. 1 (2007): 51–66. https://doi.org/10.3366/prg.2007.0013.

– "Writing Trauma: Narrative Catharsis in Homer, Shakespeare, and Joyce." In *In the Wake of Trauma: Psychology and Philosophy for the Suffering Other*, edited by Eric Severson, Brian Becker, and David M. Goodman, 77–90. Pittsburgh: Duquesne University Press, 2016.

Keller, Patricia M. *Ghostly Landscapes: Film, Photography, and the Aesthetics of Haunting in Contemporary Spanish Culture*. Toronto: University of Toronto Press, 2016.

– Review of *The Ghost in the Constitution: Historical Memory and Denial in Spanish Society*, by Joan Ramon Resina. *Revista de Estudios Hispánicos* 53, no. 2 (2019): 803–5. https://doi.org/10.1353/rvs.2019.0048.

Kidd, Natalia. "Eva Perón se transforma en un personaje de dibujos animados." *La Informacion*, 13 October 2011. https://www.lainformacion.com/arte-cultura-y-espectaculos/eva-peron-se-transforma-en-un-personaje-de-dibujos-animados_g2mKIyV0cTaJQ1vgDUK4X/.

King, Edward, and Joanna Page. *Posthumanism and the Graphic Novel in Latin America*. London: UCL Press, 2017. https://doi.org/10.14324/111.9781911576501.

Kriger, Judith. *Animated Realism: A Behind-the-Scenes Look at the Animated Documentary Genre*. Waltham, MA: Focal Press, 2012.

L'Ami, Jean-Charles, dir. *Mi historia es tu historia*. 2005. Vimeo video, 21:41, 20 July 2013, https://vimeo.com/70675656.

Labanyi, Jo. "Historias de víctimas: La memoria histórica y el testimonio en la España contemporánea." *Iberoamericana* 6, no. 24 (2006): 87–98. https://doi.org/10.18441/ibam.6.2006.24.87-98.

– "History and Hauntology; or, What Does One Do with the Ghosts of the Past? Reflections on Spanish Film and Fiction of the Post-Franco Period." In *Disremembering the Dictatorship: The Politics of Memory in the Spanish Transition to Democracy*, edited by Joan Ramon Resina, 65–82. Amsterdam: Rodopi, 2000. https://doi.org/10.1163/9789004483224_006.

– "Introduction: Engaging with Ghosts; or, Theorizing Culture in Modern Spain." In *Constructing Identity in Contemporary Spain: Theoretical Debates and Cultural Practices*, edited by Jo Labanyi, 1–14. Oxford: Oxford University Press, 2002.

– "The Languages of Silence: Historical Memory, Generational Transmission and Witnessing in Contemporary Spain." *Journal of Romance Studies* 9, no. 3 (2009): 23–36. https://doi.org/10.3828/jrs.9.3.23.

– "Memory and Modernity in Democratic Spain: The Difficulty of Coming to Terms with the Spanish Civil War." *Poetics Today* 28, no. 1 (2007): 89–116. https://doi.org/10.1215/03335372-2006-016.

– "The Politics of Memory in Contemporary Spain." *Journal of Spanish Cultural Studies* 9, no. 2 (2008): 119–25. https://doi.org/10.1080/14636200802283621.

Landesman, Ohad, and Roy Bendor. "Animated Recollection and Spectatorial Experience in *Waltz with Bashir*." *Animation* 6, no. 3 (2011): 353–70. https://doi.org/10.1177/1746847711417775.

L'Hoeste, Héctor Fernández, and Juan Poblete, eds. *Redrawing the Nation: National Identity in Latin/o American Comics*. New York: Palgrave Macmillan, 2009. https://doi.org/10.1057/9780230103184.

Lind, Jacob. "The Duality of Children's Political Agency in Deportability." *Politics* 37, no. 3 (2016): 288–301. https://doi.org/10.1177/0263395716665391.

Locuviche, Samuel. "Latin American Animation Leaders Are Gathering for a Big Meeting at the Quirino's Co-production Forum." *Cartoon Brew*, 2 April 2018. https://www.cartoonbrew.com/business/latin-american-animation-leaders-are-gathering-for-a-big-meeting-at-the-quirinos-co-production-forum-157563.html.

López Zúñiga, Antares A. Tepeu. "Oscar Andrade codirector Pequeñas Voces." *LOOP*, 15 September 2011. https://web.archive.org/web/20220121080104/https://www.loop.la/noticia.php?noticia_id=93.

Loureiro, Ángel G. "Pathetic Arguments." *Journal of Spanish Cultural Studies* 9, no. 2 (2008): 225–37. https://doi.org/10.1080/14636200802283746.

Magnussen, Anne, ed. *Spanish Comics: Historical and Cultural Perspectives*. New York: Berghahn Books, 2021. https://doi.org/10.1515/9781789209983.

–, ed. "Spanish Comics, Part I." Special issue, *European Comic Art* 11, no. 1 (2018).

–, ed. "Spanish Comics, Part II." Special issue, *European Comic Art* 11, no. 2 (2018).

Marr, Matthew J. "Building a Home for Crisis Narrative: Intermediality and Comic(s) Pedagogy in Aleix Saló's *Españistán* Project." In Amago and Marr, *Consequential Art*, 137–63. https://doi.org/10.3138/9781487531386-007.

– *The Politics of Age and Disability in Contemporary Spanish Film: Plus Ultra Pluralism*. London: Routledge, 2016.

Martí López, Emilio. "*MAKUN (No llores)*: Recreando realidades vetadas por medio de la animación documental y la animación periodística." *Con A de Animación*, no. 11 (2020): 16–41. https://doi.org/10.4995/caa.2020.13978.

Martín, Antonio. "Para iniciar el despegue." In *El arte de volar*, by Antonio Altarriba and Kim, 5–10. Alicante: Edicions de Ponent, 2010.

Martín, Manuel H., dir. *30 años de oscuridad*. Seville: La Claqueta, 2012. DVD.

Martínez, Tomás Eloy. *Santa Evita*. Buenos Aires: Planeta, 1995.

Marziotta, Gisela. "María Seoane: 'Evita era más feminista que muchas mujeres de hoy.'" *Infobae*, 7 May 2019. https://www.infobae.com/sociedad/2019/05/07/maria-seoane-evita-era-mas-feminista-que-muchas-mujeres-de-hoy/.

McKinney, Collin, and David F. Richter, eds. *Spanish Graphic Narratives: Recent Developments in Sequential Art*. Cham: Palgrave Macmillan, 2020. https://doi.org/10.1007/978-3-030-56820-7.

Méndez, Germán Labrador. "The Cannibal Wave: The Cultural Logic of Spain's Temporality of Crisis (Revolution, Biopolitics, Hunger and Memory)." *Journal of Spanish Cultural Studies* 15, nos. 1–2 (2014): 241–71. https://doi.org/10.1080/14636204.2014.935013.

Merino, Ana. *El cómic hispano*. Madrid: Cátedra, 2003.

Mickwitz, Nina. *Documentary Comics: Graphic Truth-Telling in a Skeptical Age*. New York: Palgrave Macmillan, 2016. https://doi.org/10.1057/9781137493323.

Mihailova, Mihaela. "The Mastery Machine: Digital Animation and Fantasies of Control." *Animation* 8, no. 2 (2013): 131–48. https://doi.org/10.1177/1746847713485833.

Mikkonen, Kai. *The Narratology of Comic Art*. New York: Routledge, 2017. https://doi.org/10.4324/9781315410135.

Misemer, Sarah M. *Secular Saints: Performing Frida Kahlo, Carlos Gardel, Eva Perón, and Selena*. Woodbridge: Tamesis, 2008.

Monroy-Hernández, Andrés, and Luis Daniel Palacios. "Blog del Narco and the Future of Citizen Journalism." *Georgetown Journal of Intational Affairs* 15, no. 2 (2014): 81–92.

Morales Rivera, Santiago. *Anatomía del desencanto: Humor, ficción y melancolía en España, 1976–1998*. West Lafayette, IN: Purdue University Press, 2017.

Muñoz-Basols, Javier, and Marina Massaguer Comes. "Social Criticism through Humour in the Digital Age: Multimodal Extension in the Works of Aleix Saló." *European Comic Art* 11, no. 1 (2018): 107–28. https://doi.org/10.3167/eca.2018.110107.

Murray, Jonathan, and Nea Ehrlich, eds. *Drawn from Life: Issues and Themes in Animated Documentary Cinema*. Edinburgh: Edinburgh University Press, 2018.

Nash, Kate, Craig Hight, and Catherine Summerhayes, eds. *New Documentary Ecologies: Emerging Platforms, Practices and Discourses*. Basingstoke: Palgrave Macmillan, 2014. https://doi.org/10.1057/9781137310491.

Nestornaut Advertising Campaign for the Luna Park Rally. *La Campora*, 20 October 2020. https://www.lacampora.org/afiches-nestor/.

"Niño Becerra: '¿Engañados? El fallo fue pensar que el banco era nuestro amigo.'" *elEconomista.es*, 30 November 2012. https://www.eleconomista.es/economia/noticias/4439935/11/12/2/Nino-Becerra-Que-todo-es-un-engano-El-fallo-fue-considerar-que-un-banco-o-una-caja-era-nuestro-amigo-.html.

Nora, Pierre. "Between Memory and History: *Les Lieux De Mémoire*." *Representations*, no. 26 (1989): 7–24. https://doi.org/10.2307/2928520.

Noriega, Gustavo. "Eva de la Argentina." *LA NACIÓN*, 20 October 2011. https://www.lanacion.com.ar/espectaculos/cine/eva-de-la-argentina-nid1416046/.

"Notas sobre la película." Booklet in *30 años de oscuridad*. Seville: La Claqueta, 2012. DVD.

Oesterheld, Héctor G., and Francisco Solano López. *El Eternauta: 1957–2007 / 50 años*. Buenos Aires: Doedytores, 2006.

Oloixarac, Pola. "A New Evita Rises in Argentina." *New York Times*, 5 December 2019. https://www.nytimes.com/2019/12/05/opinion/argentina-cristina-fernandez-de-kirchner.html.

Orozco, Victor, dir. *Reality 2.0*. Vimeo video, 10:57, 7 April 2012, https://vimeo.com/39942381.

Ortiz, Alicia Dujovne. *Eva Perón: A Biography*. New York: St. Martin's Press, 1996.

Ortiz de Urbina, Jesús Cantera. *Diccionario Akal del refranero sefardí: Colección de refranes y frases hechas del judeoespañol, con su correspondencia o traducción en español y francés*. Madrid: Akal, 2004.

Ospina, María. "Natural Plots." In *Territories of Conflict: Traversing Colombia through Cultural Studies*, edited by Andrea Fanta, Alejandro Herrero-Olaizola, and Chloe Rutter-Jensen, 248–66. Rochester, NY: University of Rochester Press, 2017.

Page, Joanna. "Intellectuals, Revolution and Popular Culture: A New Reading of *El Eternauta*." *Journal of Latin American Cultural Studies* 19, no. 1 (2010): 45–62. https://doi.org/10.1080/13569321003589963.

Palacios, Cristian. "'The Nestornaut,' or How a President Becomes a Comic Superhero." Translated by Mariana Casale. In Scorer, *Comics beyond the Page*, 177–94. https://doi.org/10.2307/j.ctv13xpstc.14.

Pano Alamán, Ana. "La negación en el discurso político-económico de Zapatero." *Revista general de derecho público comparado*, no. 8 (2011): 1–34.

Paz-Mackay, María Soledad, and Omar Rodríguez, eds. *Politics of Children in Latin American Cinema*. Lanham, MD: Lexington Books, 2019.

Pelegrinelli, Daniela. "La República de los Niños. La función de los juguetes en las políticas del peronismo (1946–1955)." *Revista del Instituto de Investigaciones en Ciencias de la Educación*, no. 17 (2000): 36–41.

Pérez, Gonzalo Agustín. *La taquilla de cine y el nivel de producción: Evidencias del caso argentino. Seminario de Investigación IV MAECO*. June 2015. https://repositorio.uade.edu.ar/xmlui/bitstream/handle/123456789/4343/A15A06%20Material%20Did%C3%A1ctico%201.pdf?sequence=1.

Pérez-del-Solar, Pedro. *Imágenes del desencanto: Nueva historieta española 1980–1986*. Madrid: Iberoamericana, 2013.

Pinotti, Luciana. "La animación no ficcional: Un análisis sobre la construcción del sentido en el documental animado Vals con Bashir." *Cine Documental*, no. 12 (2015): 142–68. https://www.cinedocumental.com.ar/revista/pdf/12/12-Art6.pdf.

– "Los documentales animados como síntoma del arte contemporáneo." *Me Manda Walt* 1, no. 1 (2016): 19–31.

Porter, Rachel. "Animation as a New Form of Journalism." *Knowledge Quarter*, 29 October 2015. https://www.knowledgequarter.london/animation-as-a-new-form-of-journalism-by-rachel-porter/.

Randall, Rachel. *Children on the Threshold in Contemporary Latin American Cinema: Nature, Gender, and Agency*. Lanham, MD: Lexington Books, 2017.

Ranzani, Oscar. "Toda la vida de Evita es cinematográfica." *Página 12*, 20 October 2011. https://www.pagina12.com.ar/diario/suplementos/espectaculos/subnotas/23251-6306-2011-10-20.html.

Resina, Joan Ramon. *The Ghost in the Constitution: Historical Memory and Denial in Spanish Society*. Liverpool: Liverpool University Press, 2017.

Rey, Debora. "Argentina's Evita Remembered through Toys for Poor Children." *National Post*, 26 April 2019. https://nationalpost.com/pmn/news-pmn/argentinas-evita-remembered-through-toys-for-poor-children.

Ribas-Casasayas, Alberto, and Amanda L. Petersen. "Introduction: Theories of the Ghost in a Transhispanic Context." In *Espectros: Ghostly Hauntings in Contemporary Transhispanic Narratives*, edited by Alberto Ribas-Casasayas and Amanda L. Petersen, 1–12. Lanham, MD: Rowman & Littlefield, 2015.

Rippl, Gabriele, and Lukas Etter. "Intermediality, Transmediality, and Graphic Narrative." In *From Comic Strips to Graphic Novels: Contributions to the Theory and History of Graphic Narrative*, edited by Daniel Stein and Jan-Noel Thon, 191–217. Berlin: de Gruyter, 2013. https://doi.org/10.1515/9783110282023.191.

Rodríguez Jiménez, Pablo, and Fernán Alvarado Vejarano. "Presentación." In *Envejecer en Colombia*, edited by Pablo Rodríguez Jiménez and Fernán Alvarado Vejarano, 19–24. Bogotá: Universidad Externado de Colombia, 2015. https://doi.org/10.2307/j.ctv13qfwsp.4.

Romano, Nick. "The Pandemic Animation Boom: How Cartoons Became King in the Time of COVID." *Entertainment Weekly*, accessed 24 February 2023. https://ew.com/movies/animation-boom-coronavirus-pandemic/.

Rosa, José María. "La popularidad de Perón." In *La jornada del 17 de Octubre: Por cuarenta y cinco autores*, compiled by Fermín Chávez, 52–3. Buenos Aires: Corregidor, 1996.

Rosen, Jonathan D., and Roberto Zepeda. "Una década de narcoviolencia en México: 2006–2016." In *Atlas de la seguridad y la defensa de México 2016*, edited by Raúl Benítez Manaut and Sergio Aguayo Quezada, 55–65. Mexico City: CASEDE, 2017.

Ruiz Bartolomé, José Luis. "Desmontando Españistán (1)." *Libertad Digital*, 29 May 2011. https://www.libremercado.com/adios-ladrillo-adios/desmontando-espanistan-1/amp.html.

Sainz Borgo, Karina. "Aleix Saló: 'Nuestra generación es como un Ferrari en un camino de cabras, completamente ineficiente.'" *Vozpópuli*, 13 September 2014. https://www.vozpopuli.com/altavoz/cultura/Culturas-Libros-Comics_0_733726669.html.

Saló, Aleix. "Aleix Saló: *Españistán* simplifica por su formato, pero no busca culpables." *elEconomista.es*, 3 June 2011. https://www.eleconomista.es/opinion-blogs/noticias/3126051/06/11/Aleix-Salo-Espanistan-simplifica-por-su-formato-pero-no-busca-culpables.html.

– "Booktrailers de mis libros." YouTube, updated 3 June 2020. https://www.youtube.com/playlist?list=PLEygubrMOUOWtG7V1P9OPjfg-Rn82PxuR.

– *Españistán, de la Burbuja Inmobiliaria a la Crisis (por Aleix Saló)*. YouTube video, 6:45, 25 May 2011. https://www.youtube.com/watch?v=N7P2ExRF3GQ.

– *Españistán: Este país se va a la mierda*. Barcelona: Glénat, 2012.

– "Important Problems Explained through Comics & Comedy." Aleix Saló (website), 20 November 2015. https://web.archive.org/web/20220629220546/http://www.aleixsalo.com/important-problems-explained-through-comics-comedy/.

Sampedro, Víctor, and Mayra Martínez Avidad. "The Digital Public Sphere: An Alternative and Counterhegemonic Space? The Case of Spain." *International Journal of Communication*, no. 12 (2018): 23–44. https://ijoc.org/index.php/ijoc/article/view/6943.

Sánchez, Samuel. "Editorial: El prestigio del Banco: Conviene aclarar del todo los criterios de inspección bancaria durante la crisis." *El País*, 3 February 2017. https://elpais.com/elpais/2017/02/03/opinion/1486140720_408790.html.

"Santiago Niño-Becerra: 'El Señor del banco nunca es tu amigo.'" *La Vanguardia*, 4 April 2013. https://www.lavanguardia.com/economia/20130402/54371924086/nino-becerra-no-suficiente-dinero-europa-garantizar-primeros-100-000-euros.html.

Sastre, Ángel, and Jon Sedano. "Videocómic: La batalla de Mosul." *El País*, 7 September 2019. https://elpais.com/elpais/2019/08/29/eps/1567094903_071360.html.

Scalabrini Ortiz, Raúl. *El hombre que está solo y espera. La manga. Tierra sin nada, tierra de profetas*. Buenos Aires: Fundación Ross, 2008.

Schlichting, Laura, and Johannes C.P. Schmid. "Introduction to Graphic Realities: Comics as Documentary, History, and Journalism." *ImageTexT* 11, no. 1 (2019). https://imagetextjournal.com/introduction-to-graphic-realities-comics-as-documentary-history-and-journalism/.

Schöb, Mia. "Memory Building within the Colombian Conflict: How Do Films Contribute? An Analysis of Three Films." IR*eflect* 2, no. 1 (2015): 29–48.

Schwarz, Shaul, dir. *Narco Cultura*. New York: Ocean Size Pictures, 2014.

Scolari, Carlos A. "El Eternauta: Transmedia Expansions, Political Resistance and Popular Appropriations of a Human Hero." In *Transmedia Archaeology: Storytelling in the Borderlines of Science Fiction, Comics and Pulp Magazines*, edited by Carlos Scolari, Paolo Bertetti, and Matthew Freeman, 55–71. London: Palgrave Pivot, 2014. https://doi.org/10.1057/9781137434371_4.

Scorer, James, ed. *Comics beyond the Page in Latin* America. London: UCL Press, 2020. https://doi.org/10.2307/j.ctv13xpstc.

– "Latin American Comics beyond the Page." In Scorer, *Comics beyond the Page*, 1–28. https://doi.org/10.2307/j.ctv13xpstc.6.

Sebreli, Juan José. *Los deseos imaginarios del peronismo*. Buenos Aires: Editorial Legasa, 1983.

Seoane, María, dir. *Eva de la Argentina*. Buenos Aires: Illusion Studios, 2011. DVD.

Seoane, María. "Ni a palos." *Caras y Caretas*, 5 October 2020. https://carasycaretas.org.ar/2020/10/05/ni-a-palos/.

– *La noche de los lápices*. Buenos Aires: Sudamericana, 1986.

Seoane, María, and Victor Santa María. *Eva Perón. Esa mujer*. 3rd ed. Buenos Aires: Octubre, 2019.

Seoane Pérez, Francisco. "'Spain Is Not Greece': Reflections of the Hellenic Crisis in Spanish Political Discourse." *Journal of Greek Media & Culture* 4, no. 1 (2018): 45–57. https://doi.org/10.1386/jgmc.4.1.45_1.

Serrano Abarca, Patricia. "La retórica de la facticidad en tiempos de hibridación: Recreación, memoria y realidad en los docudramas y documentales animado." *Boletín del Centro de Investigación de la Creatividad*, no. 1 (2019): 20–7.

"Short Film Reality 2.0." Victor Orozco's website. Accessed 28 February 2023. https://www.victororozco.com/reality.html.

Skelton, Tracey. "Young People, Children, Politics and Space: A Decade of Youthful Political Geography Scholarship 2003–13." *Space and Polity* 17, no. 1 (2013): 123–36. https://doi.org/10.1080/13562576.2013.780717.

Sköld, Johanna, and Ingrid Söderlind. "Agentic Subjects and Objects of Political Propaganda: Swedish Media Representations of Children in the Mobilization for Supporting Finland during World War II." *Journal of the History of Childhood and Youth* 11, no. 1 (2018): 27–46. https://doi.org/10.1353/hcy.2018.0002.

Sommerland, Ylva, and Margareta Wallin Wictorin. "Writing Comics into Art History and Art History into Comics Research." *Konsthistorisk tidskrift /Journal of Art History* 86, no. 1 (2017): 1–5. https://doi.org/10.1080/00233609.2016.1272629.

Soto, Álvaro. "Retrato de la generación de 'Guatepeor.'" *Sur*, 13 September 2014. https://www.diariosur.es/culturas/libros/201409/13/retrato-generacion-guatepeor-20140913002824-rc.html.

Suárez Vega, Carla. "Memoria histórica en viñetas: Representaciones de la Guerra Civil Española a través de la narrativa gráfica y los testimonios familiares." *Caracol*, no. 15 (2018): 286–307. https://doi.org/10.11606/issn.2317-9651.v0i15p286-307.

Sullivan, John P. "Criminal Insurgency: Narcocultura, Social Banditry, and Information Operations." *Small Wars Journals*, 3 December 2012. https://smallwarsjournal.com/jrnl/art/criminal-insurgency-narcocultura-social-banditry-and-information-operations.

Sullivan, John P., and Adam Elkus. "Barbarization and *Narcocultura*: Reading the Evolution of Mexico's Criminal Insurgency." *Small Wars Journal*, 31 August 2011. https://smallwarsjournal.com/jrnl/art/barbarization-and-narcocultura.

Sullivan, John P., and Carlos Rosales. "Ciudad Juárez and Mexico's 'Narco-culture' Threat." *Mexidata*, 28 February 2011. https://www.academia.edu/8727000/Ciudad_Ju%C3%A1rez_and_Mexicos_Narco_Culture_Threat.

Tahmassian, Lena. "*Espacios en blanco*: Historical Memory, Defeat, and the Comics Imaginary." In McKinney and Richter, *Spanish Graphic Narratives*, 29–46. https://doi.org/10.1007/978-3-030-56820-7_2.

Tekiner, Uğur. "Back-to-Roots Again? Kirchnerismo as a Reclaiming of Classical Peronism." *METU Studies in Development*, no. 47 (2020): 257–80.

Theimer, Kate. "What Is the Meaning of Archives 2.0?" *American Archivist* 74, no. 1 (2011): 58–68. https://doi.org/10.17723/aarc.74.1.h7tn4m4027407666.

30deoscuridad. *Trailer 30 años de Oscuridad HD Ed. Goyas*. YouTube video, 2:28, 16 January 2012, https://www.youtube.com/watch?v=Fy_dwp90kFo.

Tobar, Hector. "Mexico's Brutality Cheered on YouTube." *Los Angeles Times*, 11 February 2007. https://www.latimes.com/archives/la-xpm-2007-feb-11-fg-mexvideo11-story.html.

Tolliday, Steven. "Enterprise and State in the West German Wirtschaftswunder: Volkswagen and the Automobile Industry, 1939–1962." *Business History Review* 69 no. 3 (1995): 273–350. https://doi.org/10.2307/3117336.

Torbado, Jesús, and Manuel Leguineche. *The Moles*. Translated by Nancy Festinger. London: Secker & Warburg, 1981.

Trombetta, Jimena Cecilia. "La ficción y su función de memoria: A propósito de Eva Perón." *Rizoma* 7, no. 1 (2019): 35–46. https://doi.org/10.17058/rzm.v7i1.12647.

– "El lenguaje de animación como herramienta poética para mitificar la historia de Eva Perón." *Fotocinema revista científica de cine y fotografía*, no. 14 (2017): 365–78. https://doi.org/10.24310/fotocinema.2017.v0i14.3605.

Tronsgard, Jordan. "Drawing the Past: The Graphic Novel as Postmemory in Spain." *Romance Notes* 57, no. 2 (2017): 267–79. https://doi.org/10.1353/rmc.2017.0023.

Uhrig, Meike, ed. *Emotion in Animated Films*. New York: Routledge, 2018. https://doi.org/10.4324/9780203731253.

Uhrig, Meike. "'Portraying Emotions Is Fundamental to Animated Film': An Interview with Felix Gönnert." In Uhrig, *Emotion in Animated Films*, 219–26.
UNHCR: The UN Refugee Agency. *Global Trends: Forced Displacement in 2015.* 20 June 2016. https://www.unhcr.org/576408cd7.pdf.
– *Global Trends: Forced Displacement in 2019.* 18 June 2020. https://www.unhcr.org/5ee200e37.pdf.
Utas, Mats. "Victimcy, Girlfriending, Soldiering: Tactic Agency in a Young Woman's Social Navigation of the Liberian War Zone." *Anthropological Quarterly* 78, no. 2 (2005): 403–30. https://doi.org/10.1353/anq.2005.0032.
van den Heuvel, Maartje. "Picturing Landscape: Contemporary Photography, Collective Visual Memory and the Making of Place in the Netherlands." PhD diss., University of Leiden, 2018.
van Gageldonk, Maarten, László Munteán, and Ali Shobeiri, eds. *Animation and Memory*. Cham: Palgrave Macmillan, 2020. https://doi.org/10.1007/978-3-030-34888-5.
Vargas, Hector D. "Qué hizo Evita el 17 de Octubre." Clarín, 24 February 2017. https://www.clarin.com/ediciones-anteriores/hizo-evita-17-octubre_0_r1ZiQl-AKl.html.
Vázquez, María Celia, coord. *Intervenciones intelectuales en el contexto del peronismo clásico*. Bahia Blanca: EDIUNS, 2011.
"Victor Orozco." *Singulares*, 16 May 2014. https://www.singulares.es/victor-orozco-director-cine-animacion-cortometrajes-mexico-reality-2-0/.
"vídeo cómico de animación explica la situación española, Un." *La Vanguardia*, 28 September 2012. https://www.lavanguardia.com/politica/20120928/54352027066/un-video-comico-de-animacion-explica-la-situacion-espanola.html.
Viñolo Locuviche, Samuel. "La animación española en 2012." *Con A de Animación*, no. 3 (2013): 24–9. https://doi.org/10.4995/caa.2013.1418.
Walden, Victoria Grace. "Animation and Memory." In Dobson et al., *Animation Studies Reader*, 81–90.
– "Animation: Textural Difference and the Materiality of Holocaust Memory." *Animation Studies*, no. 9 (2014). https://journal.animationstudies.org/victoria-grace-walden-animation-textural-difference-and-the-materiality-of-holocaust-memory/.
Ward, Paul. "Animated Documentary, Recollection, 'Re-enactment' and Temporality." In Murray and Ehrlich, *Drawn from Life*, 69–83.
– "Animated Documentary: Viewer Engagement, Emotion, and Performativity." In Uhrig, *Emotion in Animated Films*, 84–103.
– "Animating with Facts: The Performative Process of Documentary Animation in *the ten mark* (2010)." *Animation* 6, no. 3 (2011): 293–305. https://doi.org/10.1177/1746847711420555.

– *Documentary: The Margins of Reality*. New York: Columbia University Press, 2012.

Weber, Wibke, and Hans-Martin Rall. "Comics Journalism and Animated Documentary: Understanding the Balance between Fact and Fiction." *ImageTexT* 11, no. 1 (2019). https://imagetextjournal.com/comics-journalism-and-animated-documentary-understanding-the-balance-between-fact-and-fiction/.

Wells, Paul. "The Animation Manifesto; or, What's Animation Ever Done for Us?" *Metro*, no. 188 (2016): 94–100.

Wells, Paul. "Never Mind the Bollackers: Here's the Repositories, Sites and Archives in Nonfiction Animation." In Murray and Ehrlich, *Drawn from Life*, 106–25.

– *Understanding Animation*. London: Routledge, 1998.

Winter, Ulrich. "'Localizar a los muertos' y 'reconocer al otro': Lugares de memoria(s) en la cultura española contemporánea." In *Casa Encantada: Lugares de memoria en la España Constitucional (1978–2004)*, edited by Joan Ramon Resina and Ulrich Winter, 17–39. Madrid: Iberoamericana, 2005.

Wright, Amarantha. "The Hand of God." *New Internationalist*, no. 277 (1996): 22–3.

Wyness, Michael. "Childhood, Human Rights and Adversity: The Case of Children and Military Conflict." *Children & Society* 30, no. 5 (2016): 345–55. https://doi.org/10.1111/chso.12171.

Ziemann, Luc-Carolin. "Victor Orozco Ramírez: Documentarist in Animation Skin." *Shortfilm.de*, 12 March 2021. https://www.shortfilm.de/en/victor-orozco-ramirez-ein-dokumentarist-im-animationspelz/.

Index

Toronto Iberic

1 Anthony J. Cascardi, *Cervantes, Literature, and the Discourse of Politics*
2 Jessica A. Boon, *The Mystical Science of the Soul: Medieval Cognition in Bernardino de Laredo's Recollection Method*
3 Susan Byrne, *Law and History in Cervantes'* Don Quixote
4 Mary E. Barnard and Frederick A. de Armas (eds.), *Objects of Culture in the Literature of Imperial Spain*
5 Nil Santiáñez, *Topographies of Fascism: Habitus, Space, and Writing in Twentieth-Century Spain*
6 Nelson R. Orringer, *Lorca in Tune with Falla: Literary and Musical Interludes*
7 Ana M. Gómez-Bravo, *Textual Agency: Writing Culture and Social Networks in Fifteenth-Century Spain*
8 Javier Irigoyen-García, *The Spanish Arcadia: Sheep Herding, Pastoral Discourse, and Ethnicity in Early Modern Spain*
9 Stephanie Sieburth, *Survival Songs: Conchita Piquer's* Coplas *and Franco's Regime of Terror*
10 Christine Arkinstall, *Spanish Female Writers and the Freethinking Press, 1879–1926*
11 Margaret E. Boyle, *Unruly Women: Performance, Penitence, and Punishment in Early Modern Spain*

12 Evelina Gužauskytė, *Christopher Columbus's Naming in the* diarios *of the Four Voyages (1492–1504): A Discourse of Negotiation*
13 Mary E. Barnard, *Garcilaso de la Vega and the Material Culture of Renaissance Europe*
14 William Viestenz, *By the Grace of God: Francoist Spain and the Sacred Roots of Political Imagination*
15 Michael Scham, Lector Ludens: *The Representation of Games and Play in Cervantes*
16 Stephen Rupp, *Heroic Forms: Cervantes and the Literature of War*
17 Enrique Fernandez, *Anxieties of Interiority and Dissection in Early Modern Spain*
18 Susan Byrne, *Ficino in Spain*
19 Patricia M. Keller, *Ghostly Landscapes: Film, Photography, and the Aesthetics of Haunting in Contemporary Spanish Culture*
20 Carolyn A. Nadeau, *Food Matters: Alonso Quijano's Diet and the Discourse of Food in Early Modern Spain*
21 Cristian Berco, *From Body to Community: Venereal Disease and Society in Baroque Spain*
22 Elizabeth R. Wright, *The Epic of Juan Latino: Dilemmas of Race and Religion in Renaissance Spain*
23 Ryan D. Giles, *Inscribed Power: Amulets and Magic in Early Spanish Literature*
24 Jorge Pérez, *Confessional Cinema: Religion, Film, and Modernity in Spain's Development Years, 1960–1975*
25 Joan Ramon Resina, *Josep Pla: Seeing the World in the Form of Articles*
26 Javier Irigoyen-García, *"Moors Dressed as Moors": Clothing, Social Distinction, and Ethnicity in Early Modern Iberia*
27 Jean Dangler, *Edging toward Iberia*
28 Ryan D. Giles and Steven Wagschal (eds.), *Beyond Sight: Engaging the Senses in Iberian Literatures and Cultures, 1200–1750*
29 Silvia Bermúdez, *Rocking the Boat: Migration and Race in Contemporary Spanish Music*
30 Hilaire Kallendorf, *Ambiguous Antidotes: Virtue as Vaccine for Vice in Early Modern Spain*
31 Leslie J. Harkema, *Spanish Modernism and the Poetics of Youth: From Miguel de Unamuno to* La Joven Literatura
32 Benjamin Fraser, *Cognitive Disability Aesthetics: Visual Culture, Disability Representations, and the (In)Visibility of Cognitive Difference*
33 Robert Patrick Newcomb, *Iberianism and Crisis: Spain and Portugal at the Turn of the Twentieth Century*
34 Sara J. Brenneis, *Spaniards in Mauthausen: Representations of a Nazi Concentration Camp, 1940–2015*

35 Silvia Bermúdez and Roberta Johnson (eds.), *A New History of Iberian Feminisms*
36 Steven Wagschal, *Minding Animals in the Old and New Worlds: A Cognitive Historical Analysis*
37 Heather Bamford, *Cultures of the Fragment: Uses of the Iberian Manuscript, 1100–1600*
38 Enrique García Santo-Tomás (ed.), *Science on Stage in Early Modern Spain*
39 Marina S. Brownlee (ed.), *Cervantes'* Persiles *and the Travails of Romance*
40 Sarah Thomas, *Inhabiting the In-Between: Childhood and Cinema in Spain's Long Transition*
41 David A. Wacks, *Medieval Iberian Crusade Fiction and the Mediterranean World*
42 Rosilie Hernández, *Immaculate Conceptions: The Power of the Religious Imagination in Early Modern Spain*
43 Mary L. Coffey and Margot Versteeg (eds.), *Imagined Truths: Realism in Modern Spanish Literature and Culture*
44 Diana Aramburu, *Resisting Invisibility: Detecting the Female Body in Spanish Crime Fiction*
45 Samuel Amago and Matthew J. Marr (eds.), *Consequential Art: Comics Culture in Contemporary Spain*
46 Richard P. Kinkade, *Dawn of a Dynasty: The Life and Times of Infante Manuel of Castile*
47 Jill Robbins, *Poetry and Crisis: Cultural Politics and Citizenship in the Wake of the Madrid Bombings*
48 Ana María Laguna and John Beusterien (eds.), *Goodbye Eros: Recasting Forms and Norms of Love in the Age of Cervantes*
49 Sara J. Brenneis and Gina Herrmann (eds.), *Spain, the Second World War, and the Holocaust: History and Representation*
50 Francisco Fernández de Alba, *Sex, Drugs, and Fashion in 1970s Madrid*
51 Daniel Aguirre-Oteiza, *This Ghostly Poetry: History and Memory of Exiled Spanish Republican Poets*
52 Lara Anderson, *Control and Resistance: Food Discourse in Franco Spain*
53 Faith S. Harden, *Arms and Letters: Military Life Writing in Early Modern Spain*
54 Erin Alice Cowling, Tania de Miguel Magro, Mina García Jordán, and Glenda Y. Nieto-Cuebas (eds.), *Social Justice in Spanish Golden Age Theatre*
55 Paul Michael Johnson, *Affective Geographies: Cervantes, Emotion, and the Literary Mediterranean*

56 Justin Crumbaugh and Nil Santiáñez (eds.), *Spanish Fascist Writing: An Anthology*
57 Margaret E. Boyle and Sarah E. Owens (eds.), *Health and Healing in the Early Modern Iberian World: A Gendered Perspective*
58 Leticia Álvarez-Recio (ed.), *Iberian Chivalric Romance: Translations and Cultural Transmission in Early Modern England*
59 Henry Berlin, *Alone Together: Poetics of the Passions in Late Medieval Iberia*
60 Adrian Shubert, *The Sword of Luchana: Baldomero Espartero and the Making of Modern Spain, 1793–1879*
61 Jorge Pérez, *Fashioning Spanish Cinema: Costume, Identity, and Stardom*
62 Enriqueta Zafra, *Lazarillo de Tormes: A Graphic Novel*
63 Erin Alice Cowling, *Chocolate: How a New World Commodity Conquered Spanish Literature*
64 Mary E. Barnard, *A Poetry of Things: The Material Lyric in Habsburg Spain*
65 Frederick A. de Armas and James Mandrell (eds.), *The Gastronomical Arts in Spain: Food and Etiquette*
66 Catherine Infante, *The Arts of Encounter: Christians, Muslims, and the Power of Images in Early Modern Spain*
67 Robert Richmond Ellis, *Bibliophiles, Murderous Bookmen, and Mad Librarians: The Story of Books in Modern Spain*
68 Beatriz de Alba-Koch (ed.), *The Ibero-American Baroque*
69 Deborah R. Forteza, *The English Reformation in the Spanish Imagination: Rewriting Nero, Jezebel, and the Dragon*
70 Olga Sendra Ferrer, *Barcelona, City of Margins*
71 Dale Shuger, *God Made Word: An Archaeology of Mystic Discourse in Early Modern Spain*
72 Xosé M. Núñez Seixas, *The Spanish Blue Division on the Eastern Front, 1941–1945: War, Occupation, Memory*
73 Julia Domínguez, *Quixotic Memories: Cervantes and Memory in Early Modern Spain*
74 Anna Casas Aguilar, *Bilingual Legacies: Father Figures in Self-Writing from Barcelona*
75 Julia H. Chang, *Blood Novels: Gender, Caste, and Race in Spanish Realism*
76 Frederick A. de Armas, *Cervantes' Architectures: The Dangers Outside*
77 Michael Iarocci, *The Art of Witnessing: Francisco de Goya's* Disasters of War
78 Esther Fernández and Adrienne L. Martín (eds.), *Drawing the Curtain: Cervantes's Theatrical Revelations*
79 Emiro Martínez-Osorio and Mercedes Blanco (eds.), *The War Trumpet: Iberian Epic Poetry, 1543–1639*

80 Christine Arkinstall, *Women on War in Spain's Long Nineteenth Century: Virtue, Patriotism, Citizenship*
81 Ignacio Infante, *A Planetary Avant-Garde: Experimental Literature Networks and the Legacy of Iberian Colonialism*
82 Enrique Fernández, *The Image of Celestina: Illustrations, Paintings, and Advertisements*
83 Maryanne L. Leone and Shanna Lino (eds.), *Beyond Human: Decentring the Anthropocene in Spanish Ecocriticism*
84 Jennifer Nagtegaal, *Politically Animated: Non-fiction Animation from the Hispanic World*

www.ingramcontent.com/pod-product-compliance
Lightning Source LLC
LaVergne TN
LVHW061748060826
844660LV00017B/987/J

9781487544423